P9-DWN-557

ALSO BY MARY J. SHAPIRO

The Dover New York Walking Guides:
    From the Battery to Wall Street
    From Wall Street to Chambers Street
    Greenwich Village

A Picture History of the Brooklyn Bridge

For children:
How They Built the Statue of Liberty
    Illustrated by Huck Scarry

GATEWAY TO LIBERTY

GATEWAY TO LIBERTY

THE STORY OF THE STATUE OF LIBERTY AND ELLIS ISLAND

MARY J. SHAPIRO

VINTAGE BOOKS
A DIVISION OF RANDOM HOUSE
NEW YORK

FOR BARRY

A VINTAGE ORIGINAL, May 1986
FIRST EDITION

Copyright © 1986 by Mary J. Shapiro

All rights reserved under International and Pan-American
Copyright Conventions. Published in the United States by
Random House, Inc., New York, and simultaneously in
Canada by Random House of Canada Limited, Toronto.

Library of Congress Cataloging-in-Publication Data

Shapiro, Mary J.
  Gateway to liberty.

  "A Vintage original"—T.p. verso.
  Bibliography: p.
  1. Statue of Liberty (New York, N.Y.)—History—
Pictorial works.   2. Ellis Island Immigration Station
(New York, N.Y.)—History—Pictorial works.   3. United
States—Emigration and immigration—History—Pictorial
works.   I. Title.
F128.64.L6S47   1986   974.7'1   85-40673
ISBN 0-394-72891-2

Cover photographs: Statue by Henry Wolf; immigrants by
Lewis W. Hine, Library of Congress

Manufactured in the United States of America
Book design by Naomi Osnos

Grateful acknowledgment is made to the following for permission to reprint excerpts
from previously published material: / "It Doesn't Cost Them a Cent" by Andy Logan,
The New Yorker, May 12, 1951. Reprinted by permission; © 1951, 1979, The New
Yorker Magazine, Inc. / *On the Trail of the Immigrant* by Edward Steiner, Fleming H.
Revell Company / *Observations of Mr. Dooley* by Peter Finley Dunne, Harper & Row
Publishers, Inc. / *The Promised Land* by Mary Antin, © 1912 by Houghton Mifflin
Company. © renewed 1940 by Mary Antin; reprinted by permission of Houghton
Mifflin Company / *Keepers of the Gate: A History of Ellis Island* by Thomas M. Pitkin.
Reprinted by permission of New York University Press, © by New York
University / *American Mosaic: The Immigrant Experience in the Words of Those Who Lived
It* by Joan Morrison and Charlotte Zabusky. © 1980 by Joan Morrison and Charlotte
Fox Zabusky; reprinted by permission of the publisher, E. P. Dutton, a division of
New American Library / *How We Lived: A Documentary History of Immigration* by Irving
Howe and Kenneth Libo. Reprinted by permission of the Putnam Publishing Group;
© 1979 by Irving Howe and Kenneth Libo / *Memories of an American Jew* by Philip
Cowen, New York, The International Press, 1932 / *The Polish Peasant in Europe and
America* by William I. Thomas and Florian W. Znaniecki, Alfred A. Knopf, Inc. / *The
Making of an Insurgent: An Autobiography, 1882-1919* by Fiorello LaGuardia. Reprinted
by permission of J. B. Lippincott Company / *Island of Hope, Island of Tears* by David
M. Brownstone, Irene Franck and Douglas Brownstone. Reprinted by permission of
Viking Penguin, Inc. / *Pillar to Post* by Henry H. Curran. Reprinted by permission
of C. Scribner's Sons / *Land of Their Choice: The Immigrants Write Home* by Theodore
C. Blegen, University of Minnesota Press. © 1955 by the University of Minnesota.

CONTENTS

ACKNOWLEDGMENTS

I have been given much help in gathering the photographs and historical documents which make up this book. I am especially grateful to Margaret Heilbrun for her untiring and expert research and her persistent resourcefulness in finding information. I thank, too, Kevin M. Crotty, who translated much primary source material from the French, and later read the entire manuscript and made many useful suggestions.

I am indebted as well to many archivists and librarians for their knowledgeable assistance, among them: Won H. Kim, Librarian, Statue of Liberty National Monument; Jennifer Bright, Museum of the City of New York; Carole L. Perrault, National Park Service; and Bara Levin, curator of the Chemical Bank Archives, which has an extensive Statue of Liberty collection including Bartholdi's diary of his trip to America in 1871.

I owe thanks to the staffs of the New-York Historical Society, the YIVO Institute for Jewish Research, the Library of Congress, and the National Archives. I am particularly grateful to the experienced staff of librarians at the New York Public Library, where the research facilities offered by the Wertheim Study were invaluable.

I thank Pierre Burger and Christian Kempf, Musée Bartholdi in Colmar, France; Geneviève Gareau, Caisse Nationale des Monuments Historiques et des Sites, in Paris; and André Desvallees, Conservatoire National des Arts et Métiers, also in Paris.

John Robbins, Historical Architect for the National Park Service, and Jean Wiart, whose team of coppersmiths from Les Metalliers Champenois sculpted Liberty's new flame, gave me cogent technical explanations on how the Statue of Liberty was constructed.

Others who generously gave of their time and effort were James E. Crotty, Rita and Robert E. Crotty, Ella Elstein, formerly librarian of the Child Welfare League of America, Herbert R. Hands of the American Society of Civil Engineers, Kevin MacCarthy, James Molloy, Huck Scarry, and William Welling, historian of photography.

Two books that were extremely helpful and should be given special mention are Marvin Trachtenburg's *The Statue of Liberty* (London:

Penguin Books, 1976), and Thomas M. Pitkin's *Keepers of the Gate: A History of Ellis Island* (New York: New York University Press, 1975).

I am indebted to Jason Epstein, whose idea it was to do this book. I thank Corona Machemer, Laura Schultz, Jayne Nomura and Naomi Osnos, all of Random House, and Joan Whitman, for their guidance and sound advice.

Finally, I thank my family: my children, Michael and Eben, for their patience as well as their impatience to have the project completed; and most of all, I thank my husband Barry for his prodigious help, constant encouragement, and infectious enthusiasm.

GATEWAY TO LIBERTY

INTRODUCTION

The office of America is to liberate, to abolish kingcraft, priest-craft, caste monopoly, to pull down the gallows, to burn up the bloody statute book, to take in the immigrant, to open the doors of the sea and the fields of the earth.
                                            —*Ralph Waldo Emerson*

The Statue of Liberty and Ellis Island have stood side by side in New York's harbor for nearly a century. Liberty was un-veiled on Bedloe's Island—now Liberty Island—in 1886, and six years later, at a time when immigration from Europe was steadily rising, the first federal landing depot for immigrants was opened on Ellis Island, situated in Liberty's shadow. Together, these two landmarks express an essential, characteristically American theme: the search for freedom from political and social oppression. The federal government officially recognized the landmarks' relationship in 1965 when it incorporated the abandoned, somewhat disreputable immigration station into the Statue of Liberty National Monument.

This book is a documentary record of Liberty and Ellis Island. Their combined histories, beginning in the 1870s, when the statue was first proposed, up to the 1950s when Ellis Island closed, give a wide view of an emerging America and its relations with the rest of the world. The photographs, prints and drawings collected here offer eyewitness testimony of that era. The narrative too is carried wherever possible by first-hand accounts: correspondence, govern-ment reports, newspaper and magazine articles, and personal mem-oirs. The history of each landmark, however, is presented separately. This is because, even though today the two share a common theme, the nineteenth-century ideas and sentiments that prompted their creations are quite different and almost completely unrelated. Lib-erty was an expression of romantic idealism commemorating a glo-rious past; Ellis Island was an attempt to cope with a world migration that was bringing to America hundreds of thousands of people every year.

3

The colossal Statue of Liberty, ingeniously fashioned from hundreds of thin copper plates, was constructed in Paris from 1875 to 1884. It was a gift from the people of France to the people of the United States to mark—albeit ten years late—the 1876 American Centennial. Originally entitled "Monument to American Independence: Liberty Enlightening the World," the statue commemorates the Franco-American alliance and the decisive role France played in the Revolutionary War. But Liberty's creators intended their monument to honor not so much a military victory as a triumph of a heroic social experiment. In a land far removed from the monarchies of Europe, the Americans had succeeded in building an enduring republic based on liberty and equality that had withstood the trials of one hundred years, including a bloody civil war. For European countries still chafing under the rule of monarchy or empire, the United States, with its Constitution and Bill of Rights, provided a potent model of representative government. This was especially true in France where the "Liberté, Fraternité, Egalité" proclaimed by the leaders of the French Revolution in 1789 had in fact remained elusive ideals, frustrated and repressed by a recurring cycle of revolution, anarchy, counter-revolution, and autocracy. Indeed, for Liberty's first patrons, a small group of influential and politically active French intellectuals, the statue paid homage to a form of government—a republic—that they dearly longed to see established in their own country.

Situated dramatically near the center of New York Bay, the gateway to the New World, Liberty soon became a revered and powerful symbol, not just of an abstract ideal, but of America itself. Throughout the past century, generations of Americans have reinterpreted her significance, adapting her image to represent the new concerns and new philosophies of each succeeding age. But the special meaning of Liberty for immigrants to the United States—those intrepid seekers of liberty from all over the world—has remained constant from the statue's unveiling to today.

One of the first, certainly the most famous, expressions of this theme was "The New Colossus" by Emma Lazarus, a young New York poet who had been encouraged in her art by Ralph Waldo Emerson. In 1883, while Liberty was still under construction in Paris, the American Committee, which had been organized to raise money to build its pedestal, asked Lazarus to write a poem for its fund-raising drive. Lazarus's sonnet ignores the symbolism assigned

Liberty Enlightening the World, ca. 1886. Photograph by Edward Bierstadt. New-York Historical Society.

to Liberty by her creators and envisions the statue as a "mother of exiles" reaching out to welcome the disenfranchised, the downtrodden, and the persecuted from the Old World. The sweeping romantic concepts of "Liberty, Fraternity, Equality" that had inspired the great statue's creation were both complemented and tempered by the motherly ideals of peace, kindness, and generosity bestowed on Liberty by the "New Colossus" and softened, at least in the popular imagination, the austerity of her Junoesque face and steady judgmental gaze.

When Lazarus wrote her poem, she had in mind the plight of Jewish men, women, and children who had been driven from their homes during the pogroms that raged in Russia following the assassination of Czar Alexander II in 1881. Over the next year, Jewish communities in 160 towns across Russia were brutally pillaged and vandalized forcing thousands to find peace and security in a new strange land. Emma Lazarus, who visited some of these homeless refugees in a resettlement center in New York, was profoundly affected by their stories of persecution and ruin and their undaunted hopes for the future.

Americans who may have found Liberty's original abstract symbolism too rarefied warmed to Lazarus's more immediate interpretation of the statue's meaning. James Russell Lowell, the American poet and essayist, told Lazarus that her sonnet gave Liberty a " 'raison d'être' which it wanted before quite as much as it wants a pedestal. You have set it on a noble one," he wrote her, "saying admirably just the right word to be said."[1] In 1903, Georgina Schuyler, an admirer of Lazarus, had "The New Colossus" inscribed on a bronze plaque and affixed to the interior of the statue's pedestal; and over the years, Liberty's beloved image as "mother of exiles" has been nurtured by the memories of many immigrants who recall their first sight of her—the applause, the weeping, the singing and dancing that broke out on the steerage decks—as their ships steamed past the mighty woman's welcoming, overwhelming figure.

As the immigrants gazed at Liberty, Ellis Island, known more familiarly to them as "Isle of Tears," would gradually come into their view. Next to the Statue of Liberty, no other place in the United States conjures up as strong an image of the immigrants—latter-day pioneers, laden with baggage, surrounded with children and filled with hope—than does this tiny island with its towered red brick buildings. While the proximity of Liberty and Ellis Island binds them together in a shared theme, their relationship is unavoidably ironic; for if Liberty symbolized the aspirations, ideals, and dreams of the immigrants, Ellis Island would come to represent the harsh realities and ordeals they would have to endure before they and their children would share in America's blessings.

Ellis Island's complex of buildings—reception hall, dormitory, restaurant and hospital—was opened in 1892. Since then, nearly 70 percent of the immigrants to the United States, about fourteen million people, were admitted through Ellis Island where they first encountered American bureaucracy and the confusing demands of the country's immigration laws. Here the new arrivals, who were often exhausted and sick from loneliness and travel, had to face the possibility of being rejected and sent back to their homelands. They were hustled through a line inspection, methodically poked and prodded by a Public Health Service doctor, then pushed forward, held back, or separated from their families, most often without an explanation, and finally questioned by an immigration officer who would decide whether they were eligible to land. Even though only 2 percent of those who came to Ellis Island were excluded, the anxiety over the inspection caused scenes of hectic emotion—a chaotic mixture of fright and despair giving way to joy and relief.

As the country's chief immigration station, Ellis Island was in the continual glare of sensational publicity. Accusations of extortion, theft, and bribery were frequent, although the worst of the corruption was cleaned up when Teddy Roosevelt became president in 1901. Ellis Island was also at the center of the government's decades-long controversy over immigration laws—whether to keep an open-door policy or impose stringent restrictions. While this debate raged in Washington, the practical concerns of providing an adequate budget for Ellis Island were shunted aside. Yet, it was obvious almost from the day this public facility was opened that the money and space provided by the government were simply not enough to carry out the task of properly inspecting and caring for the thousands of immigrants who came to New York every day.

By World War I, when Liberty's image was being used to urge Americans to support the war effort and buy Liberty bonds, Congress was pushing to impose strict limitations on immigration. In 1917, it passed the Literacy Act, which required immigrants to be able to read at least forty words in their native language. When this failed to cut immigration significantly, the First Quota Act was passed in the early 1920s. This law drastically reduced the number of immigrants who could be admitted according to nationalities. It was followed by the even more restrictive National Origins Act of 1924, which effectively stopped the flood of immigration at America's door.

Gradually, Ellis Island was no longer needed as a reception station but was kept in service as a deportation center until it was finally and quietly closed in 1954. Today, it has emerged from its years of obscurity to become a national symbol, together with the Statue of Liberty, of the long procession of immigrants who settled in and built up America. For many of our parents, grandparents and great-grandparents, Liberty and Ellis Island marked the end of a long, hard, and often heart-breaking journey, and the beginning of a new life in a land of freedom and great promise.

On the Statue of Liberty's fiftieth anniversary in 1936, President Franklin D. Roosevelt paid special tribute to that "steady stream of men, women and children (who) followed the beacon of liberty" to America. "They brought to us," he said, "strength and moral fiber developed in a civilization centuries old but fired anew by the dream of a better life in America. They brought to one new country the cultures of a hundred old ones. . . . They adopted this homeland because in this land they found a home in which the things they most desired could be theirs—freedom of opportunity, freedom of thought, freedom to worship God. Here they found life because here there was freedom to live. It is the memory of all these eager seeking millions that makes this one of America's places of great romance. Looking down this great harbor I like to think of the countless number of inbound vessels that have made this port. I like to think of the men and women who—with the break of dawn off Sandy Hook—have strained their eyes to the west for a first glimpse of the New World."[2]

The New Colossus

Not like the brazen giant of Greek fame,
With conquering limbs astride from land to land;
Here at our sea-washed, sunset gates shall stand
A mighty woman with a torch, whose flame
Is the imprisoned lightning, and her name
Mother of Exiles. From her beacon-hand
Glows world-wide welcome; her mild eyes command
The air-bridged harbor that twin cities frame.
"Keep, ancient lands, your storied pomp!" cries she
With silent lips. "Give me your tired, your poor,
Your huddled masses yearning to breathe free,
The wretched refuse of your teeming shore.

Emma Lazarus, 1849–1887. Wood engraving from The Century Magazine, *1888. National Park Service.*

In 1883, Emma Lazarus, who came from a wealthy New York family, wrote "The New Colossus" to help raise money for the Statue of Liberty pedestal fund. Tragically, Lazarus would never see Liberty. She went to Europe in 1885 before the statue was reconstructed on Bedloe's Island and, when she returned two years later, her ship sailed into New York at night. By this time, very ill with cancer, Lazarus was taken directly to her home where she died shortly thereafter, on November 19, 1887, at the age of thirty-eight.

Opposite.
"Liberty's torch as it will appear when completed on Bedloe's Island." Frank Leslie's Illustrated Newspaper, June 20, 1885.

Long before Liberty was actually completed, this wood engraving illustrated an article urging readers to contribute to the pedestal fund. In extolling the virtues of the statue, the paper stressed the thrill of being able to "look down upon the magnificent panorama of New York City and harbor" from a height of over three hundred feet. The torch was open to tourists until 1916.

The Statue of Liberty

The Statue of Liberty Enlightening the World, Paris, ca. 1885. Musée Bartholdi, Colmar.

From 1878 to 1884, Liberty was under construction at the workshop of Gaget, Gauthier et Cie. at 25 rue de Chazelles in Paris. Its gleaming red-copper form, the color of an American penny, towered 151 feet over the surrounding neighborhood of diminutive four- and five-story houses. It must have been an improbable, somewhat surrealistic sight. The statue was to be a gift from the people of France to the people of the United States.

Frédéric-Auguste Bartholdi (1834–1904), photograph by Paul Nadar. Caisse Nationale des Monuments Historiques et des Sites.

Bartholdi was born to a prosperous family in Colmar, Alsace, a province of eastern France. He later studied painting and sculpture in Paris, and when he was nineteen years old, opened his own sculpture studio. That year, 1853, he exhibited his first sculpture at the Paris Salon and received a commission to create a larger-than-life statue of one of Napoleon I's generals. Bartholdi had a passion for the colossal that was undoubtedly encouraged by the nineteenth-century enthusiasm for monument-building. He drew his artistic inspiration, however, from ancient sources, most notably from Egypt, a land he visited in 1856 to view the Sphinx, the pyramids, and the giant granite statuary of Abu Simbel and Thebes.

LIBERTY ENLIGHTENING THE WORLD

I n 1865, Edouard de Laboulaye, a prominent professor of law, gave an informal dinner party at his home in Versailles, France. His guests, politicians and writers well known for their liberal sympathies, also included a young sculptor named Frédéric-Auguste Bartholdi. During the evening, according to an account written years later by Bartholdi, the conversation turned to relations between France and the United States. Laboulaye, a fervent admirer of America, remarked that the participation of France and of Lafayette and his volunteers in the American Revolution formed an indestructible basis for a lasting friendship between the two countries—a friendship that was unusual in world relations.

"The Frenchmen who fought in the United States spilled their blood for the principles they hoped to see prevail in France and the world . . ." Laboulaye said. "In that struggle for independence [there was] a fraternity of feelings, a community of efforts and of emotions, and when hearts have beaten together, something always remains among nations as among individuals."[1]

He finished by saying that ". . . if a monument were to be built in America as a memorial to their independence, I should think it very natural if it were built by a united effort, if it were the common work of both nations."

This idea captured Bartholdi's imagination. It remained, as he later wrote, "fixed" in his memory and would inspire him to undertake the immense task of creating Liberty Enlightening the World or, as we know her today, the Statue of Liberty.

The creation of Liberty would commemorate the centennial of America's independence and a hundred years of friendship between the American and French people. But more than that, it would express the political ideals of French republicans who had become increasingly restive under a long succession of monarchs and emperors. Since the French Revolution and the First Republic, there had been two more attempts (in 1830 and 1848) to establish representative government, but these were ill-fated efforts and were inevitably followed by a return to autocracy. The latest of these autocrats was Louis Napoleon, who was elected president of the Second Republic in 1848, then in 1851 declared himself emperor and called himself Napoleon III. His coup d'état outraged the French intellectuals, whose feelings were expressed by Alexis de Toqueville, author of *Democracy in America.* "We cannot bear to be deprived of the power of speaking or writing," he said shortly after Napoleon's takeover, "We cannot bear that the people which carried liberty through Europe should now be employed in quenching all its lights."[2]

Both Laboulaye and Bartholdi were deeply opposed to the empire and, for Laboulaye especially, the theme of liberty became all-consuming. As a renowned professor at the Collège de France, he exerted a moral influence that was felt despite the government's policy of strict censorship. An unabashed admirer of everything American, he expressed his political hopes though his lectures and writings on American democracy and he became France's leading authority on the United States Constitution.

Napoleon III remained in power until 1870 when the disastrous Franco-Prussian War plunged France into a nightmare of humiliation and defeat. In August the Germans crossed the border into eastern France, and by September the emperor was a prisoner of war, his army of eighty thousand surrounded and captured at Sedan. The Third Republic was joyously, though somewhat prematurely, declared in Paris; but more bloodshed followed. France did not surrender to Germany until five months later; and then, shortly after the armistice was signed, a bitter socialist uprising broke out in Paris that was brutally crushed two months later by French regular troops.

The postwar provisional government, although nominally a republic, was unstable and seriously endangered by the efforts of monarchists and conservatives to reassert their own power and restore the old order. In May of 1871, while this political drama was just beginning in the National Assembly, Bartholdi wrote to Laboulaye that he intended to go to America and asked for letters of introduction:

"I hope to get in touch with art lovers," Bartholdi wrote, "and to find important work to do, but above all, I hope to realize my project of a monument in honor of American independence. I am

Edouard-Réné Lefebvre de Laboulaye (1811–83). Photograph by Félix Nadar. Caisse Nationale des Monuments Historiques et des Sites.

By 1865, Laboulaye's name was already well known in the United States from his pamphlets and articles published during the American Civil War. At a time when most Europeans openly sympathized with the seceding southern states, Laboulaye, who was chairman of the French Anti-Slavery Society, vigorously defended the Union cause. John Bigelow, who was appointed American minister to France by Abraham Lincoln, recalled that Laboulaye's writings, which were circulated all over France (and, in translation, in the United States), were crucial in persuading the French government not to recognize the Confederate government. "His pen and his influence were always at our service," Bigelow wrote.
". . . M. Laboulaye's value as a friend of the Union, and of representative government was not long in being recognized in the United States. The press proclaimed his sympathetic utterances wherever the Federal mails could carry them; the Union League Club of New York ordered his portrait . . . a bronze bust of him was placed in the Union League Club of Philadelphia, and at the close of our war, his name was more widely and more generally known in the United States than in Europe."[4]
Laboulaye's celebrity would later be instrumental in gaining the support of Americans to build the Statue of Liberty as a joint venture with the people of France.

re-reading your works on that subject and hope I can do honor to your friendship and patronage. I will try to glorify the republic and liberty over there and await the day when they may be found here with us!"[3]

Laboulaye encouraged Bartholdi to go—to talk to as many Americans as he could and drum up support for the Liberty project as a part of the 1876 American centennial.

Bartholdi arrived in New York on June 21, 1871 and saw at once that Bedloe's Island, a tiny parcel of land in the middle of the harbor, would be a perfect site for his monument. Every ship that sailed into New York, the busiest port in America, passed this island. From New York, he traveled to Philadelphia, Boston, and Washington. With letters of introduction from Laboulaye, who was known in the United States through his writings, Bartholdi met many important personalities including Henry Wadsworth Longfellow, Senator Charles Sumner, Horace Greeley, and President Ulysses S. Grant.

The artist then traveled across the country by train to Chicago, Omaha, Salt Lake City, and San Francisco. He returned by way of St. Louis and Cincinnati. In a letter to Laboulaye, he described his

Senator Charles Sumner and Henry Wadsworth Longfellow, ca. 1860. Collection of William Welling.

With Laboulaye's letters of introduction, Bartholdi was able to meet some of America's most prominent citizens. He wrote to his patron, "Thanks to your letters I have met with the most cordial welcome. Mr. Sumner gave me a warm welcome and showed me a lively sympathy."[5] And of his stay in Boston, he wrote: "Mr. Longfellow very enthusiastic, asked me to tell you he will do everything you wish for the success of this demonstration of friendship during the centenary."[6]

transcontinental journey as a "missionary's pilgrimage . . . Not always fun, but always very interesting. In each town I look for some people who might wish to participate in our enterprise. Up until now, I've found them everywhere. Things will be prepared; it will only need a spark from France."[7]

France, however, was still in a state of political unrest, and Laboulaye, who had been elected to the National Assembly, took no immediate action to publicize the statue. He was deeply involved in the struggle of moderate republicans to establish the Third Republic and devoted all his time to his new senatorial office. In 1874, however, after his party had won a series of significant legislative battles, Laboulaye organized the Franco-American Union to raise money for building the Statue of Liberty. An appeal for contributions was immediately published "to elevate in commemoration of the glorious anniversary of American independence an exceptional monument."[8] A colossal statue would be raised ". . . at the entrance of that vast continent, full of life, where ships meet from all points of the world, it will look as springing up from the bosom of the deep representing: Liberty Enlightening the World." The monument, so casually proposed in 1865, would become in the 1870s a forceful rallying point for Laboulaye and his party's fight to secure a republic for France. The Franco-American Union was made up mostly of men who were moderate republicans. Their espousal of the liberal cause would give the statue its meaning; Bartholdi's colossal vision would give it its form.

Bartholdi had actually started working on drawings and models of Liberty as early as 1870, before his trip to the United States, and by August 1875 he had completed a four-foot model showing Liberty as we know her today. The Franco-American Union enthusiastically approved Bartholdi's design and showed it on November 6, 1875, at a lavish fund-raising banquet at the Hôtel du Louvre in Paris. Two hundred guests attended and pledged forty thousand francs. As news about Liberty spread throughout France, more contributions followed and by the end of the year the Franco-American Union had raised 200,000 francs.

Bartholdi set to work immediately in his own studio on the rue d'Orléans in Paris. It would be impossible to have the entire monument completed for America's 100th anniversary in 1876, but working with a crew of artisans Bartholdi hoped to complete at least a representative portion—the arm and torch—for display at the

Study for Suez Lighthouse. Watercolor by Bartholdi, ca. 1867. Musée Bartholdi, Colmar.

Liberty is a direct descendant of this earlier project, Egypt Bringing the Light to Asia, *which Bartholdi designed for Ismail Pasha, the young Khedive of Egypt. The seventy-five-foot-high lighthouse was to be erected at the entrance to the Suez Canal, then under construction. In 1869, when Ismail lost interest in building the lighthouse, Bartholdi turned his attention to creating a monument to American independence. Bartholdi later hotly denied that there was any connection between the two projects: "Everyone had seen the models of the Statue of Liberty made at Paris," he said on one occasion, "and only evilly disposed persons are ignorant of what it has cost me. . . . My Statue of Liberty was a pure work of love, costing me the sacrifice of ten years and twenty thousand dollars—little perhaps for Americans but a great deal for me . . . The Egyptian affair would have been purely a business transaction. I declare most emphatically, and I defy anyone in the world to contradict me, that the Statue of Liberty was offered to any other government."[9]*

Philadelphia Centennial Exhibition. Throughout the beginning of 1876, the interior of Bartholdi's studio was the scene of intense activity as a team of sculptors and coppersmiths hammered and shaped the copper plates following an ancient technique of metal-working called repoussé—meaning literally "push back." In sculpture, it means to hammer thin sheets of metal from the inside surface

The final model for Liberty, ca 1875. Library of Congress.

Bartholdi started working on Liberty in 1870 and continued to refine his design over the next five years. The final model for Liberty, completed some time during the early part of 1875, was a bit over four feet high. Heavily draped in Roman-style robes, Liberty strides forward out of the shackles and chains of tyranny, which lie broken at her feet. In her right hand she carries aloft a torch of freedom. Her left arm cradles a tablet, representing the law, inscribed July 4, 1776—the date on which America declared its independence. On her head rests a crown with seven rays for the seven continents and the seven seas of the world.

to create a finished image on the outside surface. The artists used a wide assortment of tools: wooden mallets, iron-headed hammers, and variously shaped anvils and mandrels. When finished, the copper sheets were riveted together and fastened to a supporting iron framework.

Although the work proceeded speedily, the massive arm holding aloft its torch of liberty was completed too late for the May opening of the Philadelphia Centennial Exhibition. But it was rushed to America in August, quickly reassembled and on display in time for the fair's busiest season. In October alone, more than two and one-half million people visited the exhibition. The arm and torch proved to be one of the most popular and unusual sights; visitors could go inside and climb a narrow ladder to the top of the torch, where they had a fine view of the fairgrounds.

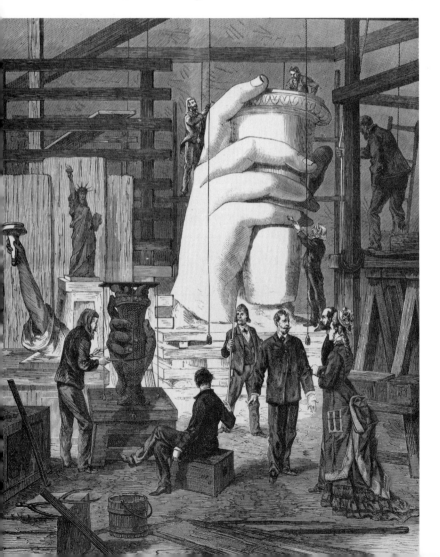

The plaster model of Liberty's hand being enlarged, May 13, 1876. L'Illustration.

The first section of Liberty to be created was the arm and torch, which the Franco-American Union wanted to show at the Philadelphia Centennial Exhibition. When completed, the arm and torch together would stand about thirty feet high. To extrapolate this gigantic piece from the original four-foot-high model of Liberty was a complicated task. First, Bartholdi made a second model of Liberty that was twice the size of the first— about nine feet tall. The forearm and torch of this model were then enlarged in successive stages. To enlarge a model, artisans first marked hundreds of reference points on contour lines drawn around the model's surface. Then the three dimensions (height, width, and depth) of each point's location were measured geometrically on two identical frames, one placed above and the other around the base of the model. Next to the model being enlarged, a set of frames four times the size of the first set was built. As measurements were taken on the first set of frames, they were applied in numbers four times as large to a model being constructed within the second set of frames. Eventually, a full-scale model would be achieved. The process, which had to be precise, demanded a good deal of skill and patience. Each reference point had to be measured six times—height, width, and depth on the model and another three on the enlargement—and each section of the statue had about fifteen hundred reference points altogether requiring nine thousand separate measurements.

Bartholdi's studio on the rue d'Orléans in Paris, ca. 1876. Musée Bartholdi, Colmar.

The completed arm and torch constructed of twenty-one copper plates stands thirty feet high in the center of Bartholdi's studio. Bartholdi chose to make the statue out of copper for several very practical reasons: it was light, easy to work, relatively inexpensive, and could be produced in sheets that were extremely thin. Liberty's shell would be a mere ³/₃₂ inch thick, about the same thickness as an American silver dollar.

Bartholdi attended the exhibition and appeared at a seemingly endless round of fund-raising events in Philadelphia and New York. His second visit to the United States lasted eight months and must be counted a great success. By January 1877, the American Committee was organized to raise funds for the statue's pedestal. The committee was made up of active members of the Republican party whose political philosophy was similar to that of the moderate republicans in France. William Evarts, the newly appointed secretary of state, was president of the new committee, and John Jay, Richard Butler, Joseph Choate, Henry Spaulding, J. W. Pinchot, and Theodore Roosevelt (father of the future president), all wealthy and prominent New Yorkers, were some of the members. On February 22, 1877, Congress adopted a joint resolution authorizing the federal government to accept the statue and provide a site as well as funds for its maintenance. After the Philadelphia Centennial Exhibition, Liberty's torch was taken to New York City and put on display in Madison Square Park (at Fifth Avenue near Twenty-third Street), where, for a fee of fifty cents, it was open to sightseers.

0035-COLOSSAL HAND AND TORCH "LIBERTY"

Liberty's arm and torch, Philadelphia, 1876. Musée Bartholdi, Colmar.

For a small fee visitors could climb up through the arm to a veranda surrounding the torch. At a souvenir stand below, brochures were handed out explaining that the arm and torch were just a small part of a colossal statue that was going to be constructed in Paris and given to the American people to commemorate the anniversary of their Declaration of Independence. The American reaction was a mixture of admiration, suspicion, and amusement. The New York Times *especially had fun lampooning the gift, writing in an editorial on September 29, 1876: "Had the French sculptor honestly intended to complete the statue of 'Liberty,' he would have begun at its foundation, modeling first the boot, then the stocking, then the full leg in the stocking. . . . Instead of doing this, the sculptor sent us an isolated and useless arm and hand . . ."*

William M. Evarts (1818–1901). Brady-Handy photograph, 1877. Library of Congress.

Evarts had just been appointed secretary of state (by President Rutherford B. Hayes) at the time he became president of the American Committee. He lent a great deal of prestige to the campaign to raise funds for the pedestal. Since 1877 when the committee was formed, Evarts was instrumental in guiding its fortunes through the whimsical labyrinth of legislative and public opinion.

chapter 2

LIBERTY RISING

Bartholdi returned to France at the end of January 1877. He immediately started the construction of Liberty's head, which he wanted to display at the Paris International Exposition of 1878. He engaged the Parisian firm of Gaget, Gauthier et Cie. to help him complete the work. The coppersmiths at Gaget, Gauthier were experts at repoussé, the metalworking technique used to shape the copper plates; they had just completed a twenty-two-foot statue of Vercingetorix in repoussé copper. They had also created the elaborate cupola of the Paris Opéra and the copper statues on the spires of Notre Dame and the St. Chapelle.

In a large workshop in the center of Paris, a team of artisans using the same methods employed for the arm and torch created a full-scale plaster model of the head and then hammered, shaped, and assembled copper plates to create the duplicate form of that model. From accounts written at that time, the scene inside the Gaget, Gauthier workshop must have been fascinating. *The World* reported in 1878:

The workshop was built wholly and solely for the accommodation of this one inmate and her attendants, some fifty workmen hammering for their lives on sheer copper to complete the toilet of her tresses for the show. The Lilliputians reached her back hair by means of ladders running from stage to stage on a high scaffolding. I mounted the scaffolding with them and stood on a level with her awful eye some thirty inches from corner to corner to be engulfed in her gaze. . . . The whole scene abounded in this curiosity of measurement. A number of pygmies of our species crawling about the inside of what appeared to be a vast cauldron used in the sugar refining trade were understood to be really at work on the crown of her head. A smaller cauldron, on which two little fellows were busy in a corner, was the tip of her classic nose. Her lips, from dimple to dimple, were as long as my walking stick, and fifteen people, I was told, might

Opposite.
Liberty's head under construction, 1877–78. Musée National des Techniques—CNAM, Paris.

sit around the flame of her torch.[1]

When Liberty's head was completed, it was hoisted onto a huge dray and pulled by thirteen horses to its site at the Paris Exposition Universelle on the Champ de Mars. A boisterous and appreciative crowd cheered Liberty as she was slowly drawn through the streets of Paris. One correspondent reported that at every turn the enormous head would pitch slightly on her thick bed of sticks and hay, giving the appearance of saluting her enthusiastic admirers. "The effect was imposing," he wrote, "and in spite of myself, I raised my hand to my hat to acknowledge the statue's greeting."[2]

Once it was placed on its pedestal, Liberty's head was open to the public. Inside this bizarre construction of copper sheets and iron framework, people could climb forty-three steps to peer out of the windows of Liberty's crown at the rest of the fairgoers.

Meanwhile, efforts to raise money to pay for Liberty's construction continued. Admission, of course, was charged to enter the head at the exposition. Bartholdi made two hundred small clay models of Liberty that were sold for one thousand francs each. The buyer's name was baked into the clay with Bartholdi's signature and registered in a book kept by the Franco-American Union. French businesses could buy the rights to Liberty to use as advertising logos, and individual contributions were encouraged by concerts, public speeches, published appeals, and newspaper articles.

Liberty's head on display at the Paris International Exposition, 1878. Library of Congress.

One person who visited Liberty often was Rudyard Kipling, who as a thirteen-year-old boy attended the exposition with his father. Kipling recalled this experience many years later in a book called Souvenirs of France: *"A feature of [the exposition] was the head of Bartholdi's Statue of Liberty which later was presented to the United States. One ascended by a staircase to the dome of the skull and looked out through vacant eyeballs at a bright coloured world beneath. I climbed up there often, and once an elderly Frenchman said to me, 'Now you, young Englisher, you can say you have looked through the eyes of Liberty Herself.' He spoke less than the truth. It was through the eyes of France that I began to see."*[3] *Kipling was speaking figuratively, of course. His view was through the windows of the crown, not the eyeballs, but he rightly surmised that Liberty was an expression of the suffering France had endured over the past eight years.*

But by the time the Paris exposition closed at the end of 1878, the Franco-American Union was still short of the amount needed to cover the full cost of the statue's construction—about two million francs ($400,000). To rekindle public interest, the Union decided to organize a lottery. Five hundred and twenty-eight prizes were donated by French businesses, and 300,000 lottery tickets were issued. The first prize, a set of silver and crystal, was worth twenty thousand francs. The hundreds of other prizes varied in value from five hundred to five thousand francs. The Franco-American Union planned to hold the drawing in December of that year, but so few tickets were sold by then that it was postponed until the following June. Despite the delay, the lottery succeeded in achieving its fundraising goal. On July 7, 1880, at a dinner at the Continental Hotel in Paris, Laboulaye was able to announce that the Franco-American Union had the necessary money in hand. An illuminated parchment stating that the statue's completion was assured was signed by the members of the Union and sent to the American Committee in New York.

© Arch. Phot. Paris/S.P.A.D.E.M.

Gustave Eiffel (1832–1923). Photograph by Félix Nadar. Caisse Nationale des Monuments Historiques et des Sites.

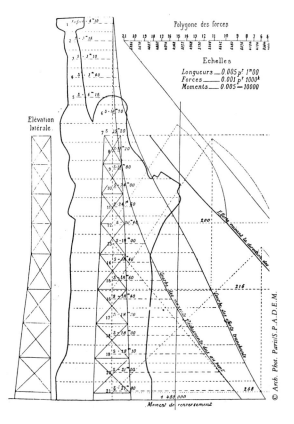

© Arch. Phot. Paris/S.P.A.D.E.M.

Eiffel's design for Liberty's central tower, 1880. Le Génie Civil, August 1, 1883.

Because of the statue's unprecedented height, the problem of supporting the copper shell and stabilizing the structure against high winds called for a radically new solution. An earlier plan proposed by Eugene Viollet-le-Duc consisted of attaching the copper plates to an iron frame and then weighting the bottom of the statue by filling it hip-high with sand. Eiffel's solution, however, was completely different and did not depend on mass for stability.

He designed a free-standing wrought-iron structure firmly braced with horizontal and diagonal bars. The construction of this ingenious load-bearing tower was precisely calculated to resist the strongest winds. American architects, though probably unaware of Eiffel's design, came up with a similar solution for building skyscrapers. A load-bearing steel skeleton was first used by William Jenney to build his ten-story Home Insurance Building in Chicago in 1885.

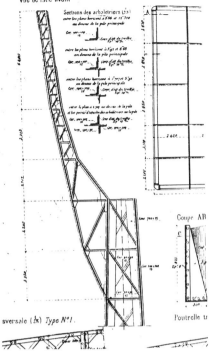

force (½s)
Vue de face avant

Sections des arbalétriers (½s)

sversale (⅛s) Type Nº1.

Coupe AB

Poutrelle tr

Eiffel's calcuations and diagrams for Liberty's right arm, 1880. Le Génie Civil, August 1, 1883.

The arm is supported by a second frame, forty feet seven inches long, which swings up and out from the main pylon. In Liberty's recent restoration it was discovered that the iron frames for both the arm and head were eighteen inches off the points specified by Eiffel. This discrepancy between the actual work and Eiffel's design remains a mystery, although several explanations have been proposed. At one time it was thought that the misplacement was the fault of the American engineers who, in 1886, were responsible for reconstructing the statue in New York. Another theory is that Bartholdi made the changes deliberately for purely artistic reasons. Moving the arm and head may have given the statue a more dynamic gesture. If such a change was authorized by Bartholdi, it was probably carried out by the artisans at Gaget, Gauthier et Cie. without Eiffel's consent. Eiffel would have recognized that shifting the framework would cause serious structural weakness in the connection of the arm and shoulder. This became Liberty's major maintenance problem which has had to be dealt with frequently since the statue's inauguration in 1886.

Building a Colossus

Construction of Liberty would present considerable difficulties simply because of her enormous size. Most of the metalworking and sculptural techniques used to build the statue were centuries old but had never before been employed on so grand a scale. When completed Liberty would stand 151 feet tall. She would be fashioned from over 350 thin plates of copper fitted together like a gigantic three-dimensional jigsaw puzzle. The copper shell would be no thicker than a silver dollar, but all together the plates would weigh 100 tons. Unquestionably, the most daunting challenge for her builders in an age before skyscrapers was simply how to hold the gigantic statue up.

Early in 1880, Bartholdi asked Gustave Eiffel (who built the Eiffel Tower in 1889 for yet another Paris exposition) to design an interior skeleton for Liberty. Eiffel was one of France's most innovative engineers. His remarkably long bridge spans, notably the Douro Bridge at Oporto (1878) and the Garabit viaduct (1884), are among the great achievements in the history of engineering. These wrought-iron spans of continuous girders were supported by broad arches and tall latticed towers. Using many of the ideas that he had developed from his experience as a bridge builder, Eiffel designed a latticed wrought-iron frame of enormous strength for Liberty. It would support the weight of her thin copper shell and withstand the high winds of New York Bay. Ironworkers constructed the skeleton in the yard outside Gaget, Gauthier; inside the workshop carpenters, sculptors, and coppersmiths—about thirty to fifty men—built the rest of Liberty's body.

To enlarge the body, Bartholdi's starting point was a nine-foot-high plaster model of Liberty. From this model he made another that was precisely four times as large—nearly thirty-eight feet tall. This was called the quarter-scale model, meaning that it was one quarter the height of the final 151-foot-high statue. Bartholdi studied this model very carefully. This was his last chance to take in Liberty's full form with his discerning eye and make whatever changes he wanted. The quarter-scale model was then reproduced in eight layers and each layer enlarged separately four times its size to achieve full-scale.

Liberty's iron skeleton under construction, 1881. Library of Congress.

Opposite.
Diagram of Liberty's skeleton, 1984.
Swanke Hayden Connell Architects.

The iron skeleton inside Liberty is actually three separate structural systems bolted together. First, there is a central ninety-six-foot-high pylon braced with an iron lattice. A secondary frame of iron angles reaches out from the central pylon and supports a third system of iron flat bars that rise up and out to the copper plates.

The flat bars are bolted to the armature—the network of horizontal and vertical ribs that back each copper plate. (These ribs were forged to duplicate the exact shape of Liberty's interior surface.) Thus, the flat bars and secondary frame transfer the weight of the copper shell back to the central pylon, which supports the entire structure.

Each copper plate is held up separately by one or more flat bars and does not weigh down in the least on the plates below it. The flat bars are angled up and act like springs allowing the shell to bend and flex without being damaged in high winds or in extremes of hot and cold temperatures.

Because iron and copper have different rates of thermal expansion, the iron ribs are not fastened directly to the copper plates. Instead, they are held in place by copper saddles. Thus the ribs can slip enough through the saddles as the two metals adjust separately to changes in temperature.

Over the years, however, some of the iron in Liberty's skeleton became badly corroded. The iron ribs had expanded and tore the saddles away from the copper. In 1984–1987 Swanke Hayden Connell, architects for the restoration of the Statue of Liberty, carried out the delicate and demanding task of replacing nearly all the corroded iron flat-bars and ribs with new ones made of stainless steel and installing new copper saddles.

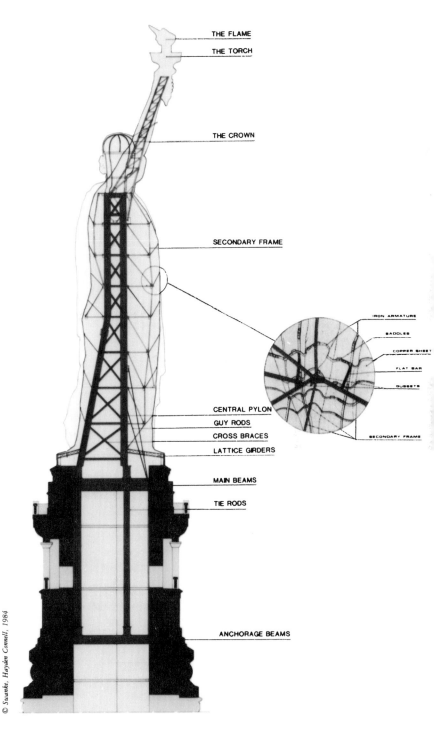

THE FLAME
THE TORCH
THE CROWN
SECONDARY FRAME
IRON ARMATURE
SADDLES
COPPER SHEET
FLAT BAR
GUSSETS
SECONDARY FRAME
CENTRAL PYLON
GUY RODS
CROSS BRACES
LATTICE GIRDERS
MAIN BEAMS
TIE RODS
ANCHORAGE BEAMS

© Swanke, Hayden Connell, 1984

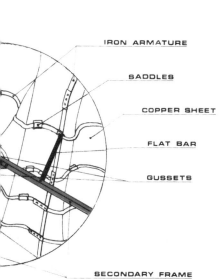

IRON ARMATURE
SADDLES
COPPER SHEET
FLAT BAR
GUSSETS
SECONDARY FRAME

The workshops of Gaget, Gauthier et Cie., 1881. Musée Bartholdi, Colmar.

Inside the workshop, massive full-scale plaster models of sections of Liberty can be seen. The body of the statue was reproduced in eight layers, each of which measured about twelve feet high and thirty feet wide. Outside, the first copper fragment, Liberty's left foot, is in place on the iron skeleton. (The skeleton is still under construction.)

Workshop yard at Gaget, Gauthier et Cie., October 24, 1881. Library of Congress.

October 24, 1881 would mark the centennial of the Battle of Yorktown. Thanks to the efforts of French forces under the commands of General Rochambeau and Admiral de Grasse, this battle marked the turning point of the American Revolution. As France was sending a delegation to the United States to take part in anniversary celebrations, the Franco-American Union decided to partake in the spirit of remembrance with its own ceremony in Paris. The new American minister to France, Levi P. Morton, was invited to Gaget, Gauthier et Cie. to help fasten the first section of copper—Liberty's left foot—to the iron armature. As Bartholdi and the members of the Franco-American Committee watched, Morton tapped a rivet into Liberty's left toe. His efforts were ceremonial because the foot had to be removed again to allow work on the skeleton to be completed.

The full-scale plaster model of Liberty's
tablet arm under construction, 1882. Library of Congress.

Bartholdi, standing at the bottom center
of the photograph, was on hand at Gaget,
Gauthier to oversee the construction of
Liberty. By 1882, the full-scale plaster
model of the tablet arm (the seventh layer
of the statue) was well under way, with
its wooden armature completed and half-
covered with plaster.

A full-scale plaster model of each layer was built up gradually
with wooden beams and lath and then covered with plaster. When
finished, these models were huge, about twelve feet high and over
thirty feet wide.

The next step was to duplicate the plaster model in copper. Liberty
would be made up of about 350 separate thin plates of copper. Since
these could not be hammered directly against the surface of the
plaster model, carpenters built large wooden molds—called garabits—that duplicated in reverse the complex shapes and curves of
the statue's surface (see illustration on page 31. Planks of wood were
carved and fitted directly against the full-scale model. Crosspieces
were inserted—like shelves—between the planks, forming pigeon-
holes. The more complex the plaster surface, the more shelves were
inserted, sometimes forming a solid wooden surface against which
to beat the copper.

Where the surface of the statue curved in deeply, the wooden
molds had to be constructed in sections so that they could be easily
removed from the plaster model and so that the copper, once hammered, could be easily removed from the mold. These separate molds

were then fastened together to form the same standard rectangular sizes as the copper plates.

Soon an entire area of the plaster model's surface was covered with these gnarled wooden frames. As each mold was completed, it was pulled away from the model and placed on its back so that the reverse copy of the statue's surface faced upward. A mold usually had to be nailed into a cradle to hold it steady against the impact of the coppersmiths' hammers.

Each copper plate, pressed into its mold with a giant lever, was held in place with vises and lead weights hung around the edge of the plate. Then the coppersmiths hammered the metal with wooden mallets to make it fit the contours of the mold exactly. As their work progressed, they would use smaller hammers with iron heads. Hammering the metal made it harder but also more brittle. To keep the copper plate from cracking, workers would often remove it from its mold and anneal it, that is, heat it with a blow torch, to increase its malleability. Most of this work of hammering and shaping was done on the inside of the plate. When a plate was completed it was turned over to reveal a smooth image on its outside surface.

Liberty's tablet arm under construction, 1882. Musée Bartholdi, Colmar.

Artisans hammering the copper plates into wooden molds, 1882. Library of Congress.

The finished full-scale plaster model of Liberty's arm stands in the background. On the right side of the photograph, the quarter-size model of the same layer and another of Liberty's head stand on their central platforms.

The last step in making the copper shell was to forge two-inch-wide iron straps or ribs to fit the exact shape of each plate. These iron ribs, attached horizontally and vertically to each plate, supported the copper and kept it from sagging. When the entire shell was put together, these ribs would form an immense network of support inside the statue.

Work proceeded on the statue from one enlargement to another. After one section was completed, the plasterers and sculptors moved on to build another while a team of carpenters would construct giant wooden molds of the first. When the carpenters finished their work, they, too, would move on to the next section, and a team of coppersmiths would continue the work of hammering and shaping the copper plates against the wooden molds. Meantime, the plasterers and sculptors started working on yet another section.

Soon the interior of the workshop was a sea of wavy wooden frames and fragments of hammered red copper. When all the copperwork from a full-size plaster enlargement was completed, that model would be demolished, its space cleared to make room for

Two views of the interior of Gaget, Gauthier et Cie., 1882. National Park Service.

Bartholdi chose to sculpt Liberty in repoussé because he wanted her shell to be as thin and as light as possible. This would cut down on the cost of material and also make it easier to transport the disassembled statue to America. If Bartholdi had wanted to cast Liberty, he would have needed hundreds of large sand molds, more expensive to produce than the wooden molds, and the resulting shell would have been much thicker and much heavier. Even with repoussé and using copper plates just 3/32-inch thick, Liberty's complete shell weighs 100 tons.

another, and so the work continued until all eight layers were completed.

When a copper plate was finished, it was carried out into the yard and hoisted up onto Liberty's skeleton with ropes and pulleys. Then the workmen would fasten it to its neighboring plates with a few temporary screws. Later, when the statue was rebuilt in America, over 300,000 copper rivets would be inserted around the edges of the plates. For now, most of the carefully drilled rivet holes were left empty.

Throughout the spring of 1882, progress was steady. Carpenters built a giant wooden scaffolding around the statue and each day a team of coppersmiths and ironworkers would climb a series of ladders to continue the demanding work of fastening the thin copper plates that made up Liberty's shell to the iron skeleton. They had to bolt the iron flat bars to the system of horizontal and vertical iron ribs, and then attach the iron ribs to each plate with copper saddles. The workers would often have to send a section of copper or a piece of iron back to the shop to be rehammered, recut, or changed in some

A full-scale plaster model of Liberty's shoulder stands in the background of this photograph. It is encased in large wooden molds, or garabits. When the carpenters completed building a mold they would pull it away from the model and set it on its back so that a reverse copy of the statue's surface faced upward. Then a rectangular sheet of copper was beaten into the mold to form one of the approximately 350 pieces that make up Liberty's shell.

way so that it would fit precisely into place on the statue.

By July 1882, Liberty was completed to her waist, and Bartholdi decided to stage a celebration for his crew. Food and wine were hauled up to a table set up on the scaffolding inside the statue in the midst of ropes, hoists and pulleys and other construction paraphernalia. Altogether twenty-six people attended, including Gustave Eiffel and Bartholdi's chief artisans: M. Simon, the master sculptor (Simon would receive the Légion d'Honneur for his work on Liberty), M. Bergeret, foreman of the metalworkers, M. Baron, head of the carpenters, and of course, several newspaper reporters.

As work progressed, Liberty's form grew, eventually dominating that section of Paris surrounding Gaget, Gauthier et Cie. By December 1882, Bartholdi wrote the American Committee; "The statue commences to reach above the houses, and next spring one will see it overlook the entire city."

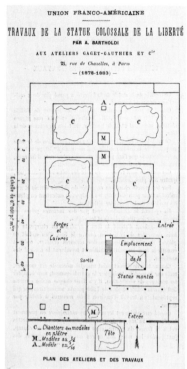

Floor plan of Gaget, Gauthier et Cie., 1883. New York Public Library.

"A" on the floor plan shows where the nine-foot-high (1/16 scale) model of Liberty stood. "C" indicates the four areas where the full-scale models were constructed. Two layers of the quarter-scale model were placed on platforms in the center of the workshop, while the entire thirty-eight-foot (quarter-scale) model of Liberty was stored outside in a shed.

Liberty under construction in Paris, ca. 1882. Library of Congress.

Opposite.
Liberty's copper skirt and scaffolding, ca. 1882. Musée National des Techniques—CNAM, Paris.

chapter 3

FUND-RAISING IN AMERICA

Although work on the statue was well under way in Paris by 1881, the French had still not received official word from the American Committee about its plans for building the pedestal. The Americans had not even acknowledged receipt of the illuminated parchment signed with great ceremony by the Franco-American Union in July of 1880, which marked the successful conclusion of the fund-raising campaign in France.

Bartholdi found this lack of response disturbing and complained to American friends living in Paris.[1] One of these, J. W. Pinchot, wrote in April 1881 to Richard Butler, secretary of the American Committee, urging him to ask William Evarts to write Laboulaye soon about the American Committee's intentions, but it was not until that fall that members of the committee finally made some preliminary plans for raising money. On November 18, 1881, Richard Butler sent copies of the American Committee's subscription appeals to Levi Morton in Paris. His accompanying letter said in part:

You will observe in looking the enclosed papers over that we have taken up the "statue" business in blood earnest. . . . Say to dear Bartholdi that I have got the work well in hand and have no doubt about prompt and good results.

Mr. Evarts is cooperating cordially and attending all of our meetings from which you will soon hear results as the various sub-committees are each doing their quota of the work.

An appeal to the country will soon be issued, and we shall expect to associate gentlemen of prominence from every state making the matter national as far as can be—New York, of course, will have to raise I fancy one half to three quarters of the whole and that whole will probably reach $200,000. . . . I shall write Bartholdi after our next meeting and try to give him some cheering words. The dear fellow has had a

Opposite.
Liberty's copper arm and torch in Madison Square Park, New York City, ca. 1877–82. Musée Bartholdi, Colmar.

When the Philadelphia Centennial Exhibition closed, the torch was dismantled and shipped to New York, where it remained on display until 1882. It was then sent back to Paris to be united with the rest of the statue.

sorry time with this noble work, and I have fully sympathized with him, but as the Committee would not go on until we could be assured of its completion at a certain time—I had to relinquish my enthusiasm and bide my time.

"All's well that ends well" and perhaps it is as well that we have deferred action until this opportune moment . . .[2]

And on December 3, 1881, William Evarts wrote directly to Laboulaye:

I assure you, my dear M. de Laboulaye, that we have no doubt that our compatriots will joyfully furnish the money for the pedestal, and that we shall be able to complete its construction in ample time for it to receive the noble statue which your genius and your generosity have offered us . . .

Early in 1882, Richard Morris Hunt, one of America's most fashionable architects, was asked to design the pedestal. Hunt had studied at the École des Beaux Arts in Paris and later worked on the construction of the Pavillon de la Bibliothèque at the Louvre during the Second Empire. After he returned to the United States in 1855, he was soon in great demand by America's newly rich. He designed mansions in a facile eclectic style that was as much admired by his clients as it was criticized by his fellow architects. Bartholdi was regularly in touch with Hunt exchanging ideas and sketches for the design of the pedestal.

The most demanding task for the American Committee, however, was raising the funds for the massive pedestal. The committee's first appeal was published in January 1882 while memories of the Victory of Yorktown Centennial celebration were still fresh in the minds of the American people. Circulated throughout the United States, the appeal invited . . . "Not only individual citizens, but Chambers of Commerce, Boards of Trade, Exchanges, Tradesmen's and Mechanics' Associations and Social Clubs, and other legal or voluntary organizations" to take part in "this grand, patriotic enterprise."[3]

"The committee feels assured," it continued, "that the American people will be only too eager to testify their grateful sense of the friendliness of this magnanimous offer on the part of the French people, and to reciprocate the kindly and liberal sentiments in which it originated, by a prompt acceptance of it and in active prosecution of the labors that may be required to give the statue an appropriate

Richard Morris Hunt, 1828–95. National Park Service.

Hunt (brother of William Morris Hunt) was the first American architect to study at the École des Beaux Arts in Paris. When he returned to New York, he brought with him a formidable reference library of books on architecture. "Those were the days," commented Henry Ives Cobb Jr., "when to be original meant having an architectural book that none of the other fellows had." Hunt soon became one of New York's most fashionable architects and is known today especially for the chateaux and "cottages" he designed for wealthy Americans (including Marble House and The Breakers at Newport, Rhode Island). One of his most famous structures, however, was one of New York's first skyscrapers. The Tribune Building, completed in 1875, at a height of 260 feet (nine stories), predates the era of the steel skeleton. Its walls were made of thick masonry.

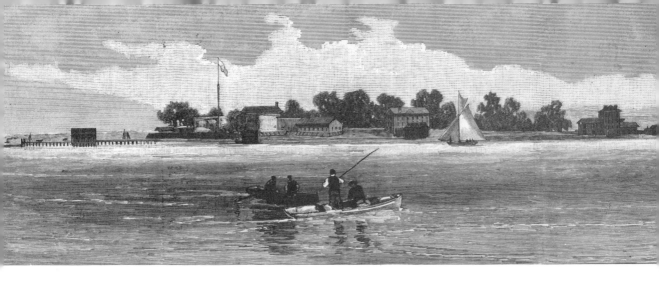

View of Bedloe's Island, May 19, 1883.
Frank Leslie's Illustrated Newspaper.

Bartholdi chose Bedloe's Island as the site for Liberty when he first visited New York in 1871. The island derived its name from the Dutch farmer, Isaac Bedloe, who acquired it in 1667. Since that time, the island had served as a site of a quarantine station, a summer resort, a pest house, and finally, an army post. Fort Wood was built over a period of three years (1808–11) in anticipation of war with Britain, which came in 1812. When this wood engraving was published, workers had just started digging up the parade ground of Fort Wood for the pedestal's foundation.

setting and pedestal."

The Americans, however, were not eager to contribute to the pedestal fund. The committee's request generated so little interest that less than $85,000 had been collected by the end of 1883. Most of the contributions from wealthy New Yorkers or local businesses were in amounts of over $100. John Jacob Astor gave $5,000; Joseph Drexel, $5,000; the Union Ferry Company, $2,000; Cornelius Vanderbilt, $500; P. T. Barnum, $250. Liberty boxes, much like poor boxes, were placed all over the city by the Sons of the Revolution, but collected a mere $2,355. In March 1883, Congress voted down a bill appropriating $100,000 for the construction of the pedestal. This was especially disappointing since earlier that month Congress had approved $400,000 for the New Orleans World Exhibition.

Despite this major disappointment, actual work on the pedestal was started. General Charles P. Stone was appointed chief engineer in charge of building the foundation and pedestal and reconstructing the statue once it arrived in New York. In April 1883, ground was broken for the foundation, and the workers proceeded to excavate a pit nearly twenty feet deep on the parade ground of Fort Wood on Bedloe's Island.

This proved to be a much more difficult task than had been anticipated. The ground beneath the fort was a beehive of stone magazines and bomb-proof shelters. These had to be broken up and leveled—a task that slowed the construction schedule and cost considerably more than had been budgeted.

The difficulty of the Americans' task, not just with fund-raising but also the actual construction of the foundation and pedestal, seems to have taken its toll on everyone involved. At one point, Joseph Drexel, chairman of the American Committee, wrote a letter to his wife describing the constant disputes between the engineer and the contractor: "I shall have to go down to Bedloe's Island at least once a week until the work is finished as I find all hands including the committee are very much inclined to quarrel."[4]

At a time when things looked particularly bleak on the American side, the sad news arrived from Paris that Edouard de Laboulaye had died on May 25, 1883. As president of the Franco-American Union, Laboulaye had been the guiding force behind the Liberty project since 1874. Many of the men who joined the American Committee did so because they felt a certain amount of indebtedness to Laboulaye for his vigorous defense of the Union cause during the Civil War. Indeed, nearly the entire membership of the American Committee was drawn from the roster of New York's Union League Club, which was organized in 1863 to counteract secessionist sympathy in the North and provide political support for Lincoln. Laboulaye was succeeded as president of the Franco-American Union by Ferdinand de Lesseps.

The Liberty campaign in America, however, was slowly gathering momentum, proving the inevitability of gradualness. Liberty found an energetic and dedicated advocate in Joseph Pulitzer, who was attracted to her cause as early as 1883. He would not, however, play a major role in raising funds for the pedestal for several more years.

Pulitzer had emigrated to the United States from Hungary in 1864. After serving a year in the Union army, he moved to St. Louis, studied law, and worked as a reporter. He managed to buy two small newspapers in the early 1870s, but he laid the foundation for his fortune when he purchased the *St. Louis Dispatch* in 1878.

He moved to New York in 1883 and purchased *The World* from J. P. Gould for $346,000. The sale was completed on May 10. Four days later, *The World* published the following editorial on its front page:

The statue, the noble gift of our young sister republic, is ready for us. And here, in the commercial metropolis of the Western world, where hundreds of our citizens reckon their wealth by millions, where our merchants and bankers and brokers are spoken of as "princes," we stand haggling and begging and scheming in order to raise enough money to

Liberty Feeding the World. Library of Congress.

Ad in Frank Leslie's Illustrated Newspaper, 1878. *Chemical Bank Archives.*

procure a pedestal on which to place the statue when it arrives in our harbor.

New York ought to blush at this humiliating spectacle. A quarter of a million dollars only needed for the base and pedestal, and the subscriptions crawling along at a snail's pace with the aid of fairs and theatrical performances given as for a local charity!

. . . As the rich citizens of New York have shown such apathy in this matter, let the poorer classes move. The World . . . offers to receive all sums of $1.00 and upwards that may be sent to its care. . . . Let us see if the people have more respect for the Statue of Liberty and the reputation of their city than the millionaires and "merchant princes."[5]

"Let the Advertising Agents Take Charge of the Bartholdi Business," a cartoon in Puck. *National Park Service.*

At one point during the fund-raising campaign, William Evarts received an offer from a company that wanted to contribute twenty-five thousand dollars to the pedestal fund if it could place its product's name, "Castoria", across the top of the pedestal for one year. This unusual proposal was declined. Other advertisers, however, made frequent use of Liberty's image without bothering to pay for permission. Liberty was enlisted to sell a gamut of American products, including thread, soda crackers, and champagne. An ad for soap showing Liberty holding high a bar of Sapolio was captioned "Liberty Enlightens the World and Sapolio Brightens It!"

Mrs. Cornelius Vanderbilt as the "Electric Light," 1883. *New-York Historical Society.*

Mrs. Vanderbilt, in a pose similar to Liberty's, was photographed at a lavish costume ball she held in March 1883. The party was her first in the new Vanderbilt mansion (Fifty-second Street and Fifth Avenue) designed by Richard M. Hunt. The ball, attended by one thousand New York socialites, cost $250,000—an amount equal to the cost of the pedestal for the Statue of Liberty.

Even this aggressive appeal, however, drew very little response. After writing a second editorial, which ran a month later, Pulitzer decided to give up the effort and to turn his attention to stories of political corruption and social reform. Two years later, he would raise the issue again and with much greater success, but for the time being the committee was on its own.

The American Committee held a Pedestal Fund Art Loan Exhibition in December, which brought in $13,674. In addition to paintings and sculpture, there was also a literary section featuring original manuscripts by Henry Wadsworth Longfellow, William Cullen Bryant, Bret Harte, Mark Twain, and Emma Lazarus, who wrote the poem "The New Colossus" especially for the occasion.

The committee also sold Bartholdi's autograph and small models of Liberty ($1 for a six-inch model, $5 for a twelve-inch model). As a last resort, Richard M. Hunt was urged to redesign the pedestal to a more modest height to save on the cost of granite. Hunt obliged

Statue of "Liberty Enlightening the World."

The Committee in charge of the construction of the base and pedestal for the reception of this great work, **in order to raise funds for its completion,** have prepared a miniature Statuette *six inches in height* — the statue bronzed; pedestal nickel-silvered — which they are now delivering to subscribers throughout the United States at **ONE DOLLAR EACH.**

This attractive souvenir and mantel or desk ornament is a *perfect fac-simile* of the model furnished by the artist.

The Statuette in same metal, *twelve inches high,* at **Five Dollars Each.** delivered.

Address, with remittance,
RICHARD BUTLER, Sec'y,
American Committee of the Statue of Liberty,
33 Mercer Street, New York.

Advertisement in a New York newspaper for Statue of Liberty models. Chemical Bank Archives.

On August 3, 1883, Bartholdi wrote to Richard Butler: "If agreeable, I will transfer temporarily to the New York Committee all royalties I am entitled to from my copyright, of which they might collect by authorizing the reproduction of the statue. This to take effect till the day that the subscription is closed at which date the committee would retransfer all contracts to me (they ought to be made, with this provision)."[6]

The Pedestal Fund Art Loan Exhibition, December 9, 1883. Harper's Weekly. Chemical Bank Archives.

The Pedestal Fund Art Loan Exhibition was held at the National Academy of Design at Twenty-third Street and Fourth Avenue in New York City. Wealthy New Yorkers lent paintings and sculptures from their private collections to be exhibited at the show. There was also a literary section that displayed writings by Henry Wadsworth Longfellow, William Cullen Bryant, Walt Whitman, Mark Twain, and Emma Lazarus. The exhibition succeeded in raising about $13,000.

Pedestal design by Richard Morris Hunt, August 3, 1883. National Park Service.

One of Hunt's first definitive designs for the pedestal specified a 114-foot-high tapered square mass of roughly textured stone with a pattern of projecting blocks and a portico with four Doric columns. The bottom of the pedestal is surrounded with a Doric frieze of round shields. Note the stamp, indicating that Hunt's office was in a building he designed, the Tribune building.

Pedestal design of Richard Morris Hunt, 1884. National Park Service.

In 1884, the American Committee asked Hunt to reduce the height of the pedestal. In addition to having genuine misgivings about the pedestal's great height overwhelming the statue, the committee was also becoming anxious about the cost of building such a large mass of granite and concrete. This model represents one of Hunt's first responses to the committee's request. It is probably the design that prompted Bartholdi to write Richard Butler: "I have recently written Hunt about the pedestal of which he has forwarded me a new design which I consider to be far inferior to the first. His first design I considered as very good, and advised him to keep as much as feasible of its general character."[8]

and reduced the height of the proposed structure by twenty-five feet. Ironically, the intricacy of the stonework in his new design actually added twenty thousand dollars to the cost of construction.

Meanwhile, the workers at Gaget, Gauthier et Cie. completed constructing the Statue of Liberty. On February 1, 1884, Bartholdi wrote to Butler that they were just finishing the interior staircase. "Let us hope," he added, "that when you receive this news from France, the patriotic spirit of America will awaken, and that funds will be coming in."[7]

That June, Governor Grover Cleveland vetoed a bill passed by the New York State Legislature appropriating fifty thousand dollars

for the pedestal fund on the ground that the bill was unconstitutional.

Despite the halting campaign to build the pedestal, the statue itself was finally presented to the people of the United States on July 4, 1884. The ceremony took place in the small yard outside the workshops of Gaget, Gauthier et Cie. The *New York Morning News* reported:

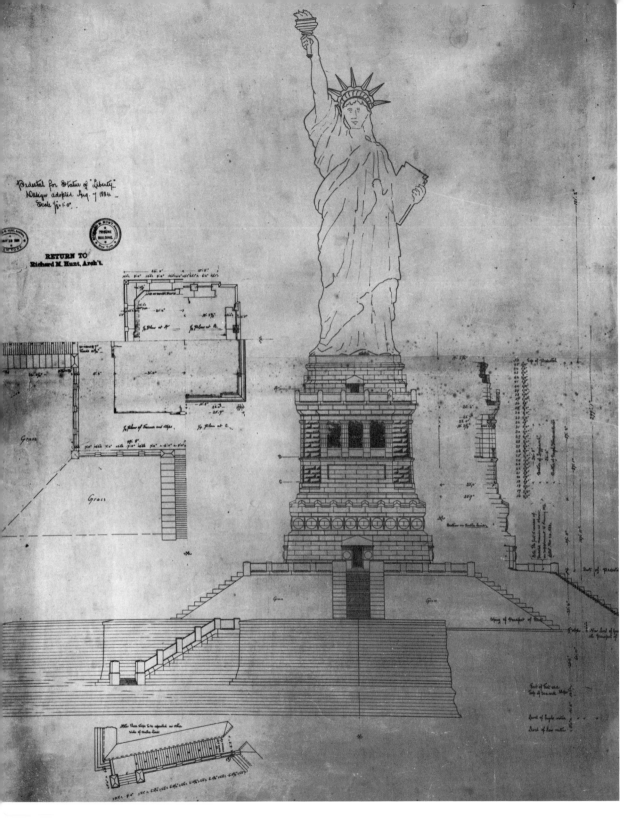

Opposite.
Pedestal design by Richard M. Hunt,
August 7, 1884. National Park Service.

Hunt submitted his final design two days
after the cornerstone of the pedestal was
laid. The rusticated stone was now limited to just the corners of the structure
and a tablet of smooth stone has been
added below the portico. The height of the
pedestal is eighty-nine feet.

*The biggest statue in creation was duly inaugurated yesterday on the big-
gest day of the American year. It was the mere formal handing over of
the statue by the representative of the French Republic to the representative
of the American Republic. If anything could have unbent the impassible
features of the statue, it would be the thought of her being "handed over"
by any of the pygmies at her feet. She towered above the yard and the
workshops and the people, and dwarfed everything into absolute insignif-
icance: even the American flag, proudly flying from the torch at the end
of her outstretched arm, seemed a mere ornament of a bride cake. It was
impossible to give oneself airs in such a presence, and the managers of the
fete seemed to have felt this, and to have arranged everything on a becoming scale of modesty of presence.*[9]

Liberty nears completion, 1884. Chemical
Bank Archives.

By August 1883, the head was raised
into place, and then over the winter, the
arm, hand, and torch were all safely installed. In February 1884, Bartholdi informed the American Committee that
"our statue is completed."[10] This wood
engraving, which appeared in Harper's
Weekly, shows the flame ready to be
hoisted to its lofty perch on top of the
torch. In the corner, a workman shows
the entrance to the statue through Liberty's foot.

The modesty of the affair was in part due to a cholera epidemic that had been raging in Paris since the beginning of the summer. Jules Ferry, the president of France, was advised by his doctor not to attend, but the venerable president of the Franco-American Union, Ferdinand de Lesseps, was present and made a gracious speech. He directed his remarks to Levi P. Morton, the American foreign minister to France:

This work, Mr. Minister, is the product of enthusiasm, of devotion, of intelligence, and of the noblest sentiments which can animate man. It is great in its conception and in its realization. It is colossal in its proportions, and we hope that it will grow still greater through its moral values, thanks to the remembrance and the sentiments which it is to perpetuate. We commit it to your care, Mr. Minister, that it may remain forever the pledge of the bonds which should unite France and the great American nation.

Morton then made an acceptance speech on behalf of the president of the United States, which sought to reassure the French that the statue would indeed be received in the same spirit of friendliness with which it was offered.

"After this," the *Morning News* reported, "the illustrious company, with M. Bartholdi leading the way, went to see the statue, entering by the door in the sole of the uplifted foot, and toiling steadily up the double staircase with nothing to guide their steps but the ten thousand little eyelets of sunlight that came through the rivet holes. Only a few persevered to the summit; most of them gave up half way; and, confounding the two staircases for the ascent and descent, were for some time lost to the world. It was the fancy of Rabelais over again—with his pygmies wandering about the interior of the monster."

Opposite.
The presentation of Liberty Enlightening the World to American minister to France, Levi P. Morton, July 4, 1884. Musée Bartholdi, Colmar.

Bartholdi's colossus remained a prominent feature on the Parisian skyline until January 1885, when the statue was dismantled for shipment to New York. In the meantime, thousands of people came to Gaget, Gauthier to see Liberty. Perhaps her most famous visitor was the aging Victor Hugo, who said: "Yes, this beautiful work aims at what I have always loved, called for: peace between America and France—France which is Europe—this pledge of peace will be permanent. It was a good thing that this should have been done."[11] Hugo later wrote an inscription for Bartholdi's history of Liberty, which read: "Form to the sculptor is all and yet nothing. It is nothing without the spirit; with the idea it is everything."[12]

c h a p t e r 4

PULITZER'S CAMPAIGN

T he cornerstone for the pedestal was laid on Bedloe's Island on August 5, 1884, just one month after the presentation ceremony in Paris. The Parisians had been blessed with sun, but the Americans were vexed with rain. Sheltered with black umbrellas against a steady downpour, an undaunted and loyal crowd gathered on the wind-swept foundation to observe the first great block of granite being lowered into place. The American Committee had hoped that an impressive ceremony covered by all the newspapers would breathe new life into its dying fund-raising campaign. These frail hopes were effectively dashed by the driving wind and rain. Two months later, with a mere two thousand dollars left in the treasury, all work on the pedestal had to be halted.

At first the American Committee was not overly concerned. Construction had to shut down for the winter anyway, and the members of the committee felt that by spring they would certainly have enough money to continue the work. In the meantime, as prominent Republicans they were very involved in the presidential campaign of James G. Blaine against Democrat Grover Cleveland. Joseph Pulitzer also had a great interest in the election and threw *The World*'s support solidly behind Cleveland.

It was a close race for the Republicans, who had been in power since Abraham Lincoln was elected in 1860, and it looked as if Blaine would prevail. Toward the end of the campaign, *The World* published (across the width of the front page), a cartoon depicting a political dinner honoring Blaine that had taken place at Delmonico's in New York. The main participants were shown feasting on "monopoly soup," "lobby pudding," and "Gould pie,"[1] while outside a poor starving family stood in a drift of snow. The guest list for that dinner included William Evarts, Levi Morton, Richard Butler, and other prominent members of the American Committee.

Also reported on the inside pages of *The World* was a speech by

Opposite.
The cornerstone laying ceremony for Liberty's pedestal, August 5, 1884. National Park Service.

WILLIAM A. BRODIE, THE GRAND MASTER

*Laying the cornerstone of the pedestal for
the Statue of Liberty, August 5, 1884.
Harper's Weekly, August 16, 1884.
Chemical Bank Archives.*

*The ceremonies were conducted in Ma-
sonic tradition and presided over by
Grand Master William A. Brodie. The
copper casket placed inside the six-ton
granite cornerstone included among other
mementos a silver fifty-cent piece struck
in 1824, the year the Marquis de Lafayette made his triumphant return to the
United States. The accompanying article
in* Harper's Weekly *reflected mixed sentiments regarding Bartholdi's statue: "We
are not perhaps more sympathetic with
French ways of thought than are the English, but distance has removed from us
the facilities for misunderstanding the
French which the English so abundantly
enjoy; and the three several efforts to establish a republic in France, including
the latest and most auspicious, though
really having little in common with our
own political ideas, could scarcely fail to
strengthen a feeling of good-will which
had its origin in the boyish espousal of
our cause by Lafayette, and the succor
brought to our arms by Rochambeau and
De Grasse. There could not be a more fitting symbol of this feeling than that
which has been devised by M. Bartholdi.
It will be extremely discreditable to New
York, now that the part of France is
fully done, if preparations for receiving
and exhibiting the gift of France are not
made as fast as they are needed."*

a New York minister, the Reverend Samuel C. Burchard, excoriating
the Democrats as "the party of rum, Romanism and rebellion."
None of the Republicans who heard Burchard speak gave his words
a second thought until they read the lead editorial in *The World* the
next day:

*Let the party of Rum, Romanism and Rebellion resent the insult at the
polls.*[2]

The two articles tipped the scales just enough to give Cleveland
a victory in New York, which gave him the state and won the

The Statue of Liberty One Thousand Years Later: Waiting. Frank Leslie's Illustrated Newspaper. *August 30, 1884.*

Work on the pedestal was completely shut down in the fall of 1884 when only two thousand dollars remained in the American Committee's treasury.

Joseph Pulitzer (1847–1911), publisher of The World.

election. Blaine reflected afterward, "The good Lord sent me an ass in the shape of a preacher."

The following spring, the American Committee was still not able to authorize new work on the pedestal. On March 13, 1885, a story in the back pages of *The World* was headlined: "Committee Acknowledges Its Inability to Proceed with the Work." The committee's treasurer, Henry Spaulding, reported that of the $182,491.40 raised, $179,624.51 had been spent, leaving just $2,866.89. "There was a general discussion in the committee after Mr. Spaulding made his report. . . . What should be done!" *The World* cried. "It looks as though the committee has reached a crisis."

As Joseph Pulitzer scanned that day's edition, he saw the story and decided *The World* would do something about it. "As Cleveland was elected, Liberty will be erected," Pulitzer said. On March 16, the first front-page editorial appeared:

Money must be raised to complete the pedestal for the Bartholdi statue. It would be an irrevocable disgrace to New York City and the American Republic to have France send us this splendid gift without our having provided even so much as a landing place for it.

Nearly ten years ago the French people set about making the Bartholdi Statue. It was to be a gift emblematic of our attainment of the first century of independence. It was also the seal of a more serviceable gift they made to us in 1776, when, but for their timely aid, the ragged sufferers of Valley Forge would have been disbanded and the colonies would have continued a part of the British dominion. Can we fail to respond to the spirit that actuated this generous testimonial?

The statue is now completed and ready to be brought to our shore in a vessel especially commissioned for the purpose by the French Government. Congress, by a refusal to appropriate the necessary money to complete preparations for its proper reception and erection, has thrown the responsibility back to the American people.

There is but one thing that can be done. We must raise the money!

The World is the people's paper, and it now appeals to the people to come forward and raise the money. The $250,000 that the making of the statue cost was paid in by the masses of the French people—by the workingmen, the tradesmen, the shop girls, the artisans—by all, irrespective of class or condition. Let us respond in like manner. Let us not wait for the millionaires to give this money. It is not a gift from the millionaires of France to the millionaires of America but a gift of the *whole people of France to the whole people of America.*

Take this appeal to yourself personally. It is meant for every reader of The World. *Give something, however little. Send it to us. We will receive it and see that it is properly applied. We will also publish the name of every giver, however small the sum given.*

Over two thousand dollars was collected during the first week, to which *The World* added its own contribution of one thousand dollars. The American Committee issued its own appeal on March 23, and Pulitzer printed it on *The World*'s editorial page:

. . . our means for carrying on the work have failed. We have made many appeals to the people of the Nation, and they have not responded. Out of the $182,000 more than 90 percent has been subscribed by the citizens of New York and its immediate vicinity. We are constrained, therefore, to look to them for the completion of the noble and magnificent enterprise which they have so gloriously begun.

. . . We cannot believe that they will fail us in this our last appeal. If the money is not now forthcoming the statue must return to its donors, to the everlasting disgrace of the American people, or it must go to some other city, to the everlasting dishonor of New York. Citizens of the State, citizens of the metropolis, we ask you once for all to prevent so painful and humiliating a catastrophe! We ask you one and all, each according to his means, to contribute what he is able; we ask you in the name of glorious memories, in the name of our country, in the name of civilization and of art, not to neglect this last opportunity for securing to yourselves and to the Nation an imperishable glory.

Subscriptions may be sent to Henry F. Spaulding, Treasurer, at the office of the Central Trust Company, corner of Nassau and Pine Streets, or to any member of the committee.

But most donations were sent not to the committee but to *The World*, which continued to run editorials every day for the next six months until the goal of $100,000 was attained.

By April 15, just four weeks after the fund was started, over twenty-five thousand dollars had been collected. Contributors were listed on a special page underneath a drawing of Uncle Sam, top hat extended, and the headline: "The World's Bartholdi Pedestal Fund." Their letters were also published and revealed donors to be young office boys, working girls, struggling artists, recent immi-

"Progress of the work on the Pedestal," Frank Leslie's Illustrated Newspaper, *May 16, 1885.*

By April 1885, enough money had been raised to continue the construction of the pedestal. The World *campaign sparked cooperation from other New York papers. This wood engraving, published in a popular weekly, was accompanied by an inspiring plea: "Let us all have some part in this undertaking. Long after we are through the voyage of this life, that conflagration of good cheer will flash light upon the voyagers from the deep; and sailors, weary with battling the tempests, will bless it as they come through the Narrows; and the homesick from other lands will feel the glow of its international welcome. Light for the oppressed of all climes. Light for the travelers returning from a far to their own homestead. Light for all ships of all ensigns. Night by night, it will put upon the grandest harbor of the world, and upon the island it holds in its arms, a baptism of fire."*

grants, school children, the poor and the elderly.

Inclosed find $1 for the Pedestal fund.

—*Poor but not mean.*

I am a little boy. Would like to help you more. I send you my first gold dollar for the Bartholdi Fund.

—*Norman Allen*

Please find inclosed $7.25 as a first subscription to the Bartholdi Pedestal Fund. We, as workmen poor in pockets, but rich in patriotism, contribute our mite in hope that the example will be followed by workingmen generally, and shame the close-fisted millionaires if that be possible.

—*The Employees,*
Douglas Taylor, printer,
80 Nassau Street

I am a young man of foreign birth and have seen enough of monarchical governments to appreciate the blessing of this Republic. Inclosed please find $2 for the Bartholdi fund.

—*Nathan Fleisch*

"Uncle Sam's Awkwardness." Frank Leslie's Illustrated Newspaper, *June 13, 1885. Chemical Bank Archives.*

The Isère *would steam into New York harbor on June 19, 1885, less than a week after this cartoon appeared. But the pedestal for Liberty would not be completed until the following year.*

Some letters were so close to Pulitzer's point of view that they could have been written by a *World* staffer:

In response to your appeal as a Democratic tribute to the "Genius of Liberty," I suggest that those whose first ballot helped to erect a monument to the perpetuity of constitutional reform in the elevation of Grover Cleveland, manifest their gratification by contributing to the unfinished pedestal on Bedloe's Island. Inclosed find $1 which please "anchor to windward" of this project.

—E Pluribus Unum.

The order to resume stone-cutting was given in April, and by the middle of May construction of the pedestal was once again under way. Bartholdi was delighted with this unexpected turn of events. He wrote Pulitzer an effusive note of thanks and told him that Liberty was ready to be shipped and would be in New York soon.

The *Isère* left Rouen on May 21 and arrived off New York's Sandy Hook on June 17. A magnificent naval parade and reception were planned for June 19, and on that day the stately *Isère* trimmed with a hundred bright-colored flags steamed through the narrows and into the bay. *Frank Leslie's Illustrated Newspaper* reported:

The Isère, *surrounded by flagships and war vessels was exceedingly picturesque with her bright white sides, black, gold-trimmed boats and lofty masts. . . . At 12:15 the* Isère *rounded Bedloe's Island and cast anchor*

Arrival of the French transport steamer Isère, *June 19, 1885. Frank Leslie's Illustrated Newspaper, June 27, 1885. National Park Service.*

The arrival of the Isère, *June 19, 1885. Frank Leslie's Illustrated Newspaper. June 27, 1885. Chemical Bank Archives.*

One reporter called the parade that accompanied the Isère *into the city's harbor, "a splendid reception . . . the like of which has not been witnessed there for many years." The World reported that the* Isère's *precious cargo consisted of 214 crates weighing from 150 pounds to 3 tons each.*

ONE HUNDRED THOUSAND DOLLARS!

TRIUMPHANT COMPLETION OF THE WORLD'S FUND
FOR THE LIBERTY PEDESTAL.

Story of the Greatest Popular Subscription Ever Raised in America—How the Republic Was Saved from Lasting Disgrace—An Event for Patriotic Citizens to Rejoice Over—A Roll of Honor Bearing the Names of 120,000 Generous Patriots—The Flags of France and the American Union Floating in Sisterly Sympathy—Over $3,300 Received Yesterday—The Grand Total Foots Up $102,006.39—A Generous Lady Pays $130 for the Washington Cent.

"One Hundred Thousand Dollars!" The World, August 11, 1885. National Park Service.

The World *was not above congratulating itself for a job well done; it often ran articles detailing the newspaper's many virtues and triumphs. But the pedestal fund must have been especially gratifying, and Pulitzer did not shrink from taking full credit.*

300 feeet offshore. The guns from Bedloe's Island crashed with a deafening noise. Fort William replied with a rapid and heavy firing. A hundred steam-whistles shrieked, and 10,000 people waved handkerchiefs and flags.[3]

The World announced on August 11 that it had reached its goal of $100,000, the amount needed to complete the construction of the pedestal, assuring the Statue of Liberty a proper home in America. On the front page of *The World* a flag-waving Liberty watched as Uncle Sam completed writing this inscription:

This pedestal to Liberty was provided by the voluntary contributions of 120,000 patriotic citizens of the American Union through the New York World. *Finis coronat opus. (The end crowns the work.)*

The pedestal was completed the following year on April 22. The jubilant workers threw a shower of silver coins into the mortar before the last granite block was lowered into place.

The work of raising Liberty's iron skeleton started immediately. Throughout May and June, an assembly of iron bars and beams rose gradually atop the pedestal. On July 12, the process of riveting the copper plates onto the skeleton began. Many of the huge pieces boxed up so long, shaken about in so many handlings and exposed to a great variety of temperatures, had flattened out of their original shape. There was a great deal of delay in reforming and realigning them so they could be fastened into their proper place on the skeleton.

The American Committee also faced serious delays in arranging the statue's inaugural celebration. First, they had to raise more money. The $100,000 from *The World* (actually $102,006.39) paid for the pedestal, but more was needed to re-erect the statue and to organize a suitable dedication. The Franco-American Union, of course, expected to be invited to New York to witness this great event, and Richard Butler was receiving letters almost weekly from Bartholdi concerning their plans.

Congress was appealed to for funds on the basis of the resolution passed in 1877, which stipulated that the United States Government, on completion of the statue, "shall cause the same, to be inaugurated with such ceremonies as will serve to testify the gratitude of our people for this expressive and felicitous memorial." The

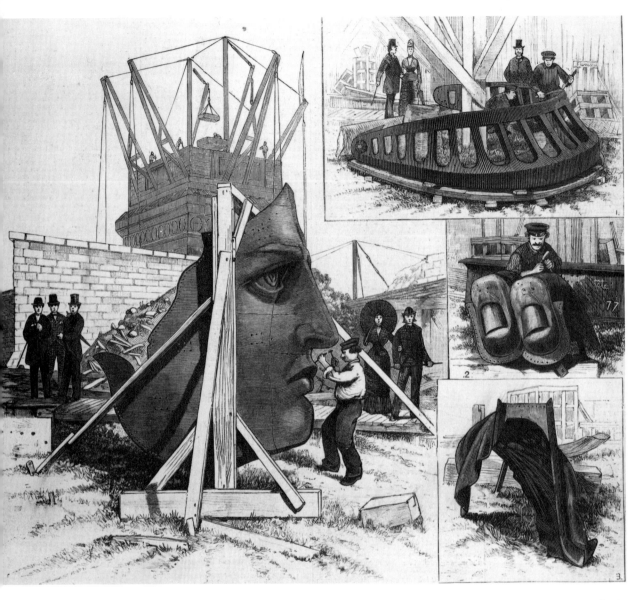

same resolution also provided for Liberty's care and maintenance as a lighthouse. Thus, reasoned the bill's sponsors, Congress would have to appropriate some money to abide by the resolution. The American Committee was asking for $106,100.

The debates in the House and the Senate were lively, particularly on the point of what refreshments would be served at Liberty's dedication. At one point, a Democrat from Pennsylvania who favored the appropriation wagged his finger at its New York sponsors saying:

Reassembling Liberty on Bedloe's Island. Frank Leslie's Illustrated Newspaper, October 17, 1885. A sort of sculpture park was created around the base of the pedestal when the copper fragments were uncrated and pieced together. One reporter called the scene highly picturesque, remarking on Liberty's iron framework, which was painted a bright vermilion. In the spot with Liberty's fingers, the iron beam in the background is marked "tête-77" showing the location of that piece in the skeleton.

The face of Liberty on Bedloe's Island, 1885–86. National Park Service.

Liberty's toes on Bedloe's Island, 1885–86. National Park Service.

The statue's pedestal and supporting iron framework. Scientific American, *June 13, 1885. National Park Service.*

The pedestal, like the foundation, was made of concrete, but faced with granite block. Inside the pedestal's shaftway, two sets of steel girders were built into the concrete walls. The first set was placed twenty-nine feet from the bottom of the pedestal; the second set was close to the top. The iron framework of the statue was attached to these top girders with giant bolts measuring five and one-half inches in diameter, and the two sets of girders were connected with chains of steel tie-bars set as close to the walls of the shaftway as possible. Thus, the statue's framework was firmly anchored through a series of massive bolts, steel girders, and tie-bars to the lower end of the pedestal.

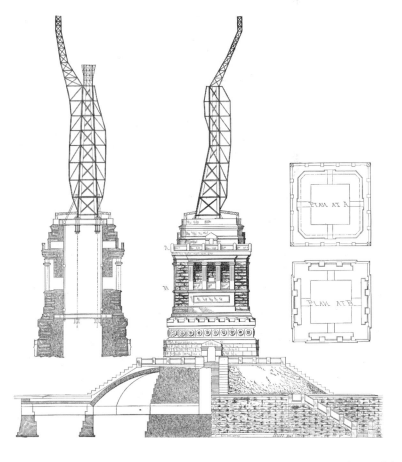

Opposite.

Liberty under construction on Bedloe's Island. Scientific American, *August 14, 1886. New York Public Library.*

The large loop of copper on the left-hand side of this wonderful wood engraving is Liberty's right foot. Note the confusing array of iron ribs laid out on a platform at the bottom of the drawing. Each rib had to be fitted into its exact place on the armature. The article that accompanied this view explained that extensive refitting had to be done because the iron and copper pieces were somewhat flattened and distorted from their year-long storage. "This, together with the drawbacks under which the men labor," said the article, "particularly the height above ground, renders the otherwise simple work of erection one of great magnitude. The thousands of rivets add most materially to the labor, as they must be so driven as not to disfigure the statue by presenting conspicuous and unseemly lines."

Liberty under construction on Bedloe's Island. Frank Leslie's Illustrated Newspaper, *August 21, 1886. National Park Service.*

An article published in The World *(July 12, 1886) gives us some idea of the difficulties encountered in reconstructing this gigantic work: "Each iron bone has its appropriate place in the skeleton and will fit no other. By carelessness several of these were improperly marked, and Mr. C. O. Long, the Superintendent, was sometimes obliged to raise and lower twenty pieces before he found the right one. As each had to be raised some 200 feet, these were no light tasks." The giant derrick mounted on top of the skeleton was driven by a steam engine located at the base of the pedestal.*

You were too mean to contribute the necessary funds and went begging and preyed upon the patriotic sentiment of the country to furnish the means of erecting a pedestal on which to set your Statue of Liberty. You have been begging throughout the length and breadth of the land for that pedestal and now you want to have a grand spree, and you want the people to go to your city to make it a success. But you think you cannot do it yourselves, and you come to the Government again and go down on your marrow bones begging for a miserable hundred thousand dollars to have this spree. I'm willing you should have it. If it's to be done at all, it should be done right. I will say, God knows if there is any place in the world that requires enlightenment it is New York City . . .[4]

An appropriation was finally passed for $56,100 with the stipulation that none of the money could be spent on hard liquor.

Liberty under construction on Bedloe's Island. Frank Leslie's Illustrated Newspaper, *October 9, 1886. Chemical Bank Archives.*

Although the drawing of the exposed skeleton is incorrect, and the rendering of Liberty's drapery a bit clumsy, this is a stunning view of the work in progress. Frank Leslie's reported: "The stupendous size and majesty of the figure are now for the first time fully apparent, and the effect is truly sublime. . . . Workmen are at present moving like industrious ants over the classic draperies and uplifted arm of the mighty figure. They remind one of the Lilliputians swarming over Gulliver in the picture-books; or if they will pardon the comparison, like New Jersey mosquitoes attacking a summer boarder." *The Americans did not build scaffolding around the outside of the statue, as the French workmen did in Paris. Instead, wooden seats, like bos'n chairs, were suspended by ropes from the iron framework and lowered over the outside edge of the copper shell.*

Opposite.
The interior of Liberty's head. Frank Leslie's Illustrated Newspaper, *October 23, 1886. Chemical Bank Archives.*

The artist "climbed amidst falling bolts and clouds of smoke and dust, to the rayed diadem . . . of the now perfect statue of Liberty" *to draw this extraordinary view of the great statue's head.*

chapter 5

THE UNVEILING

By October 10, 1886, the statue was virtually finished. The arm and torch were in place, and the workmen were busy putting the final touches on the seams and rivets. The last piece of copper—the sole of Liberty's right sandal—was riveted into place on October 25, 1886. Throughout construction workmen had entered the great statue by way of her foot. Now, the opening was sealed off in preparation for the inauguration on October 28.

Apart from the statue itself, the most talked about topic on the day of Liberty's unveiling was the weather. The *Evening Post* said:

Many anxious glances were cast skyward early this morning, and little consolation could be derived from the threatening aspect of the heavens . . . the sky was still heavy with drifting clouds, the wind blew with abominable persistency from the northeast, and a mist veiled the Statue of Liberty and almost everything else in a most effective but dispiriting manner.

There was however one solid bit of ground for satisfaction. It was not raining. . . . It was plain enough from the earliest hours of the morning that the great mass of the people had made up their minds to celebrate the unveiling of the colossal statue of Liberty with something of a general holiday. The rush to New York from all quarters was wonderful. It was probably as great as it was on the memorable day of Gen. Grant's funeral. Excursion trains brought thousands of country visitors here yesterday and the day before, and the influx continued this morning. . . . The hurrying crowds were made gay by flashes of bright uniforms here and there. The red shirts of veteran firemen, the glitter of polished metal on some old hand-engine, the gold epaulettes, and an occasional white feather all helped to give color to the scene, to say nothing of the flags which flaunted themselves bravely everywhere in complete defiance of any attempt of the elements to dispirit them. [1]

Unveiling of the Statue of Liberty, October 28, 1886. Photograph by H. O'Neill. Library of Congress.

Shrouded in fog, mist, and smoke, Liberty towers over the clusters of paddle-wheel steamers packed with spectators. For fifty cents, each passenger got a box lunch and a choice view of one of America's most thrilling celebrations.

At 10:30, President Grover Cleveland and the American officials met Bartholdi, Ferdinand de Lesseps, and the French delegation at the reviewing stand at Madison Square. Cleveland clasped Bartholdi's hand warmly saying, "You are the greatest man in America today."

The parade started at Fifth Avenue and Fifty-seventh Street and wended its way over a three-and-one-half-mile route down to the Battery. Over twenty thousand marchers took part. Fife and drum corps played a medley of the "Marseillaise," "Yankee Doodle," and

Edward Moran 1886

"Hail to the Chief." The American brigades were followed by the
Rochambeau Grenadiers and the French societies. Then came the
city officials in their carriages—judges, aldermen, and the mayor.

Richard Hunt and August Bartholdi on Bedloe's Island, n.d. Musée Bartholdi, Colmar.

Opposite.
Unveiling of the Statue of Liberty, oil painting by Edward Moran, 1886. Museum of the City of New York.

"*Liberty, it is thine hour of arrival!*" wrote the Cuban patriot José Marti for *La Nacion of Buenos Aires.* "*Flags are reflected on faces, heartstrings are plucked by a sweet love, a superior sense of sovereignty brings to countenances a look of peace, nay of beauty. And all these luckless Irishmen, Poles, Italians, Bohemians, Germans redeemed from oppression or misery, hail the monument to Liberty because they feel that through it they themselves are uplifted and restored. . . . In her presence, eyes once again know what tears are. She seemed alive, wrapped in clouds of smoke, covered by a vague brightness, truly like an altar with steamers kneeling at her feet!*"[2]

The police departments from New York, Brooklyn, and Philadelphia marched, as did the volunteer firemen, the Knights of Pythias and Templar, and the Italian Rifle Guards.

George Washington's carriage was included in the procession. Drawn by eight dappled gray horses, it was escorted by the Continental Guards. There were uniformed cadets from the military schools and students dressed in black academic gowns and mortarboards from Columbia University and the University of the City of New York. Three little girls marching in the parade presented a silk flag to Bartholdi and flowers to the president.

Throughout it all, reported the newspapers, Cleveland stood at his post on the reviewing stand. Despite a steady drizzle, he "religiously removed his hat in response to every salute tendered him."

As the last of the land parade passed Madison Square, the president's party hurried across Twenty-third Street to board the *Dispatch,* the presidential yacht, to take part in the naval procession.

Then, a flotilla of ships forming a naval parade swept like nautical ghosts toward the mist-shrouded and gigantic statue that loomed up through the fog to the southward. . . . The flotilla was inside of the warships, which were anchored in the following order: Yantic, Alliance, Tennessee, Portsmouth, Saratoga, and Jamestown. The tugs and steamers were crowded so close together that every one said, "How like an international yacht race." The calm weather, the dreary, foggy day and the crowd of boats did indeed make one expect to see the Galatea and Mayflower drift down the bay.

But over all and above all, towering grand through the mist, the gigantic statue with its veiled face made one realize that a grander procession was at hand. Presently, a spectral ship with ghostly flags flying from its rigging came steaming by the fleet. At the main flew the President's flag . . . and as the Dispatch passed along, flame and smoke bursting through the mist from the ports of the men-o-war saluted it and a grand chorus of steam whistles from the other boats shook the heavy wreaths of fog. The President landed on the island while this earsplitting chorus was going on and for a time comparative quiet reigned over the fleet. Every eye now watched the flag that enveloped the colossal face of the statue that towered up so grandly above. The clouds of mist and smoke and steam rolled around and enveloped it like the smoke of the battles in which its prototype was born. Suddenly the tricolor vanished and looking down through the fog and rain was that mighty human face. At that moment the guns from the men-of-war and from the mist-wreathed walls of Castle William burst forth a tremendous salvo of artillery and all the steam whistles in the flotilla blew as they never blew before.

On Bedloe's Island itself, a platform had been built next to the pedestal. The president arrived shortly after two o'clock when the unveiling program of speeches was scheduled to begin. Ferdinand de Lesseps, president of the Franco-American Union, spoke first and was followed by William Evarts, his American counterpart. Bartholdi meanwhile was standing on a separate platform out of view of the speaker, waiting to pull a cord that would draw the French tricolor from Liberty's face. Through a mix-up in signals, this was done in the middle of Evarts's address. He tried to continue speaking through the roar of cannon and blowing of whistles but eventually gave up; the tremendous din that greeted Liberty's unveiling persisted for fifteen minutes. When the noise level dropped to something approaching normal, President Cleveland rose to make his speech accepting the statue on behalf of the American people. He said in part:

Instead of grasping in her hand thunderbolts of terror and death, she holds aloft the light which illumines the way to man's enfranchisement. We will not forget that Liberty has made here her home nor shall her chosen altar be neglected. Willing votaries will constantly keep alive its fires, and there it shall gleam upon the shores of our sister republic in the East. Reflected thence and joined with answering rays, a stream of light shall pierce the darkness of ignorance and man's oppression until liberty enlightens the world.[3]

In stories about the Statue of Liberty, these words of Grover Cleveland are almost always included. Of all the verbiage produced that day, this one paragraph seems to express most eloquently the idea behind Liberty's creation—that the alliance of two great republics exerted a powerful, proselytizing influence on all other governments. This at a time when most of the world was still ruled by kings, and the United States and France stood virtually alone at the threshold of a new age of democracy.

The unveiling of the Statue of Liberty called forth a celebration that *The New York Times* said was like "a hundred Fourths of July

The Statue of Liberty fireworks display. Harper's Weekly, November 6, 1886. Chemical Bank Archives.

Because of the heavy rain on October 28, the fireworks had to be postponed, finally taking place three nights later. The statue was illuminated with floodlights and the light from the torch projected through two rows of circular windows cut into the flame. The effect was very disappointing, however, and even Bartholdi remarked that the torch was no brighter than a glowworm.

broke loose" at the same time. There was at least one dissenting opinion, however—that of the New York State Women's Suffrage Association. The Suffragettes were denied permission to take part in the formal ceremonies on Bedloe's Island as were all women except the wives of the French officials. However, the undiscouraged Suffragettes hired their own boat and observed the ceremonies from the water in a prime spot in front of the reviewing stand. Later, they issued a statement declaring:

. . . in erecting A Statue of Liberty embodied as a woman in a land where no woman has political liberty, men have shown a delightful lack of consistency which excites the wonder and admiration of the opposite sex.[4]

American women finally won the right to vote in 1920, but French women had to wait until 1945 to cast their first ballots.

Across the Atlantic, *The Times* of London called the unveiling "a curious festival" and asked why "Liberty should be exported from France, which has so little thereof, to America, which has so much."[5]

The unveiling of Liberty Enlightening the World presented other ironies as well. In the United States in 1886, thousands of black citizens freed from slavery just two decades before found themselves cut off from America's promise of liberty by violent and vicious bigotry. In the North, powerful industrialists were quickly creating a new system of near slavery as nonunionized workers labored long and hard for subsistence wages. In the West, tribes of American Indians were being systematically uprooted, subdued, and herded onto reservations.

Yet to the rest of the world America was the land of liberty, a new world where Providence had given mankind a second chance to create a civilization—this time free of monarchy and based on democratic ideals. Sited at the gateway of a young, brash nation, Liberty expressed this message of redemption in a way that was vivid and moving, especially for people coming to America for the first time.

The drama of the statue's presence was recognized by nearly everyone who witnessed the unveiling; and the next day the following editorial appeared in *The New York Herald*:

Amid the uproar and excitement that succeeded the consecration of the statue, there glided through the Narrows a huge steamship crowded with European immigrants. From her decks the eyes of the strangers were fixed upon the wonderful drama in progress before them. The cannon smoke and the vapor rolled up, and ringed in a huge, fire-fringed semi-circle, they saw before them the mighty figure of Liberty. Imagination can hardly conceive what to their tired eyes, weary with the hardships, the hopelessness and the cruelties of the Old World, this apparition must have conveyed; but surely, whatever else it signified, it could not have meant less to them than

> *Such glories as the Patriarch viewed, when, through the darkest skies,*
> *He saw above the ruined world the Bow of Promise rise.*

Opposite.
Immigrant family on dock at Ellis Island, 1912. Photograph by Underwood & Underwood, Library of Congress.

Father points out the New York skyline to his family while they await the ferry to take them away from Ellis Island.

Ellis Island

chapter 6

THE GREAT MIGRATION

Emigration from Europe during the nineteenth and early twentieth centuries represents the largest mass movement of people in world history. Nearly sixty million people packed up their belongings and traveled thousands of miles to seek new opportunities in new lands, to find political or religious freedom. Not all the emigrants came to the United States. Australia, New Zealand, Argentina, Brazil, and Canada attracted about one third of the total emigrant population, and millions more moved from one country to another within European boundaries. Of the overseas alternatives, however, the United States was the land of choice for most emigrants. Throughout the hundred years previous to 1924 when America's open-door policy was abruptly halted, over thirty-four million Europeans were admitted to this country.

This great migration was spurred in large part by the effects of the Industrial Revolution—a term so familiar that it no longer seems to express adequately the phenomenal changes and social upheaval that took place during the nineteenth century. New technology, new inventions, and new materials, new concepts of self-government and the rights of man wrenched the centuries-old European culture from its traditional mainstays of land, church, and aristocracy and thrust it headlong into a modern age. The effects of this great revolution, along with a steady growth in Europe's population, displaced an ancient social system and induced millions to leave their homes, and attempt to find their livelihoods elsewhere.

The migration to America started to gain momentum after the Napoleonic Wars. During the 1820s and 1830s, six hundred thousand—primarily English and Irish—entered the United States. Then, over the next two decades, immigration exceeded three million. This tremendous surge in numbers is attributable to disastrous circumstances in both Ireland and Germany. The first of several potato famines occurred in Ireland in 1845. Thousands died of outright

Opposite.
Immigrants on deck of S.S. Amerika, 1907. Library of Congress.

"The parents of some of our splendid citizens went through a life of hardship and sacrifice. It is no wonder that so many of their children have made valuable contributions to American life, for they valued what they and their parents got after such effort . . . Look around you in any part of this country: the immigrants have contributed more than their share to building its power and its wealth."—Fiorello H. LaGuardia.[1]

starvation and over one and a half million persons were forced out of their homeland. Many Irish, desperately poor, came to the United States on tickets paid for by landlords wanting to clear their land of tenants. In Germany, the brutal suppression of the 1848 revolution prompted political refugees to emigrate, as well as many more seeking economic opportunity. During the next ten years nearly one million Germans came to America. The financial depression of 1857 and then the Civil War brought about a temporary decline in immigration. By the 1870s, however, Scandinavians who had been arriving in small numbers in previous decades were now arriving in the hundreds of thousands.

These groups from the northern European countries came to be known as the "old" immigrants. The "new" immigrants from Italy, Russia, Austro-Hungary, and Poland arrived in great numbers starting in the 1880s and continuing for the next five decades. A large percentage of the eastern Europeans were Jews who had been cruelly driven from their homes by a series of pogroms and discriminatory laws passed by the Czarist government. Other nationalities were compelled to emigrate by a combination of economic forces that had been developing and gathering strength since the first decades of the nineteenth century. A marked growth of Europe's population and a serious shortage of arable farmland reduced many farmers, craftsmen, and laborers to extreme poverty. The Industrial Revolution and expansion of the railroad brought local craftsmen into competition with large manufacturers who could transport their goods to every corner of Europe quickly and cheaply. The new demands of a modern industrial age coupled with the burdens of a semifeudal society—high taxes, old debts, and oppressive military requirements—led many to think seriously about making a dramatic break with the past and starting over in the new world.

"I inform you that I intend to emigrate to America," wrote one young Pole to the Emigrants Protective Association in Warsaw. "I know only one handicraft, carpenter's. I practiced with a country carpenter, but at the present time it is very difficult to find material, and therefore difficult to earn. We have little land, and I have a sister and two brothers. I am eighteen years old; so if I can go to America and get work . . . before the call to the army I could earn still more money." Another Polish peasant wrote, "I have a very great wish to go to America. I want to leave my native country because we are six children and we have very little land. . . . Here

Greek immigrants embarking in small boat for steamship to America. Patras, Greece, 1910. Library of Congress.

Many Greek, Italian, and Slavic men followed a pattern of migration that brought them to the United States in the spring and returned them home in time for Christmas. Immigration officials called them "birds of passage." These immigrants left their tiny villages to work in American factories, or on railroad construction, or in textile mills. When they had saved enough money, they could either go home or send for their families to join them here. As time passed, more and more chose to stay.

in our country one must work plenty and wages are very small, just enough to live, so I would like to go in the name of our Lord God; perhaps I would earn more there." Craftsmen, whose work depended on a prosperous agricultural economy, also suffered. "I am a blacksmith," wrote one, "a specialist in agricultural machine work, and even a good one, in the opinion of my superiors. I should like to sell my strength in a profitable way, which is impossible among us. In England even a farm-laborer earns 500 rubles a year, whereas here a capable factory worker can barely vegetate. If he earns 350 rubles a year it is considered good."[2]

While many of the "old" immigrants were attracted by the chance to own their own land, the "new" immigrants were drawn by the promise of high wages. America, too, was undergoing enormous growth in its manufacturing and transportation industries and would outstrip European competitors by the end of the century. The last half of the nineteenth century saw the settling of half the American continent, the construction of over 150,000 miles of railroad, the production of record-breaking amounts of coal and steel, and the amassing of enormous personal fortunes. By 1900, despite two great depressions in the 1870s and 1890s, caused by reckless speculation and overexpansion, the United States was the wealthiest country in the world, far surpassing England, France, and Germany in manufacturing and trade. One of the critical factors in America's growth was the seemingly endless supply of cheap labor that came from the impoverished districts of European countries.

Life in the United States, apart from its economic benefits, had other appealing aspects for those in Europe who were contemplating emigration. America had a strong tradition as a haven for the oppressed. As Thomas Paine wrote in *Common Sense* one hundred years before, it was "the asylum for the persecuted lovers of civil and religious liberty from every part of Europe." These liberties were guaranteed and protected by the Constitution and the Bill of Rights. Ethnic minorities were not barred by law from owning property, going to school, practicing their religion, or reading or writing what they pleased. In Europe, many had felt the sting of discrimination because of their religion or nationality: Jews living in Rumania, Russia and Poland; Poles in Germany; Croats and Serbs in Hungary; the Irish under English rule. For some immigrants the flourishing foreign-language press in America provided their first opportunity to read a newspaper in their own language, a language that may have been banned in the old country.

Letters from those who had already emigrated often gave glowing reports of the freedom and opportunity enjoyed by all social classes living in the United States: "I am living in God's noble and free soil," wrote a Swede who had settled in Iowa in 1850. "I have now been on American soil two and a half years, and I have not been compelled to pay a penny for the privilege of living. Neither is my cap worn out from lifting it in the presence of gentlemen."[3] Letters like this were read aloud to friends and family still at home and sometimes published in the local newspapers. Successful emigrants also described the abundance of food, the quality of the soil, the comfortable homes, the variety of jobs, and the cost of living. They also gave advice to those who might be thinking about coming to America.

Returned emigrants were able to tell their stories first-hand. Sometimes they had saved up enough money to buy a farm or open a business once they had come back to their home country. "Here at home the savings of the American emigrant practically works miracles," observed one Hungarian in 1911. "It makes the villages bloom, covers the lovely thatched houses with tile roofs, brings machinery to an agricultural production that earlier had subsisted on the most primitive tools."[4]

Emigrant guide books, newspaper articles, and promotional brochures from states in the Midwest and West seeking settlers, steamship lines selling ocean passage, and railway companies selling transcontinental tickets all spread the good word about America as a new "promised land." The big trans-Atlantic steamship companies looking for trade (White-Star, Cunard, Hamburg-America, La Compagnie Générale Transatlantique) were especially aggressive in promoting an extravagant and inviting image of the United States. They had thousands of agents throughout Europe distributing posters and brochures and selling tickets. *Scribner's Monthly* wrote of this phenomenon in 1877:

There is scarcely a hamlet in all England which has not been invaded by the emissaries of one of the great steamship lines. Either in the tavern, the reading room, or the apothecary's shop, a bold red-and-black placard is displayed, bearing the names of half a dozen vessels and the dates of their sailings. Honest Giles, sitting of an evening in his accustomed place by the fire-side of the village inn, has it constantly before him, and makes it the text of many long chats with his neighbors about the wonderful land in the west. . . . Letters often come to the village . . . with small amounts of money or photographs which represent the writers as brighter-looking and in better dress than they ever appeared at home.[5]

After an initial few from a village had been persuaded to embark for America, it was only a matter of time before others followed. By the turn of the century, the majority of immigrants to the United States were traveling on tickets sent to them by relatives or friends who were already more or less comfortably settled in the New World.

Group of Italian street laborers working under Sixth Avenue elevated, New York City, 1910. Photograph by Lewis W. Hine. New York Public Library.

At a Russian boarding house, Homestead, Pa., 1909. Photograph by Lewis W. Hine. New York Public Library.

Slavic immigrants pouring steel, Ft. Pitt Steel Co., 1909. Photograph by Lewis W. Hine. New York Public Library.

Lewis Wickes Hine, one of America's foremost documentary photographers, recorded the experiences of immigrants on Ellis Island as well as in their new worlds of pick-and-shovel labor, on the streets, and in mines and factories. His straightforward images express, with compassion and concern, the hard struggle of the immigrant worker to succeed in the United States.

Slavic family living in a shack in western New York, 1912. Photograph by Lewis W. Hine. New York Public Library.

Backyard playground in Boston, 1912. Photograph by Lewis W. Hine. New York Public Library.

Assimilation of immigrants and their children into the American mainstream occurred little by little, generation by generation. This gradual transformation from European to American led one Norwegian writer Bjornstjerne Bjornson, who visited the United States in 1880, to comment: "To see a Norwegian peasant again as an American citizen and a member of the county board—I saw them by the hundreds—, that's a beautiful sight; but to see his grandson as an American gentleman . . . that is bound to silence all defamation; because here you have in front of you the finished result, that which in America is the idea and the aim of all endeavor through its institutions."[6]

chapter 7

THE JOURNEY

The decision to leave was not an easy one, and once made, was beset again and again by a variety of obstacles. The emigrant had to apply for identity papers, visas, and medical documents for himself and his family; he had to choose a destination and plan a route of travel based on second-hand information from often unreliable sources. If he lived far inland he would also have to arrange transportation to a port on the Atlantic or Mediterranean. To finance his journey, the emigrant would sell all his property—all, that is, that he could not carry with him—and pack up the rest in makeshift boxes and bundles. He might also have to borrow money, which he could not pay back until he had established himself in his new country.

Those who came during the early part of the nineteenth century knew they would probably never see their homelands again or the friends and family they left behind. Their journey aboard wooden sailing ships in cramped, usually filthy quarters, would take two or sometimes three months. It was an experience that few would ever have the forbearance to repeat. Just the overland journey to a port of embarkation was disheartening for those who had a long distance to cover. In the days before the railroad, the emigrants traveled by wagon, carriage, barge, or on foot. They were often victimized by dishonest innkeepers and border guards.

Once at port they were harassed by hordes of land-based pirates—swindlers selling counterfeit tickets and unscrupulous agents selling passage on ships that were barely seaworthy. High-pressure jobbers would buttonhole emigrants and take them to disreputable inns or other places where they could be fleeced, by a lively assortment of thugs, prostitutes, and thieves.

The trans-Atlantic voyage was the next ordeal for the emigrant, and was probably his worst. During the first half of the nineteenth century, emigrants had to provide their own food and bedding.

Opposite.
Steerage bunks. Every Saturday, *March 26, 1870.*

Of his experience sailing as a second-class passenger, Robert Louis Stevenson wrote in The Amateur Emigrant *that through the thin partitions of the cabins ". . .you can hear the steerage passengers being sick, the rattle of tin dishes as they sit at meals, the varied accents in which they converse, the crying of their children terrified by this new experience, or the clean flat smack of the parental hand in chastisement."[1]*

Provisions had to be chosen carefully and wisely since they would have to last for the full journey. If a ship were blown off course, the voyage might be extended by a week or several weeks. With provisions low, the emigrants would often plunder each other's supplies, or the ship's captain would sell food at exorbitant prices. Death by starvation, especially among young children, was not an unusual occurrence.

Even if there was enough food, there was hardly any means for cooking and preparing it. A typical galley consisted of two small rooms, each with one stove or fire. According to Friedrich Kapp, a commissioner of emigration in New York State in 1870:

These were all the arrangements for preparing meals for several hundred passengers. The result was that, except when they had nothing to cook or were sick, there was constant fighting for room near the caboose, and not one of the passengers could be sure of getting his food well-cooked. The sufferings which they endured in this way embittered the emigrants one against another, and their quarrels ended when in the evening the fires were extinguished, but only to revive in the morning.[2]

In steerage—so-called because it was on the bottom decks where the steering mechanism was located—tiers of bunks filled long, low, wide spaces. These spaces sometimes ran the full breadth and length of the ship. Steerage five feet high was considered fully sufficient for making two tiers of beds. Some ships had two steerage decks, the lower one receiving what little light and ventilation it had from the open hatchway above the upper steerage compartment. In stormy weather, when passengers sometimes had to be confined to their quarters for days at a time, the hatchways above steerage were closed, creating an unbearably hot, fetid, and nauseating atmosphere. Severe seasickness, a raging storm, and the terror of shipwreck shared by several hundred people confined in a small, dark, damp space complete as near an image of hell as one can imagine. The emigrants' quarters aboard these old ships became increasingly filthy as the voyage continued. The death rate from such disease as typhus, dysentery, and cholera was notoriously high. The worst cases occurred in 1847, when emigrant ships brought to America and Canada thousands of Irish who were fleeing the potato famine. In many cases these emigrants were near starvation even before boarding their ships. The difficult voyage on old, unsanitary ships and the lack of

Quarter-Deck of an Emigrant Ship. The Roll-call, ca. 1850. Library of Congress.

The behavior of the crew on an emigrant ship was often dictatorial and sometimes abusive. One Scandinavian who traveled on an English packet in 1853 wrote that some of the passengers had been "beaten about the head so badly that there was reason to fear for their lives . . . [another] had his breastbone broken by an inhuman English mate who kicked him in the chest with his heavy sea boots because the passenger did not understand how to comply with the orders of this monster."[4]

provisions on board resulted in incredibly high mortality rates. Kapp repeated:

To give an adequate idea of recent losses of human life on board ill-provided, ill-ventilated vessels, it may be stated here that out of 98,105 poor Irish immigrants shipped to Canada by their landlords after the great famine of 1846, during the summer of 1847, there died 5,293 at sea, 8,072 at Gross Isle (Quarantine) and Quebec, and 7,000 in and above Montreal, making 20,365, besides those who afterward perished whose number will never be ascertained.[3]

Conditions, of course, varied from ship to ship, depending on the number of steerage passengers, the weather, the captain, and the crew. There are, however, enough first-hand accounts of these voyages under sail, from passengers as well as government officials, to demonstrate convincingly that passage in steerage was usually an appalling and dangerous experience. But it was the outrageously high mortality rates among the Irish pasengers on the emigrant ships of 1847 that finally compelled England and the United States to enact legislation to protect passengers.

By the 1850s, shipowners or agents were required by law to provide food for the emigrant. This usually consisted of daily rations of biscuits, oatmeal, wheat flour, rice, molasses, sugar, and tea. In later years, meat, fish, and vegetables were added to the list of provisions. Legislation passed in England and the United States also required steerage quarters to be a certain height and be equipped with at least two ventilators and protected hatchways that could be left open even during storms. The ship had to provide an adequate number of toilets, separate compartments for men and women and children, and competent medical care. The law required that if the ship were carrying over three hundred passengers, a doctor had to be on board.

The penalties prescribed by these laws, however, were not nearly severe enough to force shipping lines to make even these minimum improvements, and ships continued to have high death rates. One notorious example was the fever ship *Leibnitz*, which arrived in New

On Board an Emigrant Ship—The Breakfast Bell, 1884. Library of Congress.

This wood engraving, showing the Dominion Line's Sarnia, *appeared in the* Graphic *on September 13, 1884. Its accompanying article remarked on the "perfect amity" that exists on board ship. "Considering the heterogeneous character of the emigrants, it is marvelous how they fraternize with each other." More than a thousand passengers were on board.*

German captain and crew, 1872. National Archives.

Aboard ship, one observer wrote, the social order is just like old Russia, Austria, Poland, or Italy. The immigrant is the peasant, "the cabin passengers are the lords and ladies, the sailors and officers are the police and the army, while the captain is the king or czar."[6]

York from Hamburg in 1868. Of the 544 passengers, all Germans, 105 died on the voyage, which lasted seventy days. Three more died shortly after the ship docked in New York. It was feared by New York State officials that an epidemic of cholera was responsible for so many of the deaths. But after inspecting the ship, they concluded "that the shocking mortality on board the *Leibnitz* arose from want of good ventilation, cleanliness, suitable medical care, sufficient water, and wholesome food." The commissioners of emigration further stated:

As to the interior of the vessel, the upper steerage is high and wide. . . . Except through two hatchways and two small ventilators, it had no ventilation, and not a single window or bull's-eye was open during the voyage. In general, however, it was not worse than the average of the steerages of other emigrant ships; but the lower steerage, the so-called orlop-deck, is a perfect pest-hole, calculated to kill the healthiest man. . . . In this place about 150 passengers were crowded for seventy days.

For each emigrant over the age of eight who died on board, the shipping line had to pay a penalty of ten dollars. This did not even equal the price of a trans-Atlantic ticket which usually cost about forty dollars.

Poor ventilation, and the powerful stench of seasickness and overused toilets remained constant characteristics of steerage. In June 1879, when Robert Louis Stevenson sailed from Glasgow to New York, he witnessed the terrible conditions that were typical of all emigrant ships. Although Stevenson traveled second class, his cabin was located next to the steerage compartments. He found the lack of air in his own cabin to be appalling, but in steerage it was worse. "To descend on an empty stomach into steerage," Stevenson wrote, "was an adventure that required some nerve. . . . The stench was atrocious, each respiration tasted like some horrible kind of cheese."[5]

The most important factor in improving steerage conditions and cutting the death rate was the gradual introduction of the steamship into trans-Atlantic shipping. By 1870, the average voyage aboard an iron-hulled steamship from Liverpool to New York took only fourteen days. By the turn of the century an Atlantic crossing could be accomplished in eight days.

The Inman Line of Liverpool was the first to try to improve emigrant service and capitalize on the ever-growing numbers of men, women, and children leaving Europe. In 1850, Inman introduced a fleet of iron-screw steamers capable of making an Atlantic crossing in three weeks. This innovation marked the end of the sailing packet in the emigrant trade. Inman's example was soon followed by North German Lloyd, Hamburg-America, and Campagnie Générale Transatlantique. By 1882, a congressional report stated that 99 percent of all the emigrants to America journeyed across the Atlantic by steam.

With the introduction of steam, the business of shipping also changed, which made it easier to regulate steerage quarters. The old sailing ships were often owned by small partnerships or individuals, who would hire agents to handle their business. Emigrants would apply for passage to the agent through a shipping broker. The broker's commission was 12½ percent of the cost of passage. Sometimes a broker would lease an entire cargo hold from the agent, fit it up with sleeping berths, and then sell space directly to the passengers. Runners who worked for the brokers got a commission of 7½ percent for each passage sold. With so many middlemen involved in a ship's business, it was nearly impossible to improve steerage conditions or enforce laws meant to protect emigrants.

Steamships, on the other hand, were owned by large companies that could be held directly responsible for conditions aboard their ships. The strong competition for the emigrant trade, which represented a big part of a shipping line's profit, also brought many

The Wreck of the Atlantic, *April 1, 1873. Lithograph by Currier & Ives. Library of Congress.*

The fierce North Atlantic storms that so terrified emigrants did indeed cause many shipwrecks. In the three decades from 1871 to 1900, about 350 steam-powered vessels were lost at sea. Not all of these ships, fortunately, carried passengers; but when disaster did strike a passenger ship the loss of life was great. The White Star steamship Atlantic *was caught in a heavy gale and driven against the rocks of Nova Scotia en route from Liverpool. Most of the nearly one thousand on board were steerage passengers; 250 men saved themselves by means of a rope that had been strung up to shore, but no women were saved and only one child survived. In all, almost 550 lives were lost. One survivor, who clung to the rigging of the ship, described a frightening scene: "It was just a gleaming day; a large mass of something drifted past the ship on the top of the waves and then was lost to view in the trough of the sea. As it passed by, a moan—it must have been a shriek, but the tempest dulled the sound—seemed to surge up from the mass, which extended over fifty yards of water. It was the women. The sea swept them out of steerage and with their children, to the number of 200 or 300, they drifted thus to eternity."* [7]

Stealing Their Way to the Land of Liberty—Three Stowaways Discovered Between Decks on an Ocean Steamer, July 6, 1886. Frank Leslie's Illustrated Newspaper. New York Public Library.

"Many readers who have crossed the ocean will recognize in our front page picture a scene painfully familiar," the accompanying article reads. "A nest of stowaways has been overhauled between decks, and the half-starved, terified little ragamuffins are brought before the captain. . . . They will be compelled to work for their passage, however, and will perhaps be landed at Castle Garden, New York, only to be shipped back to Liverpool by the next steamer."

improvements to steerage. In 1873, a report submitted to the Senate by Dr. John M. Woodworth, the supervising surgeon of the United States Marine Hospital Service, said:

With the gradual supplanting of sailing vessels by steamers have come shorter voyages, increased space, improved accommodations, more light, better ventilation, more abundant supplies of more wholesome food and water, and superior morale of officers and crews; though in this latter respect there is still much to be desired.[8]

There was vast room for improvement in the care of passengers as well. Another part of this same report stated:

The profit of the immigrant traffic is greater to the steamship companies than any other portion of their traffic, and if emigrants themselves knew the value of it, and were sufficiently informed to understand the fact, the abuses would soon correct themselves. Six guineas (about $40), the price of a steerage ticket, is nearly half the cost of cabin passage; but, in this, as in all the wants of the poor and ignorant, they pay much larger prices in proportion to what they get than the rich . . . Steerage passengers are obliged to furnish their own bed to sleep upon; a plate, cup, knife and fork to eat with, and also to keep clean for use. The very limited room allowed each person, and often the scarcity of water renders the care of these utensils a great burden, and in case of sickness almost an impossibility. Especially women who have children clinging to them for care and attention, themselves sick, in a strange place, terrified by the motion of the ship and the state of confusion the first few days of the voyage, it is found to be a great tax.[9]

The Augusta-Victoria steams past the Statue of Liberty on her way back to home port in Hamburg, Germany, 1889. National Archives.

The Augusta-Victoria, built in 1888, was one of the first twin-screw ships of the Hamburg-America Line. Her first trans-Atlantic crossing was completed in seven days and two hours—much faster than most ships, which still took around two weeks to make the same journey.

chapter 8

PASSAGE BY STEAM

I
n 1882, the United States enacted legislation requiring steamship companies to provide more service and larger accommodations for steerage passengers. One hundred cubic feet of space had to be allotted for each adult passenger on the upper steerage deck, and 120 cubic feet on the lower. An equipped infirmary was required as well as a doctor if over fifty passengers were on board. Three meals a day had to be served at table and adequate hygiene and sanitation provided for.

During the debate in Congress that led up to the bill's passage, one representative, in recognizing the need for immigration to bolster America's growth, said the welfare of these future citizens must be protected:

They come here and buy and settle our lands, they convert the wilderness into green pastures and productive fields, and thereby add so vastly to our national wealth. . . . We, the representatives of the American people, who receive the benefits of this immigration, a people which is ever ready to stand by those who need our help, always willing to correct all abuses of human beings, should not now hesitate to pass a law which is so urgently required . . .[1]

This law, well-meaning though it was, was poorly written and difficult to enforce and overcrowding and unsanitary conditions prevailed in steerage well up into the twentieth century.

Ironically, it was the immigration restriction laws, making steamship lines responsible for the care of those denied entry to the United States, that improved the treatment of steerage passengers. The Immigration Act of 1882 was the first in a long series of laws that required steamship companies to assume the expense of deporting immigrants who could not meet the physical or mental requirements for admission to the United States.

Opposite.
The S.S. Angelo, leaving Christiana, Norway, with emigrants for America, 1905. Library of Congress.

"*I remember the day I left home. Mother had prepared some home-baked beans and salt pork. She was very quiet when I left. Maybe she cried later. Father went with me to the railroad station. He looked pretty sad, and I saw tears in his eyes as he wished me well.*

"*After two days, I arrived in Gothenburg. There I stayed in a dark room the steamship company had rented for me. I had to wait for the trans-Atlantic ship to come. It was raining, and I just sat there in the room. Just sat watching heavy raindrops falling on the window.*

"*Finally, the big ship came and I walked on board. I had a suitcase and a trunk in the hold and I also had the tickets, besides thirty-five dollars. By and by the ship lifted anchor, and we left—left the harbor of Gothenburg, heading out west to a stormy sea. I was on my way to a faraway country, to strange people who spoke a language I did not know. I stood on the steerage deck, silently looking back at the coast of my native land.*"[2] *(Walter Lindstrom, from Sweden, 1913)*

By 1903, when all steerage passengers had to be inspected at Ellis Island, steamship companies were obliged to pay for the food, accommodations, and medical care of all immigrants who had to be detained for observation. Companies were also fined ten dollars for each prospective immigrant who was excluded by law. In 1905, this fine was raised to $100. Rather than incur these extra expenses, steamship companies were more selective about taking passengers and more solicitous in their care both at port and aboard ship.

From the 1880s to the 1920s, over twenty million emigrants came to the United States. A growing percentage of them—over 80 percent by 1907—were from the eastern European and Mediterranean countries: Russia, Italy, Poland, Austria, Hungary, Greece, Turkey and Spain. By the time these new emigrants came, the transportation companies had developed an efficient system to get them to port as expeditiously as possible. A local steamship agent would plan the journey from an emigrant's small isolated village to a nearby railroad station where a special train chartered by the steamship company could be boarded and taken to a port of embarkation. The Compagnie Générale Transatlantique, for example, had trains pick up emigrants in Germany and transport them directly to Le Havre, where they would board ship. The major shipping lines gradually built up little villages at ports where emigrants could bathe, eat, rest, and sometimes stay a few days until their ship was ready to sail. All these services were provided either free or at a reasonable cost. Kosher meals were available for the many Jews

Arrival of train at Hamburg-America Line's emigrant village, ca. 1910. National Archives.

"The day I left home, my mother came with me to the railroad station. When we said good-bye, she said it was just like seeing me go into my casket. I never saw her again."[3] (Julia Goniprow, from Lithuania, 1899)

traveling from Russia and eastern Europe.

A United States Immigration Commission Report in 1911 included the experience of a reporter who pretended to be an emigrant and stayed at one of the emigrant hotels in Liverpool operated by Cunard. He described the Cunard Hotel system as "a village by itself in the center of Liverpool," consisting of several buildings that could house over two thousand guests. The accommodations were free. He wrote:

At the Hotel Cunard, where we stayed, we were welcomed by a matron and a hotel keeper in the uniform of the Cunard Steamship Company. We were asked most kindly to eat something before we retired. I said I did not care for anything, but they insisted that I should eat something or at least drink a glass of milk. Then my room was shown to me. It held 10 beds and was well ventilated and provided with steam heat and electric lights. Both beds and floor were clean. . . . Women were strictly separated from the men in the sleeping rooms.

There are two dining rooms, one with a seating capacity of about 500, one with 200. The meals are wholesome. A printed menu was found in several conspicuous places. The Hebrews who stay in a separate hotel get kosher cooked meals.

The toilet and bathrooms were strictly sanitary and every part of them is marble and tile-lined. The water-closets have running water. The hotel provided towels and soap.[4]

Entrance to main hall at Hamburg-America Line's emigrant village, ca. 1910. National Archives.

Some of the major shipping lines set up little villages for their steerage passengers: Cunard, in Liverpool, Holland-America in Rotterdam, and Hamburg-America in Hamburg. Emigrants could rest, eat, and await the day of their departure. They were also given a medical inspection and an antiseptic bath. Men and boys were given short haircuts and their scalps were scrubbed with a shampoo of soft soap, creolin, carbolic acid, and petroleum. Women, too, had to have their hair carefully washed and combed although they were spared the indignity of having it cut.

Medical inspections at border crossings interrupted the journey from eastern Europe to ports on the Atlantic. The German border with Russia and Austria was dotted with control stations run by the shipping lines where emigrants had to show their papers, submit to a physical, wash themselves thoroughly, and have their clothes and baggage fumigated. These control stations were set up in the early 1890s after several severe outbreaks of cholera in Russia. The disease was brought through Germany and onto many ships by Russian emigrants. To stop the ensuing epidemic the German government ordered the borders closed to the emigrants. They relented later when the steamship companies offered to establish inspection stations to turn away cholera cases. But even after the cholera scare was over, the control stations were kept in operation. In 1907, nearly half a million intended emigrants were inspected at these stations and nearly twelve thousand were rejected.

The inspection routine was vividly described by Mary Antin in her book *The Promised Land*. In 1894, when she was thirteen years old, Antin traveled from Polotzk, Russia, across Europe with her mother and brothers and sisters to Hamburg, where there was an emigrant village similar to Cunard's run by the Hamburg-America

Under the inscription "My Field is the World," Hamburg-America Line clerks register emigrants, ca. 1910. National Archives.

"Well, we're off for America. Where it is, I don't know. I only know it's far. You have to ride and ride until you get there. And when you get there, there's a Kesten Garten where they undress you and look you in the eyes.

"So you are going, really going to America?" says our neighbor Pesi. "May God bring you there safe and sound, and help you strike luck. With God everything is possible. Just last year our Rivele went to America with her husband, Hillel. The first few months we heard nothing from them. We thought they had fallen, God forbid, into the sea. Finally they write us, "America is a free country where everyone is miserable making a living."[5] (Sholom Aleichem)

Hamburg-America Line's emigrant village, ca. 1910. National Archives.

Line. From there they sailed to Boston to meet her father, who had emigrated in 1891. En route to Hamburg they were stopped at a German control station:

The plight of the bewildered emigrant on the way to foreign parts is always pitiful enough, but for us who came from plague-ridden Russia the terrors of the way were doubled.

In a great lonely field, opposite a solitary house within a large yard, our train pulled up at last, and a conductor commanded the passengers to make haste and get out. He hurried us into the one large room which made·up the house, and then into the yard. Here a great many men and women, dressed in white, received us, the women attending to the women and girls of the passengers, and the men to the others.

This was another scene of bewildering confusion, parents losing their children, and little ones crying; baggage being thrown together in one corner of the yard, heedless of contents, which suffered in consequence; those

white-clad Germans shouting commands, always accompanied with
"Quick! Quick!"—the confused passengers obeying all orders like meek
children, only questioning now and then what was going to be done with
them.

And no wonder if in some minds stories arose of people being captured
by robbers, murderers, and the like. Here we had been taken to a lonely
place where only that house was to be seen; our things were taken away,
our friends separated from us; a man came to inspect us, as if to ascertain our full value; strange-looking people driving us about like dumb
animals, helpless and unresisting; children we could not see crying in a
way that suggested terrible things; ourselves driven into a little room
where a great kettle was boiling on a little stove; our clothes taken off,
our bodies rubbed with a slippery substance that might be any bad thing;
a shower of warm water let down on us without warning; again driven
to another little room where we sit, wrapped in woolen blankets till
large, coarse bags are brought in, their contents turned out, and we see
only a cloud of steam, and hear the women's orders to dress ourselves,—
"Quick! Quick!"—or else we'll miss—something we cannot hear. We are
forced to pick out our clothes from among all the others, with the steam
blinding us; we choke, cough, entreat the women to give us time; they
persist, "Quick! Quick!—or you'll miss the train!"—Oh, so we really

The dining hall at Hamburg-America
Line's village, ca. 1910. National Archives.

Complete with hotels, shops, and a
church, the village was large enough to
house a population of four thousand emigrants. Band concerts were given nearly
every afternoon, and emigrants were fed
in spacious dining halls. There was a
separate kosher dining hall for Jewish
passengers.

Steerage passengers boarding their ship at Hamburg, ca. 1910. National Archives.

won't be murdered! They are only making us ready for the continuing of our journey, cleaning us of all suspicions of dangerous sickness. Thank God!

We arrived in Hamburg early one morning after a long night in the crowded cars . . . [We were taken to] the outskirts of the city, where we were once more lined up, cross-questioned, disinfected, labelled, and pigeonholed. This was one of the occasions when we suspected that we were the victims of a conspiracy to extort money from us; for here, as at every repetition of the purifying operations we had undergone, a fee was levied on us, so much per head. My mother, indeed, seeing her tiny hoard melting away, had long since sold some articles from our baggage to a fellow passenger richer than she, but even so she did not have enough money to pay the fee demanded of her in Hamburg. Her statement was not accepted, and we all suffered the last indignity of having our persons searched.

This last place of detention turned out to be a prison. "Quarantine" they called it, and there was a great deal of it—two weeks of it. Two weeks within high brick walls, several hundred of us herded in half a dozen compartments—numbered compartments—sleeping in rows, like sick people in a hospital; with roll-call morning and night, and short rations three times a day; with never a sign of the free world beyond our barred windows; with anxiety and longing and homesickness in our hearts, and in our ears the unfamiliar voice of the invisible ocean, which drew and repelled us at the same time. The fortnight in quarantine was not an episode; it was an epoch, divisible into eras, periods, events.

The greatest event was the arrival of some ship to take some of the waiting passengers. When the gates were opened and the lucky ones said good-bye, those left behind felt hopeless of ever seeing the gates open for them. It was both pleasant and painful, for the strangers grew to be fast friends in a day, and really rejoiced in each other's fortune; but the regretful envy could not be helped either.

Our turn come at last. We were conducted through the gate of departure, and after some hours of bewildering manoeuvres . . . we found ourselves—we five frightened pilgrims from Polotzk—on the deck of a great big steamship afloat on the strange big waters of the ocean.

For sixteen days the ship was our world . . .[6]

Conditions aboard ship had improved in many respects since the early days of steam travel, but steerage still meant large dormitories filled to capacity with bunk beds, poor sanitation, poor ventilation, and next to no service.

The United States Immigration Commission of 1911 dispatched undercover agents to report on conditions in steerage on fourteen ships representing nearly all the major trans-Atlantic lines. Here are excerpts from one investigator's report:

All the steerage berths were of iron, the framework forming two tiers and having but a low partition between the individual berths. Each bunk contained a mattress filled with straw and covered with a slip made of coarse white canvas, apparently cleaned for the voyage. There were no pillows. Instead, a life-preserver was placed under the mattress at the head of each berth. A short and light-weight white blanket was the only covering provided . . .

The floors of all these compartments were of wood. They were swept every morning and the aisles sprinkled lightly with sand. None of them was washed during the twelve days' voyage nor was there any indication that a disinfectant was being used on them. The beds received only such attention as each occupant gave to his own. When the steerage is full, each passenger's space is limited to his berth, which then serves as bed, clothes and towel rack, cupboard, and baggage space. There are no accommodations to encourage the steerage passenger to be clean and orderly. There was no hook on which to hang a garment, no receptacle for refuse, no cuspidor, no cans for use in case of seasickness . . .

Steerage passengers may be filthy, as is often alleged, but considering the total absence of conveniences for keeping clean, this uncleanliness seems but a natural consequence. Some may really be filthy in their habits, but many make heroic efforts to keep clean.

Polish emigrant boarding the President Grant of the Hamburg-America Line, November 18, 1907. Geo. G. Bain Collection, Library of Congress.

"Waiting for the ship to take us to America, we meet Goldele, a girl with bad eyes. People tell her family to go to the doctor. So they go to the doctor. The doctor examines them and finds they are all hale and hearty and can go to America, but she, Goldele, cannot go because she has trachomas on her eyes. At first her family do not understand. Only later do they realize what it means. It means that they can all go to America but she, Goldele, will have to remain behind. So there begins a wailing, a weeping, a moaning. Three times her mama faints. Her papa wants to stay with her but he can't. All the ship tickets would be lost. So they have to go off to America and leave her, Goldele, here until the trachomas will go away from her eyes."[7] (Sholom Aleichem)

Steerage bunks aboard the S.S. Duca Degli Abruzzi, Italian Line, 1908. The Byron Collection, Museum of the City of New York.[8]

Photographs of steerage are rare. This one shows just a corner of what was probably a large open compartment holding three hundred bunks.

*Eastern European woman and child
aboard the S.S. Amsterdam, ca. 1910.
photograph by Frances Benjamin Johnston. Library of Congress.*

*Seasickness was the scourge of emigrants
in steerage. On stormy days they were
confined to their cramped quarters on the
lower decks. Many were hardly able to
leave their bunks. "But when the sun
shines upon the Atlantic," wrote Edward
Steiner, "and dries the deck space allotted
to the steerage passengers, they will come
out of the hold one by one, wrapped in
the company's gray blankets . . . [and]
await the return of the life which seemed
'clean gone' out of them."⁹*

*Each steerage passenger is to be furnished all the eating utensils neces-
sary. These he finds in his berth, and like the blanket they become his
possession and his care. They consist of a fork, a large spoon, and a
combination workingman's tin lunch pail. . . . These must serve the passenger throughout the voyage and so are generally hidden away in his
berth for safe-keeping, there being no other place provided. Each washed
his own dishes, and if he wished to use soap and a towel, he must provide his own.*

*Dish washing is not easy as there is only one faucet of warm water,
and when there is no chance to use this, he has no other choice than to
try to get the grease off of his tins with cold salt water. . . . The quality of the tin and this method of washing is responsible for the fact that
the dishes are soon rusty, and not fit to eat from.*

*The food was brought into the dining room in large galvanized tin
cans. The meat and vegetables were placed on the tables in tins resembling smaller-sized dish-pans. There were no serving plates, no knives, or
no spoons. Each passenger had only his combination dinner pail, which is
more convenient away from the table than at it. This he had to bring
himself and wash when he had finished . . .*

*The daily medical inspection of the steerage was carried on as follows:
The second day out we all passed in single file before the doctor as he
leisurely conversed with another officer, casting an occasional glance at
the passing line. The chief steerage steward punched six holes in each
passenger's inspection card, indicating that the inspection for six days was
complete. One steward told me this was done to save the passengers from
going through this formality every day. The fourth day out we were
again reviewed. The doctor stood by. Another officer holding a Cablegram blank in his hand compared each passenger's card to some writing
on it. There was another inspection on the seventh day, when we were
required to bare our arms and show the vaccinations. Again our cards
were punched six times and this completed the medical examination . . .*

*To sum up, let me make some general statements that will give an
idea of the awfulness of steerage conditions on the steamer in question.
During these twelve days in the steerage I lived in a disorder and in
surroundings that offended every sense. Only the fresh breeze from the sea
overcame the sickening odors. The vile language of the men, the screams of
the women defending themselves, the crying of the children, wretched because of their surroundings, and practically every sound that reached the
ear irritated beyond endurance. There was no sight before which the eye
did not prefer to close. Everything was dirty, sticky, and disagreeable to*

the touch. Every impression was offensive. Worse than this was the general air of immorality. For fifteen hours each day I witnessed all around me this improper, indecent, and forced mingling of men and women who were total strangers and often did not understand one word of the same language. People can not live in such surroundings and not be influenced . . .[10]

The steamship companies generally depended on steerage to turn a large profit. For a small investment in iron frame bunks, horse blankets, straw mattresses, and cheap tin cups and utensils, a shipping line could charge about forty dollars per passage; and often over a thousand passengers could be transported in steerage in one crossing.

Emigrant couple from eastern Europe aboard the S.S. Amsterdam, ca. 1910. Photograph by Frances Benjamin Johnston. Library of Congress.

One of the most vocal critics of steerage was Edward A. Steiner, an immigrant from Austria. Steiner arrived in America penniless while still in his teens and worked as a farmhand in New Jersey, a laborer in Chicago, and a miner in Pennsylvania. He later completed a course of theological studies at Oberlin College, and in 1903, when he was thirty-seven years old, he was appointed professor of Applied Christianity at Grinnell College in Iowa.

Emigrant women and children from eastern Europe sitting on the deck of the S.S. Amsterdam, ca. 1910. Photograph by Frances Benjamin Johnston. Library of Congress.

Captain Leithauser and officers inspecting steerage aboard the S.S. Patricia, *1902. The Byron Collection, Museum of the City of New York.*

An emigrant reads a letter he has received aboard the S.S. Patricia, *1902. The Byron Collection, Museum of the City of New York.*

Children playing on the steerage deck aboard the S.S. Patricia, 1902. The Byron Collection, Museum of the City of New York.

Dancing on the steerage deck on the S.S. Patricia, 1902. The Byron Collection, Museum of the City of New York.

"For sixteen days the ship was our world. . . . The perils of the sea were not minimized in the imaginations of us inexperienced voyagers. The captain and his officers ate their dinners, smoked their pipes and slept soundly in their turns, while we frightened emigrants turned our faces to the wall and awaited our watery graves.

"All this while the seasickness lasted. Then came happy hours on deck, with fugitive sunshine, birds atop the crested waves, band music and dancing and fun. I explored the ship, made friends with officers and crew, or pursued my thoughts in quiet nooks. It was my first experience of the ocean, and I was profoundly moved."[11] (Mary Antin)

Steiner made the voyage across the Atlantic in steerage several times and wrote passionately about the need to protect the rights and welfare of immigrants. In his book, *On the Trail of the Immigrant*, published in 1906, he describes steerage on board the *Kaiser Wilhelm II*, one of the North German Lloyd line's largest and fastest ships. It was capable of making a trans-Atlantic journey in less than six days. Yet Steiner was not impressed with the ship's performance or its luxurious staterooms for the first-and second-class cabin. The steerage quarters had not been improved; if anything, they were worse than steerage conditions on the older ships. He described them as follows:

Clean they are, but there is neither breathing space below nor deck room above, and the 900 steerage passengers crowded into the hold of so elegant and roomy a steamer as the Kaiser Wilhelm II, *of the North German Lloyd line, are positively packed like cattle, making a walk on deck when the weather is good, absolutely impossible, while to breathe clean air below in rough weather, when the hatches are down is an equal impossibility . . .*

On the whole, the steerage of the modern ship ought to be condemned as unfit for the transportation of human beings; and I do not hesitate to say that the German companies, and they provide best for their cabin passengers, are unjust if not dishonest towards the steerage. Take for example, the second cabin which costs about twice as much as the steerage and sometimes not twice so much; yet the second cabin passenger on the Kaiser Wilhelm II *has six times as much deck room, much better located and well protected against inclement weather. Two to four sleep in one cabin, which is well and comfortably furnished; while in the steerage from 200 to 400 sleep in one compartment on bunks, one above the other, with little light and no comforts. In the second cabin the food is excellent, is partaken of in a luxuriantly appointed dining-room, is well cooked and well served; while in the steerage the unsavory rations are not served, but doled out, with less courtesy than one would find in a charity soup kitchen.*

The steerage ought to be and could be abolished by law. It is true that the Italian and Polish peasant may not be accustomed to better things at home and might not be happier in better surroundings or know how to use them; but it is a bad introduction to our way of life to treat him like an animal when he is coming to us. He ought to be made to feel immediately that the standard of living in America is higher than it is abroad, and that life on the higher plane begins on board ship. Every cabin passenger who has seen and smelt the steerage from afar, knows that it is often indecent and inhuman; and I, who have lived in it, know that it is both of these and cruel besides . . . .[12]

Another eyewitness to steerage was Broughton Brandenburg, a young American journalist who, in 1902, traveled to Italy and back disguised as an immigrant. He wrote about his experience in his book *Imported Americans.* Before the journey Brandenburg and his wife lived for four months in a New York Italian neighborhood where they learned to speak Italian fluently. They then booked passage aboard the *Lahn,* one of the better immigrant ships, to Naples. They returned from Naples on the *Prinzessin Irene.*

We had chosen the Prinzessin Irene *because she is the largest and best immigrant carrying ship in the trade. . . . People who have crossed many times and know all the ins and outs of steerage travel prefer the* Lahn *or the* Prinzessin Irene, *so that we knew we should find the minimum of abuse in her.*[13]

But what they found was typical steerage, where 214 women and children were crowded into a space meant for 195 people; where the only ventilation came from the companionway and not from the deck; where mattresses were burlap-covered bags of straw or grass. Dinner was served from gigantic twenty-five-gallon tanks. Passengers had to get the food themselves and then wash their own dishes. For breakfast, Brandenburg wrote:

. . . the steerage cooks and stewards served "biscuits" and coffee. The latter was what might be expected. The first named was a disk of dough, three-quarters of an inch thick, and a hand-length broad. It was hard as a landlord's heart, and as tasteless as a bit of carpet . . . half the biscuits were moldy. About some 3,000 were served out, and for the next half hour disks went sailing high in the air over the sides and into the sea. . . . If conditions aboard the Lahn *and the* Prinzessin Irene *were so bad what must it be like aboard the cheaper ships running from Mediterranean ports?*[14]

Social reformers wanted steerage abolished altogether and replaced with third-class accommodations. Many of the major shipping lines

Opposite.
The Steerage, 1907. Photogravure by Alfred Stieglitz. Library of Congress.

Stieglitz's famous photograph, one that he considered his finest, was taken on an eastbound voyage to Europe aboard the S.S. Kaiser Wilhelm II. *This was the same ship Edward Steiner traveled on and described several years later in* On the Trail of the Immigrant.

had already done so on their newer ships. Other companies offered both steerage and third class, while the older ships still had steerage compartments that were primitive and unclean. On the newer ships, the difference in cost between the two classes was slight—sometimes only seven or eight dollars. For just this little bit of money, third class offered services and accommodations that provided decently for human needs. According to an Immigration Commission report:

The third-class on the——, proved to be an idealized steerage. The passengers were treated with care and consideration. There was every attempt to give satisfaction. Where cabins were for any reason unsatisfactory, a new arrangement was attempted and made wherever possible. All actual human needs were supplied, with cleanliness, order, and decency. The third class was confined to the stern of the vessel.

The sleeping quarters were situated on the second deck, below the main deck. A large space extending the width of the ship was subdivided into cabins containing two, four, and six berths. Families and friends were lodged together. Men had cabins on one side, women on the other. The beds were arranged in two tiers and consisted of an iron frame work, very simple but clean. Each bed was supplied with a mattress, white sheet, and a blanket and pillow having a colored gingham covering. These were clean at the outset, but were not changed during the voyage. Each cabin was furnished with a wash-basin, drinking glasses, towels, sick cans, and was cleaned every day and supplied with fresh water . . .

Meals were served in a large dining room seating 300 persons and situated on the first deck below the main deck. The tables accommodated 14 persons each for the most part and each was the special charge of one steward. There were red covers, white napkins (which were changed once during the journey), heavy white porcelain dishes, and good cutlery. There was a double supervision and a thorough one by two higher officers of the dining room, as well as of the sleeping quarters and promenade deck. In consequence of this the stewards performed their duties carefully and thoughtfully, and so gave splendid service. The food, though it offered practically only actual necessities, was sufficient in quantity and properly prepared and decently served . . .

The stewards cleaned and scrubbed all day and everything was kept clean. The floors were swept as often and washed when necessary . . .[15]

On board this ship, the steerage quarters, which stretched the entire length and width of the ship on a lower deck, were described

Broughton Brandenburg, 1904. Photograph from his book, Imported Americans. *New York Public Library.*

Third-class smoking room on the S.S. President Lincoln *of the Hamburg-America Line, ca. 1910. The Byron Collection, Museum of the City of New York.*

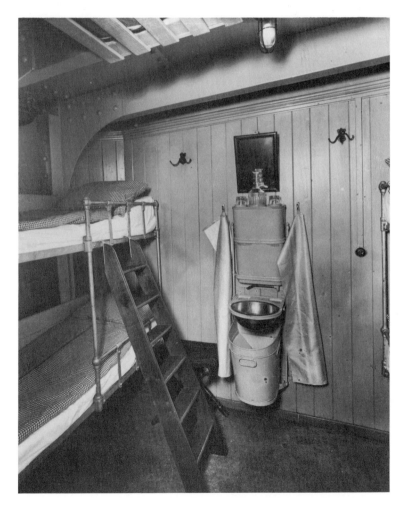

Third-class stateroom on the S.S. President Lincoln *of the Hamburg-America Line, ca. 1910. The Byron Collection, Museum of the City of New York.*

The S.S. President Lincoln *could accommodate 324 first-class passengers, 125 in second class, and 1,000 in third class. But in the open steerage compartments there were bunks for 2,320 passengers—nearly 900 more than in all the upper classes combined.*

by the same observer as "dismal, damp, dirty, and [a] most unwholesome place. The air was heavy, foul, and deadening to the spirit and the mind. Those confined to these beds by reason of sickness soon lost all energy, spirit, and ambition. . . . Such surroundings could not produce the frame of mind with which it is desirable that newcomers approach our land and receive their first impressions of it . . ."

By 1911, when the Immigration Commission published its report, steerage was slowly being phased out as new ships were being built and old ships were taken out of service. But so long as immigration to the United States remained unrestricted, and carrying large groups of passengers was so profitable, steerage remained a problem. It was not until immigration was sharply limited by the Quota Laws of 1921 and 1924—when the large open steerage compartments became financial liabilities instead of assets—that steamship companies were moved to abolish steerage and replace it with third-class cabins.

On the S.S. Patricia, steerage passengers with manifest tags pinned to their clothes wait to be transferred to Ellis Island, 1902. The Byron Collection, Museum of the City of New York.
". . . A sudden, great excitement breaks out: passengers begin to be ordered downstairs to their little cages. At first politely, then roughly. If you don't hurry up you get a good whack from behind. All the steerage passengers are here. It is stifling. They have locked the door and hung an iron chain across it. We have never felt so miserable as we do now. In our own eyes we look like prisoners. 'For what? For when?' my chum Mendel keeps saying, while his eyes blaze and shoot fire. Come to find out, we have arrived in America.
" 'What will they do, pickle us?' I ask.
" 'No,' someone answers back, 'but they will take us to a certain place called Ellis Island. There they will shut us up in a stall like calves until our friends and relatives get good and ready to take us out!' "[16] (Sholom Aleichem)

chapter 9

CASTLE GARDEN

New York was the major destination for immigrants coming to America. It was the country's largest port and had been since the 1820s. It was the home of the fast clipper ships and of the Black Ball Line, the first to schedule regular crossings to Liverpool. South Street, which ran along the east side of lower Manhattan, was legendary for its thick forest of masts and bowsprits formed by hundreds of ships moored in the East River. Shipping agencies, chandler's shops, and other businesses catering to the shipping trade lined the other side of the street. This is where the immigrant was landed before 1855—before New York had an immigrant landing depot. At this time, ships and passengers were inspected at Quarantine. A doctor stationed on Staten Island rowed out and boarded each ship before she sailed into the harbor to make sure there was no sign of contagious disease aboard. Once the ship had been cleared by the doctor, she could land and her passengers merely had to pass through customs before being at liberty in the city. As in the embarkation ports of Europe, runners and agents for railroads, steamboats, boarding houses, and money exchanges accosted the immigrant and tried to dun him into buying tickets or other services at exorbitant prices. If the immigrant objected he was likely to be bullied by thugs who often accompanied runners. One witness told a State investigating committee in 1847:

One of the common frauds practiced by the emigrant boarding house keepers is that they generally have five or six persons about their establishments, who, if they cannot prevail on the emigrant to accompany them to the boarding-house they represent, when coming from the Quarantine to the city, on their arrival at the dock seize their baggage by force, and have it carried by cartmen, who are privy to their operations, to the boarding houses. With the baggage once in the house, the emigrant, if dissatisfied with the accommodations and wishes his things removed to

DESK FOR INFORMATION.

EMIGRANT DEPOT

INTERIOR

CASTLE GARDEN

R.R. TICKET OFFICE.

OF DEPOT.

another place, is met by the landlord with a charge for either storage or one day's board, compelling him to put up with the accommodations offered him, or pay five or six dollars without an equivalent. . . . The keepers of emigrant boarding houses are invariably foreigners, the native of each nation preying upon their own countrymen.[1]

The immigrant business was one that lent itself easily to swindling, extortion, and outright robbery. In time, it became a very well organized racket. An agent's success involved the cooperation not only of boardinghouse keepers and cartmen but also of other agents, customs officials, police, and politicians. An agent's influence could stretch from New York to destinations as far west as a railroad, canal boat, or Great Lake steamer could go. An agent's much used code-line to out-of-town accomplices was "run the *O.P. line* strong." The *O.P. line*, according to one witness, meant "rob the passengers all you can and divide the money with me."[2]

In 1847, the terrible year when thousands of immigrants died in steerage, New York State appointed a commission to inspect ships and protect the immigrant from the network of swindlers that had a stranglehold on New York City docks. The following year another law was passed requiring boarding house owners as well as ticket agents and runners to be licensed. In 1855, as a further protection for America's future citizens, Castle Garden, the first immigrant landing depot in the world, was set up in Battery Park on the southern tip of Manhattan.

Castle Garden was originally a fort called Castle Clinton, which was completed in 1811 when the United States was preparing for war with England—a war that came in 1812. The fort, which stood three hundred feet offshore, was connected to the Battery by a wooden causeway. Its red sandstone walls were eight feet thick. The federal government ceded Castle Clinton to New York City in 1823, and the city added a lofty roof, renamed it Castle Garden, and turned it into a concert hall and reception center for visiting dignitaries. The Marquis de Lafayette and President Andrew Jackson were once entertained there; and Jenny Lind, the Swedish opera star, gave a concert there that made Castle Garden famous across the United States. Her appearance was hailed as the sensational event of the 1850s by her impresario, P.T. Barnum.

The Battery was still quite a wealthy and fashionable neighborhood at that time. The mansions along State Street, which bounded

Previous page.
Interior of Castle Garden. Harper's Weekly, *September 2, 1865.*

Registering immigrants inside Castle Garden, January 20, 1866. Frank Leslie's Illustrated Newspaper. *Library of Congress.*

Harper's New Monthly Magazine *described the routine at Castle Garden in 1871:*

"The steamer Holland, from Liverpool, had just arrived, and the steerage passengers were being landed. It was a motley, interesting throng. Slowly, one by one, the new-comers passed the two officers whose duty it is to register every immigrant's name, birthplace, and destination in large folios . . .

". . . On they passed, one by one, in single file, till a few steps farther down they came to the desk of the so-called "booker," a clerk of the Railway Association, whose duty it is to ascertain the destination of each passenger, and furnish him with a printed slip, upon which this is set forth, with the number of tickets wanted, and their cost in currency. Having received this, the passenger is passed over to the railway counter, where, if he so desires, he purchases his ticket. It is left to his own option what road he will patronize, and whether he will go by the first-class or the immigrant train. This arrangement is productive of much good, as by buying his ticket here he will be only charged the just price, and get the full value for his money, if he pays with a foreign exchange. It is too often the case that passengers, buying their tickets in outside offices, are shamefully swindled; the daily press exhibits numerous instances of this fact.

". . . Directly opposite the railway counter are the desks of the exchange brokers, which are at present occupied by four firms, each working in its own interest. A blackboard conspicuously displayed announces the current rates at which foreign and domestic coin are exchanged—a rate that is but a trifle below the Wall Street quotation.

"Having got his money changed and his railway ticket purchased, if he is a traveler, our citizen in embryo proceeds to have his baggage weighed and checked through to his point of destination."[3]

Battery Park on the north, were among the finest in the city. But Manhattan dwellers were gradually moving uptown and the southern portion of the island was being abandoned by its wealthier inhabitants. Their exodus was hastened by the city's decision to enlarge the park with landfill. Giant heaps of dirt and refuse and gangs of workmen made the park a much less appealing place to take children to play or to go for a pleasant walk.

It was around this time that the commissioners decided the Castle Garden would be a perfect landing depot for immigrants and it was so designated in 1855. Now immigrants would be taken directly to Castle Garden after they had passed through customs. After being registered by an immigration clerk, they could, in the words of one observer in 1856:

. . . enjoy themselves in the depot by taking their meals, cleansing themselves in the spacious bath-rooms, or promenading on the galleries or on the dock. The utmost order prevailed throughout; every requisite information was given passengers by officials conversing in different languages; letters from friends were transmitted to landing passengers, bringing them money or directions on how to proceed, etc.[4]

REGISTERING EMIGRANTS

Immigrants who were sick or needed medical attention were cared for at the commission's hospital on Ward's Island. All these services were supported by a head tax of one or two dollars for each immigrant. The amount of the tax was added to the price of the trans-Atlantic passage and paid to the commission by the ship's captain. For those immigrants who were likely to need care in a public institution—the poor, the infirm, or the aged—a three hundred dollar bond good for five years was required from the shipping company. In 1867, the German and Irish immigration societies established a labor exchange inside Castle Garden to help new arrivals find employment.

Through 1855 and 1856, immigration increased steadily and Americans were gratified to learn that the newcomers were bringing a good amount of money with them. On May 15, 1856, *The New York Herald* wrote:

The Battery presents a lively scene about these days. Since the first of the present month immigrants have been arriving at the rate of five thousand

Immigrants in Battery Park with the Castle Garden Labor Exchange in the background. Harper's Weekly. *August 15, 1868. Library of Congress.*

The article that accompanied this wood-engraving said: "The Labor Exchange is a free market for emigrant labor, open to employers from all parts of the United States. . . . Farm laborers may be hired for wages varying from $6 to $10 per month in winter; from $12 to $18 in summer (besides board and lodging) . . . Female domestic servants obtain from $6 to $10 per month. Professed cooks have been engaged from $12 to $20 per month. Families consisting of husband and wife, and sometimes including one or more small children have been hired for $15 to $24 per month."

per week. This will be still further increased. The [Crimean] war is over, and the disbanded armies will have no employment, and will come here to seek it. The Know-Nothing excitement has died away, and the attempt to make Canada a resort for immigrants has fizzled out. It is pleasant to learn that the immigrants who have lately arrived have been a better class than usual. They have brought with them an average of seventy-two dollars per head. Let them come, but let them keep out of politics for five years. There's plenty of room out West yet.

The authority of the state commission was challenged and seriously undermined in 1875, when the Supreme Court ruled that the state had no power to levy a head tax or require bonds from shipping companies. It ruled that this was the sole right of the federal government. The court's decision left New York State without funds to support its immigrant services except by raising state taxes. At the same time, many politicians and government officials were changing their views of immigration. While Castle Garden was set up to serve the interests of the immigrant, the prevailing sentiment during the 1880s favored restricted immigration. Social reformers were often quoted as saying that the state poorhouses, hospitals, and lunatic asylums were filled with immigrants who had just recently arrived and that their care cost the state millions of dollars a year.

In 1882, Congress passed two immigration restriction laws. The first, in May, was the Chinese Exclusion Act, which banned Chinese immigrants from entering the United States and denied citizenship to those Chinese already here. The second law, adopted several months later, excluded "any convict, lunatic, idiot or any person unable to take care of himself or herself without becoming a public charge." This was known as the First General Federal Immigration Law. It was to be executed by state officials—the same registry clerks at Castle Garden—but under contract to the Department of the Treasury. A federal head tax of fifty cents was levied to defray the costs of taking care of the immigrants. The inspection routine was further complicated by the Alien Contract Labor Law, passed under pressure from the unions in 1885. This law was intended to thwart the padrone system under which American businessmen would pay a contractor or padrone to supply cheap labor for their factories. Padrones were notorious for ruthlessly exploiting the immigrant workers they brought to America to fill their contracts. In addition

to witholding a percentage of the immigrant's wages, the padrones charged exorbitant rates for sub-standard room and board, and often ran over-priced company stores which their workers were expected to patronize. Unions contended that padrones accepted lower wages than were paid to American workers and that contract laborers were often used as strike-breakers. The Alien Contract Labor Law, however, did little to stop the padrones, who could recruit workers just as easily after they had passed through immigration and were safely admitted to the United States.

The Alien Contract Labor Law was administered by federal inspectors who were supposed to work side by side with the New York State registry clerks at Castle Garden. With this mixture of state and federal inspectors, there were unavoidable conflicts, with many responsibilities either being claimed by or slipping between the two authorities. The resulting chaos was further aggravated by a tremendous increase in immigration during the 1870s and 1880s.

For many years, the humanitarian services provided at Castle Garden gave the immigrants, if not a warm and friendly welcome, at least one that was free of extortion and physical abuse. Beyond

Health officers vaccinating Russian and Polish immigrants on board the steamship Victoria, *at Quarantine.* Frank Leslie's Illustrated Newspaper. *May 14, 1881. Library of Congress.*

An outbreak of smallpox on board ship was the cause of this scene. Before the Victoria *was allowed to enter New York harbor, Quarantine officers ordered that all smallpox victims be removed to a hospital on Blackwell's Island and that the rest of the passengers be vaccinated. When two health officers boarded the ship to administer the injections, the passengers, who feared the shots more than the disease, strongly protested. "About one hundred Russians and Poles threatened the doctors with violence if they persisted and for a time there was a scene of great excitement. . . . After the passengers had been vaccinated, their bedding was burned and the vessel thoroughly fumigated."*

its doors, however, the criminal influence of agents and runners remained in force. In the absence of a strong authority regulating immigration affairs, it was only a matter of time before the predators outside would find their way inside Castle Garden itself.

Joseph Pulitzer ran a series of articles on Castle Garden in 1887, charging that the immigrant landing depot had become a hotbed of swindles. *The World*'s exposé was triggered by the story of an unmarried young Norwegian woman who, according to *The World*, "arrived at this port en route to a comfortable home {in Minnesota} to live with her sister, her brother-in-law, her brother and her uncle." She was accompanied by her four-year-old son. *The World* reported:

Her brother-in-law had sent for her and her relatives expected her. Upon the question of her support being raised these relatives promptly came forward with an offer to give ample bonds that she should not be an object of public charity. The question of the legitimacy of her child was one which the Commissioners had no legal right to consider. Her detention by them, therefore, upon the ground that she was an unmarried woman with a child was as unlawful as it was frivolous. . . . The Commissioners decided that she must go back. They virtually imprisoned her in Castle Garden, compelled her and her child to sleep upon the naked benches in the rotunda (there were no sleeping arrangements at Castle Garden for detained immigrants) and live only upon bread and milk, which they furnished twice daily.

During the unlawful imprisonment, Ingjerd Jonson swore that she had been criminally assaulted by George Ivers—one of the employees of the Garden . . .

In the examination of this woman's accusations against the wretch who assaulted her, Commissioners Stephenson and Starr, gloating and chuckling like satyrs over the shameful details, plied her with obscene questions wholly irrelevant to bringing out the facts and were uproariously merry over their own indecency and brutal sallies.

After being kept imprisoned for more than a fortnight a writ of habeas corpus and an order from Secretary {of the Treasury} Fairchild for her release simultaneously came to her relief, and she was released and sent to her home.[5]

The World published its accusations on the front page. Other stories followed: a pregnant woman was detained and forced to scrub floors at the immigrant hospital on Ward's Island, two Italian women were sent back despite the pleas of their families, and a Polish woman was detained, even though she had every right to land.

The World proceeded to make a full investigation of all the activities of the commissioners at Castle Garden. It wrote that while the commission was appointed to protect immigrants from the "swarms of vicious thieves and jobbers," it had, in fact, installed its own system of swindling. Castle Garden had become a "place of unlawful detention, a place for tyranny and whimsical rule, a place for the abuse and insult of helpless women, for the inhuman treatment of mothers and children, for the plunder of the poor, for the lecherous pursuits of shielded employees, for the disgrace of the nation in the eyes of those who desire to become citizens, and for the exercise of the maudlin caprice of two brutal and self-aggrandizing old men."[6]

The two old men were Commissioner Stephenson and "his henchman," Commissioner Starr. *The World* charged that they allowed a railroad pool to divide the immigrant trade, that immigrants were charged an inflated ticket price, were sent by roundabout routes, and were packed into ramshackle and overcrowded immigrant trains. The pool (made up of a dozen or so companies) was run by a "joint agent" who would divide the business among the companies as equally as possible. This sometimes meant that groups of immigrants traveling together, or even families, were split up. The immigrants could not choose what line they wanted to travel by but were assigned to whatever company whose turn it was to get passengers.

The baggage concession also overcharged and swindled the immigrant in a variety of ways. An immigrant could retrieve his baggage only after giving the baggage handler some "drinking money—trinkgelt," in short, a tip. This usually amounted to about twenty-five cents. Cartmen working for Castle Garden overcharged for transporting baggage within the city.

At the restaurant, the prices for food were usually twice as much as outside Castle Garden. The money exchange, too, was corrupt. It paid several fractions below the market rate of a given currency; and the clerks of the money exchange were negligent about giving receipts for their transactions. The behavior of all the personnel at Castle Garden was described as surly and brusque at its best, downright brutal, cruel, and dishonest at its worst.

The World called for a thorough investigation. This was finally carried out by the Treasury Department, which had jurisdiction over

Castle Garden Emigrant-Catchers. Puck, June 14, 1882. New York Public Library.

The Free and Boundless West. A hard road for the honest emigrant to travel. Harper's Weekly, August 6, 1881.

All immigrants had to run the gauntlet of predators outside Castle Garden. But only those who followed the advice of The New York Herald to go west had to brave the frontier violence of yet uncivilized parts. By the 1880s, 60 percent of the immigrants arriving at Castle Garden went west, settling in such places as Minnesota, Illinois, Wisconsin, and Missouri.

immigration affairs. Though its report was never made public, and no legal charges of criminal misconduct were ever brought against the commissioners, there was strong sentiment in the Treasury Department that the federal government should take over the whole business of immigration, not simply to stop the alleged corruption of the various state immigration authorities, but also to limit immigration and exclude those who might wind up depending on charity. The following year, a House select committee headed by Representative Melbourne Ford of Michigan conducted a study of immigration that included an investigation of Castle Garden. That report said in part:

During the fiscal year 1888 the number of immigrants landing at the different seaports of the United States was 546,889. Of this number, 418,423 (or about 76 percent) came via the port of New York, and the greater portion of them arrived between the months of April and September; and during this period the daily arrival of immigrants is exceedingly large, sometimes amounting to as many as 9,000.

The committee visited Castle Garden on several occasions and witnessed the arrival and inspection of immigrants, and it was very obvious to them that it was almost impossible to properly inspect the large number of persons who arrive daily during the immigrant season with the facilities afforded; and the testimony taken puts it beyond question that large numbers of persons not entitled to land in the United States are annually received at this port. In fact, one of the commissioners of immigration himself testified that the local administration of affairs at Castle Garden, by the method and system now followed, was a perfect farce.

Upon this subject the committee invited attention to the testimony of Dr. Hoyt, for twenty years connected with the board of charities and corrections, who testified that every charitable institution in the State of New York is now not only filled with occupants, but overflowing, and that the State annually expends in taking care of paupers, insane persons, etc., $20,000,000, and that this condition of affairs is largely due to improper immigration.[7]

That same year, Secretary of the Treasury William Windom also issued a report stating that the federal government could not efficiently regulate immigration through state agencies. Another year, and yet another report, confirmed that the best course for the federal government would be to cancel its contract with the New York

Castle Garden, ca. 1890. New York Public Library.

The high wooden walls that surround Castle Garden would soon be torn down and the old fort transformed into the New York Aquarium.

State commissioners and assume the full responsibility for inspecting immigrants.

In February 1890, Windom sent a letter to the state commissioners informing them that as of April 18 their contract with the federal government was canceled. Windom was determined to move the entire business of inspecting immigrants out of New York City and away from the corruption that had hounded Castle Garden. He considered several islands in New York Harbor—Governor's, Ellis, and Bedloe's, all owned by the federal government.

Governor's Island was his first choice, but the War Department refused to give up even a portion of it as a landing depot for immigrants. His second choice, Bedloe's Island, stirred up a public furor. *The World* was horrified and published a series of articles

The Proposed Emigrant Dumping Site. Statue of Liberty—"Mr. Windom, if you are going to make this island a garbage heap, I am going back to France." Judge, March 22, 1890. New York Public Library.

Windom was unmoved by the public furor over building the new immigrant depot on Bedloe's Island. "Liberty Island is our only refuge in the harbor," he explained to a World reporter, "the editor of The World *is in error, I think, in assuming that the carrying out of the Government's purpose will interfere with the attractiveness of Liberty Island. The very contrary, in my judgment, will be the result. The intention is to erect sightly and commodious buildings there, and assist thus in finishing off and beautifying the spot. The island, indeed, so far as appearances go, will be benefitted by the transfer of the immigrant station to that point."[8]*

opposed to the "desecration" of the Statue of Liberty. "The Goddess Frowns" one headline ran, "she wants her pretty little isle kept sacred."[9] *The World* published remarks from many prominent New Yorkers, who were in most cases "highly indignant." "It is simply scandalous and outrageous," said one, while another warned, "Keep the immigrants off Liberty Island, it is no place to land them."

Bartholdi himself was horrified when he learned of Windom's proposal. Once Bedloe's Island was safely out of the secretary's clutches, Bartholdi wrote his old friend Richard Butler:

PUCK.

Boss Platt's Latest Outrage. T.C.P.—"I've spoiled your Fair, and I'll ruin Liberty's Island. A Democratic City has no Rights that Republicans are bound to Respect!" Puck, ca. 1890. *Chemical Bank Archives.*

New York Senator Tom Platt, who was head of the Republican party machine, was blamed not only for losing New York's World Fair (it went to Chicago in 1893), but also for scrapping Liberty and turning her island into an immigrant station. Inside the walls of Fort Wood, the cartoonist has placed an immigrant boardinghouse, a steamship company office, and a baggage express owned by Barney Biglin. Biglin, an important Republican, held the baggage concession at Castle Garden and later at Ellis Island.

. . . I have been glad to hear that the Island has escaped once more becoming a sanitarium! My idea has always been that it would be in the future a kind of Pantheon for the glories of American Independence, that you would build around the monument of Liberty the statues of your great men, and collect there all the noble memories. [10]

Bartholdi's vision was not to be, but Congress was at least able to shift the proposed immigration depot to Ellis Island, a spot of land barely three acres in size. A much less desirable choice than either Governor's or Bedloe's Island, Ellis Island was not only small but low—almost on a level with the water. The surrounding water was too shallow for a boat to even approach the island, much less dock there. Nevertheless, Ellis Island was approved as the new home of the federal immigration station.

c h a p t e r **10**

ELLIS ISLAND

When New York City was Dutch and called New Amsterdam, Ellis Island was known as Oyster Island. Named for its surrounding oyster beds, the island was a favorite spot for day excursions and picnics. The oysters found there were enormous— some as large as ten inches across. Later, in the 1760s, the island was used as an execution site and became known as Gibbet Island. At least one pirate was hanged there and probably several more. Sometime later, the island was acquired by Samuel Ellis, who left it to his grandson and namesake. The title to the island becomes obscure at this point and several descendants of the original Samuel Ellis laid claim to it. In 1807, when the federal government was planning the defense of New York City against British attack, the War Department directed New York State to buy up the various titles to Ellis Island. New York did so and then sold Ellis Island to the federal government for ten thousand dollars. A small fort was built there, but like its counterparts around New York harbor— Castle Williams on Governor's Island, Castle Clinton on the Battery, and Fort Wood on Bedloe's Island—the fort never saw action. Indeed, during the War of 1812, New York's fortifications were of no help against the British blockade, which sealed the harbor for over a year, although their presence probably deterred any thought of attacking the city.

After the war, Ellis Island with its little fort—named Fort Gibson after a hero of the battle of Fort Erie in 1813—was used as a munitions dump, and during the Civil War large amounts of powder and ammunition were stored there. When peace came, nothing was done to deplete this store of munitions, and neighboring people in New Jersey and New York became increasingly alarmed at the danger of an accidental explosion. There was a flurry of protests in 1868, which went unheeded, and again in 1876 when Representative Augustus A. Hardenburg of New Jersey charged that "if it were struck by lightning, the shock would destroy Jersey City, Hoboken, and parts of New York." But it wasn't until 1890 that Congress adopted legislation directing the War Department to clear Ellis Island of munitions. Before the bill was passed, however, it was amended to provide an initial appropriation of seventy-five thousand dollars for "improving Ellis Island for immigration purposes." President Benjamin Harrison signed the bill into law on April 11, 1890.

Within a month the munitions dump was removed. Then the island was doubled in size with landfill, and the construction of a two-story reception hall made of Georgia pine was started.

Immigration officials hoped that all this work could be accomplished in one year, but it took two years to complete all the necessary buildings. In the meantime, immigrants were landed at a small granite structure on the Battery called the Barge Office. This building, which had once been used by customs officials, was now abandoned and was surplus federal property.

The Immigration Service quickly converted it into a temporary landing depot, and federal inspection of immigrants started in April 1890. Most of the personnel were former clerks from Castle Garden, who brought with them the accepted petty corruption that had prevailed when New York State was in charge of immigration.

New York was not the only city in the United States where federal control was established. By the following year, the Treasury Department had taken over the responsibility for inspecting and admitting immigrants to all ports in the country—Philadelphia, Boston, New Orleans, etc. The Immigration Act of 1891 created the office of superintendent of immigration under the Treasury Department, and provided for the appointment of immigration commissioners for the major ports. It also contained more restrictions on immigration that would change the inspection routine. The law excluded ". . . all idiots, insane persons, paupers, or persons likely to become a public charge, persons suffering from a loathsome or a dangerous contagious disease, persons who have been convicted of a felony or other infamous crime or misdemeanor involving moral turpitude, polygamists and . . . contract laborers."

Boards of Special Inquiry made up of four men decided cases whenever there was a doubt about an immigrant's eligibility to land. The board's decision could, in turn, be appealed to the Secretary of the Treasury in Washington.

In 1892, the first commissioner of immigration in New York,

Colonel John B. Weber, worked with steamship companies to devise a ship's manifest, or list of its passengers. By the following year, ships were required by law to record the vital statistics of all passengers on these manifests.

Each completed manifest sheet listed thirty passengers and their answers to a series of questions: what is your nationality, married or single, how many in your family, what's your final destination, how much money do you have, do you have tickets to your destination, have you ever been an inmate of an asylum or prison, what is the state of your health, what is your occupation, etc. These sheets were filled out by the steamship representative at the port of embarkation and then given to the immigration inspectors once the ship arrived at its destination. The answers on the sheets were used as a basis for cross-examining the immigrant to determine whether he should be allowed to land. A representative of the steamship line had to swear that the information on the manifest was true to the best of his knowledge, and steamship companies had to pay a ten dollar fine for every passenger improperly manifested. Congress hoped that this requirement would prevent shipping agents from selling tickets to emigrants who were not qualified to enter the United States.

Recently landed immigrants in Battery Park, ca. 1890. Museum of the City of New York.

Immigrants outside Castle Garden in Battery Park, ca. 1890. Museum of the City of New York.

The new wooden immigration building on Ellis Island was opened in January 1892, and was described in *Harper's Weekly*:

It looks like a latter-day watering place hotel, presenting to the view a great many-windowed expanse of buff-painted wooden wall, of blue-slate roofing, and of light and picturesque towers. It is 400 feet long, two stories high, and 150 feet wide, and with its adjuncts, will cost about $200,000. It is devised to permit of the handling of at least 10,000 immigrants in a day, and the first story, which is 13 feet in height, is sufficiently capacious for the storage and handling of the baggage of 12,000 new comers. When a ship comes into port she will go to the wharf, as usual, to land her cabin passengers, and the steerage people will then be put off upon a barge and taken to Ellis Island. There they will enter the new station, and ascend to the second story by means of a double staircase. The medical inspectors will watch them as they climb the stairs, and whenever they see an invalid, a cripple, or one blind of an eye, or otherwise unfitted for an immigrant's future, they will stop such a person, and send him or her to one side into the physician's detention room. The others will continue on and into the great second story

room, to be separated into ten lines and to march through that number of aisles between the desks of the so-called "pedigree clerks," who will cross-examine them as the law requires. Beyond the aisles and the desks of the questioning inspectors they will find two great pens or enclosures, one 58 feet wide and 144 feet long, and the other 72 x 110 feet. Into one will go those whose destination is New York city or its suburbs; into the other will be put the greater number who are about to begin another journey to distant States and Territories. In time those whose journey is practically at an end will be taken by a government steamer across the water to be landed at the Barge Office, while the others will be carried by barges to the wharves of the railways on which they are to travel.

On this second floor, conveniently arranged, are spaces for the railroad ticket-sellers, the clerks of the information bureau, for the telegraph and broker's counters, and the lunch stand. Colonel John B. Weber, the Commissioner of Emigration (sic), will have his office in one corner on that floor, and General O'Beirne, the assistant Commissioner, will occupy a similar office in another corner. A great brick vault for the safe-keeping of records makes another small division of the space. Two little buildings on the grounds will be used for a lock-up and hospital; another building, to be constructed, will be a bath for both men and women, the sexes being separated, of course. Other separate buildings, either finished or projected, are the power-house for steam-heating and electric lighting, the kitchen and restaurant, and the doctor's quarters. The customs men will have their headquarters on the first floor, which is otherwise to be used for the baggage that these officials are to examine.[1]

The new Immigrant Landing Station under construction on Ellis Island, 1891. Library of Congress.

Ellis Island, which was officially opened in January 1892, would burn to the ground just five years later.

With the passage of the 1891 Immigration Act and the construction of the Ellis Island facilities, the federal government embarked on a policy of restriction that was intended to "sift" the newcomers

Looking Backward. They would close to the new-comer the bridge that carried them and their fathers over. Lithograph by J. Keppler in Puck, *January 11, 1893. Library of Congress.*

Although German, Jewish, and Irish societies all lobbied strenuously for liberal immigration laws, other children and grandchildren of the "old" immigrants favored restriction. This self-protective attitude was ridiculed in 1906 by Finley Peter Dunne in his Observations by Mr. Dooley: *"He was in yisterday an' says he:' 'Tis time we done something to make th' immigration laws sthronger,' says he. 'Thrue f'r ye, Miles Standish,' says I; 'but what wud ye do?' 'I'd keep out th' offscourins iv Europe,' says he . . . 'But what ar-re th' immigrants doin' that's roonous to us?' I says. 'Well,' says he, 'they're arnychists,' he says; 'they don't assymilate with th' counthry,' he says. 'Maybe th' counthry's digestion has gone wrong fr'm too much rich food,' says I; 'perhaps now if we'd lave off thryin' to digest Rockefellar an'thry a simple diet like Schwartzmeister, we wudden't feel th' effects iv our vittels,' I says. 'Maybe if we'd season th' immygrants a little or cook them thurly, they'd go down betther,' I says."[2]*

to make sure that only strong, able-bodied men and women were admitted. Even though immigration at this time was less than half a million per year, there was a growing feeling among Americans that the United States could not assimilate these newcomers whose numbers seemed to increase every year. There was, to be sure, a nativist zeal to protect the American Yankee race from foreign intruders. But most Americans who favored restriction were reacting to the impoverished conditions under which the immigrants lived in cities, which teemed with foreign populations. Jacob Riis's *How the Other Half Lives*, published in the late 1880s, presented an image of squalor rarely seen before by middle-class Americans. Riis's photographs contrasted sharply with the extraordinary wealth and power enjoyed by America's big businessmen and strongly suggested the inevitability of a violent clash between the poor and the rich. America viewed the overcrowded slums and tenements of large cities as impenetrable pockets of violence, criminal activity, and graft— virtual powder kegs of class conflict. Unrestricted immigration was blamed for these dreadful conditions.

Labor unions, too, wanted some restriction on immigration. The struggling labor movement strongly objected to employers hiring immigrants as cheap labor and as strike breakers. It was at the insistence of labor leaders that the Alien Contract Labor Law was

passed in 1885. Their view was expressed by Henry Hood in an article in *Forum* magazine in September 1892:

When a stranger visits the anthracite regions of Pennsylvania, he is filled with sympathy for the poor Italian and Slav. He considers the American residents heartless in the extreme. He is amazed at the way the foreigners are regarded. But a single year spent in that land will show him the truth, no matter how tender-hearted he is. He will then know that disgust should take the place of surprise. He sees a thousand idle Americans and a like number of foreigners slaving for 80 or 90 cents per day. He sees the Americans sending their children to school, supporting churches, living in decent houses, trying to be cleanly, and to wear presentable clothing. He also sees the scum of Europe taking the place of the former, content to swarm in shanties like hogs, to contract scurvy by a steady diet of the cheapest salt pork, to suffer sore eyes and bodies rather than buy a towel and washtub, to endure typhoid fever rather than undergo the expense of the most primitive sanitary apparatus.[3]

Hood's remarks were later quoted in an 1895 report made by a congressional committee investigating immigration problems. The report further observed that ". . . during the ten years ending January 1895, 10,000 immigrants have been given employment in Pennsylvania alone, gradually supplanting the practical miners who have found it impossible to live at the low rate of wages established by the immigrants."[4]

It was only a matter of time, however, before immigrant workers would become active members of the unions and provide labor with its most outspoken and aggressive leaders. This, too, would frighten some American legislators. Now, in addition to equating immigration with poverty, they saw a rising specter of worker-capitalist conflict emerging from immigrant-controlled labor unions. The revolt of the Molly Maguires, the bloody railroad strike of 1877, the Hungarian coal miners strike in 1886, the Haymarket bombing in Chicago the same year, lent credence to the fear that labor with its socialist and anarchist overtones was in effect undermining the American "way of life," a phrase that was just becoming current. Fear of the labor unions would persist into the early twentieth century when the Justice Department arrested thousands and deported hundreds of union members in the "Red Scare" of 1919.

Despite these fears of immigration as a "menacing eruption,"

A Kind of Freedom We Will Not Tolerate. Columbia—"You are welcome. But, understand. I'll have no trifling with the peace and security of any member of my household." Frank Leslie's Illustrated Newspaper, August 20, 1881.

Columbia's gentle admonitions are in response to the assassination of Czar Alexander II of Russia by members of a terrorist group called The People's Will. America's portal, although marked "no sympathy for political assassins," was open to political refugees so long as they did not preach or try to implement their radical theories on government here. Two years following the assassination of William McKinley in 1901, however, anarchists were barred by law from entering the United States.

there was still considerable sentiment in America for maintaining an open-door policy. Industrialists from the northeast states were willing to risk capitalist-worker conflict in order to maintain a free influx of cheap labor for their factories. Congress, too, was mindful of a growing block of foreign-born voters who favored liberal immigration policy, especially when that policy affected the admission of their family members and friends.

This liberal view was shared by Commissioner John B. Weber, who went to Europe as head of a fact-finding committee in the summer of 1891 to investigate rumors that countries of southern and eastern Europe were getting rid of their criminals, paupers, and other undesirables by sending them to the United States on "prepaid" tickets. Weber did not find any evidence of this and in an article for the *North American Review* of April 1892, he wrote that the new immigrants came to the United States for much the same

reasons as the old immigrants—to seek economic opportunity and greater freedom:

The general character of eligible immigrants arriving here is substantially the same as that of past years, the larger percentage of "prepaids" furnishing on this point evidence of an unmistakable nature. Prepaid tickets and tickets purchased in the United States and sent to relatives and friends on the other side, who, it is fair to assume, being members of the same family, are in a manner vouched for as desirable . . .

It is charged that foreigners furnish a larger percentage of paupers and criminals than the native element. This is probably true, but it is hardly because they are foreigners, but because they are the poorer half of society, and consequentially less able to cope with misfortune or to withstand temptation. It is not so creditable to a rich man to refrain from stealing a loaf of bread as it is to a hungry one. Wealthy Americans would not be so numerous if it had not been for the immigration of so many Europeans.[5]

Weber closed his article by saying that when nationalities are blended, the best characteristics of each are "retained and a high type of physical strength [is] produced, the most desirable foun-

And we open our arms to them!" Life, July 12, 1883. Library of Congress.

A gaggle of monarchs sweep away from their teeming shores not just the undesirable poor but also opera singers, destitute royalty, the Salvation Army, and at least two celebrities, Oscar Wilde and Lily Langtry. This cartoon appeared the summer before Emma Lazarus completed her memorable sonnet welcoming Europe's "wretched refuse" to America.

Liberty as guardian of the Constitution. Puck, October 27, 1886. Chemical Bank Archives.

The cartoonist from Puck *depicts the statue in the guise of Columbia, wearing the tradinal Phrygian cap of liberty and carrying a tablet inscribed "Life, Liberty and the Pursuit of Happiness." Columbia upholds the Constitution—her torch—and stands firm against the snares of a wide variety of radicals mounted on ramshackle platforms. Along with the movements that were seen as foreign imports—socialism, anarchism, and communism—the fair-minded cartoonist from* Puck *includes "intolerance," a universal malady, and "georgeism," the single-tax doctrine of Henry George, who was candidate for Mayor of New York in 1886.*

dation of mental quality."

Weber's conclusions were exactly opposite those drawn by a group of wealthy Bostonians who founded the Immigration Restriction League in 1894. They called the new immigrants "off-scourings" of Europe, illiterates, paupers, criminals, and madmen. These aliens, they said, would not enrich the American race but degrade it.

One of the Restriction League's most outspoken members was Henry Cabot Lodge, who proposed the "literacy test" bill to Con-

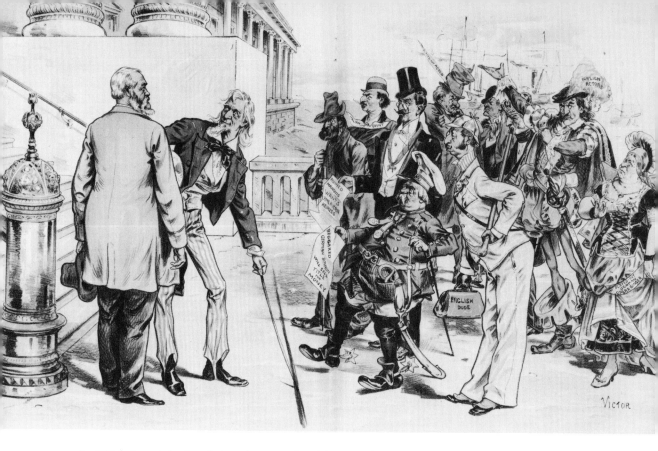

gress in 1896. It required each immigrant to be able to read at least twenty-five words of the Constitution in his or her own language in order to be admitted to the United States. Three attempts to pass the bill failed, but it passed finally in 1917 over President Woodrow Wilson's veto.

In 1896, the restrictionists pled their case for a literacy test by pointing to the sudden arrival at Ellis Island of thousands of Italian men fleeing conscription during their country's war in Abyssinia. Throughout the month of April there was an average of five hundred detained immigrants on the island every night, although there were sleeping accommodations for only 250. The overflow was kept in temporary outdoor pens. When riots threatened, the new commissioner of immigration, Joseph Senner, telegraphed to Washington for extra guards. *The New York Tribune* reported:

On Sunday, small riots that threaten to develop into trouble of a more serious nature are occurring daily among the many immigrants on Ellis Island . . . the steamship Bolivia *brought into this port 1,376 of these people, and* Alesia *followed with over one thousand. The steamships*

President Harrison Recommends Restriction of Immigration. Uncle Sam—"If we must draw the line, let us draw it at these immigrants!" Judge, *July 1889. Library of Congress.*

"We should not cease to be hospitable to immigration," Harrison said in his inaugural address, "but we should cease to be careless as to the character of it. There are men of all races whose coming is necessarily a burden upon our public revenues or a threat to social order. These should be identified and excluded." The cartoonist from Judge *suggests that the exclusion of fortune-seekers should be America's first concern.*

Victoria and Belgravia *are now on the way here with . . . 2,820 more . . .*[6]

A few days later, a *Tribune* reporter went out to Ellis Island and described the recent arrivals:

A forlorn looking lot they are, restless, depressed and penniless, and it is pitiable indeed to watch their longing looks, hoping against hope, as they do for freedom. The most sympathetic could but exclaim, as they looked upon the group, "We don't want them; send them back."[7]

Meanwhile, Francis Walker, a Yale professor of economics, wrote in the *Atlantic Monthly*:

The entrance into our political, social and industrial life of such vast masses of peasantry, degraded below our utmost conceptions, is a matter which no intelligent patriot can look upon without the gravest apprehension and alarm. These people have no history behind them which is of a nature to give encouragement. They have none of the inherited instincts and tendencies which made it comparatively easy to deal with immigration of olden times. They are beaten men from beaten races; representative of the worst failures in the struggle for existence.[8]

Senator Lodge, in his congressional speech on behalf of the literacy test, called attention to the "Russians, Hungarians, Poles, Bohemians, Italians, Greeks, and even Asiatics" who were "pouring into the United States." These aliens, Lodge warned, threatened the "very fabric of our race," adding:

The danger has begun. It is small as yet, comparatively speaking, but it is large enough to warn us to act while there is yet time and while it can be done easily and efficiently. There lies the peril at the portals of our land; there is pressing in the tide of unrestricted immigration. The time has certainly come, if not to stop, at least to check, to sift, and to restrict those immigrants. In careless strength, with generous hand, we have kept our gates wide open to all the world. If we do not close them, we should at least place sentinels beside them to challenge those who would pass through. The gates which admit men to the United States and to citizenship in the great republic should no longer be left unguarded.[9]

President Grover Cleveland vetoed the bill and in his message to Congress made it clear that he thought the literacy test was an unfair and unreliable way of determining an immigrant's worthiness.

A radical departure from our national policy relating to immigration is here presented. Heretofore we have welcomed all . . . we have encouraged those coming from foreign countries to cast their lot with us and join in the development of our vast domain, securing in return a share in the blessings of American citizenship.

A century's stupendous growth, largely due to the assimilation and thrift of millions of sturdy and patriotic adopted citizens, attests the success of this generous and free-handed policy, which while guarding the people's interests, exacts from our immigrants only physical and moral soundness and a willingness and ability to work.

. . . It is said, however, that the quality of recent immigration is undesirable. The time is quite within recent memory when the same thing was said of immigrants who, with their descendants, are now numbered among our best citizens.

I cannot believe that we would be protected . . . by limiting immigration to those who can read and write in any language twenty-five words of our Constitution. In my opinion, it is infinitely more safe to admit a hundred thousand immigrants who, though unable to read and write, seek among us only a home and opportunity to work, than to admit one of those unruly agitators and enemies of governmental control, who can not only read and write but delights in arousing by inflammatory speech the illiterate and peacefully inclined to discontent and tumult. [10]

The crush of arrivals at Ellis Island was short-lived, and the restriction controversy eventually quieted down. An economic depression in America effectively discouraged immigration; over the next several years, inspectors at Ellis Island had no difficulty in processing the less than 200,000 aliens who arrived annually.

It was fortunate that the island was not overcrowded on June 15, 1897. Early that morning a fire broke out in one of the towers of the wooden complex and quickly swept through all the buildings. *The New York Sun* reported:

Within five minutes after it was first seen more than half the building appeared to be in flames, and within fifteen minutes the whole building was going . . .

The flames were then shooting a hundred feet in the air, and by their light hundreds of people could be seen on the island rushing hither and thither . . .

From the main building the fire swept over the ferryhouse and the docks and yard, and caught, apparently on all the buildings on the island. A few minutes past one o'clock the roof of the main building was seen to fall in and a great shower of sparks shot up into the air . . .

For a few minutes after this crash the crowds that had been seen on the island running around were lost sight of but when the smoke that followed the falling of the walls cleared away it could be seen that a hundred or more tugs had reached the island, were crowding close to the shore, and appeared to be taking the people aboard.[11]

One hundred and forty immigrants and a large force of employees were on the island when the fire broke out. Miraculously there was no loss of life. Commissioner Senner said later, "Ever since I have been in office, the fear of something like this fire has haunted me, and now that it has come and no lives were lost I am glad of it. A row of unsightly, ramshackle tinderboxes has been removed, and when the Government rebuilds we'll be forced to put up decent fireproof structures."[12]

The government announced almost immediately that Ellis Island would be rebuilt with new fireproof buildings. In the meantime, the inspection of immigrants was moved back to the cramped quarters of the Barge Office. Detained immigrants were kept in an old passenger steamer, the *Narragansett*, which was moored at Ellis Island.

William McKinley, elected president in 1896, appointed a new commissioner, Thomas Fitchie, who was known as an energetic foe of corruption when he was a Republican leader in Brooklyn. But Fitchie was not a vigilant commissioner, and perhaps the worst scandals ever connected with the Immigration Service occurred during his tenure.

The affairs of immigration were actually overseen by the assistant commissioner, Edward McSweeney, who had also been Senner's assistant. The blame for a great deal of the corruption was later placed on McSweeney's shoulders. By 1900, rumors of fraud, extortion, abuse, and even murder assailed the immigration inspectors at the Barge Office. Victor Safford, who was a medical officer in the Immigration Service at that time, recalled in his memoir that one

unfortunate immigrant was found dead under a staircase at the Barge
Office with his throat cut.

*It was evidently a suicide. It certainly did seem rather remarkable how-
ever that a man could crawl under a public passageway of this character,
kill himself and the body remain there undiscovered two or three days
even though the place was rather dark and partly occupied by rubbish. It
was not hard to make it appear that even if the man had not been murdered by the Barge Office employees and his body hidden there the delay*

*The Barge Office, ca. 1900. Library of
Congress.*

*After the wooden registry building on El-
lis Island burned down on June 15,
1897, the Immigration Service moved
back into a "stuffy and ill-smelling shed"
attached to the Barge Office, according to
Harper's Weekly. "In this narrow space
six thousand aliens a week were herded.
They were gathered into pens, sent to
sleep under the rafters with layers of hot
air for coverlets, and hurried about by
frantic persons who waved papers and
scowled."*[13]

Marine Hospital Service doctors standing outside the Barge Office, ca. 1900. National Archives.

These were the men in charge of examining all steerage passengers landing in New York.

Immigrant standing outside the Barge Office, 1900. Photograph by R.F. Turnbull. Library of Congress.

in discovering the body indicated that supervision over the building was not what it should be.[14]

One of the most disgraceful episodes of Fitchie's term involved the case of Isidore Termini, who disappeared from immigration custody in May 1900. His son, who lived in Buffalo and was awaiting his father's arrival, asked an immigration official in Buffalo to trace his father's whereabouts. The inspectors at the Barge Office discovered that the father had been under detention, classed as likely to be a public charge. This was strange because the father had ninety dollars plus a ticket on the Erie Railroad to Buffalo.

After several days the old man still had not arrived in Buffalo. In reply to the son's letter, Commissioner Fitchie reported that the immigrant had apparently escaped illegally from the Barge Office, and he intimated that the son's inquiries were a pretext to keep the old man from being found. Weeks later, the father's body washed up on the New Jersey shore. It was thought that he had been pushed overboard while en route from the Barge Office to detention quarters on Ellis Island. Safford admitted in his recollection that Termini's death strongly indicated that immigrants were being murdered for their money and that the management of the Barge Office was grossly negligent.

In June 1900, *The New York Times* ran a series of stories on the treatment of immigrants at the Barge Office.

"Why do they treat those people like dogs," one article began. "People who visit Battery Park for the first time and see the big

crowd in front of the Barge Office cuffed about by policemen ask this question. The policemen, if the question is put to them, inform the inquisitive ones that it is none of their business, while the Barge officials themselves are wont to treat any complaints with silent and contemptuous disdain . . ."[15] Inside the Barge Office, *The Times* continued, immigrants were roughly hustled about: "All the while the air echoes with shouts of 'Move on, move on' and gradually the confused group of temporary prisoners is pushed and shoved upstairs to the 'pens.' "

The following month, a story appeared in *The London Express* written by a reporter who came to New York disguised as an immigrant. He called the Barge Office a prison where "immigrants are beaten and abused worse than cattle." The Ellis Island exami-

Immigrants and cartman waiting outside the Barge Office, ca. 1900. The Byron Collection, Museum of the City of New York.

Relatives and friends waiting for immigrants to land outside the Barge Office, ca. 1900. The Byron Collection, Museum of the City of New York.

Arrivals in New York traveled to their new homes in the city via wagon, or, if they were adventurous, on the elevated railroad, which can be seen in the background of our photograph.

nation of immigrants, he charged, was made without any regard to the ordinary principles of hygiene. Here is how he described the supper he had when detained on Ellis Island:

We passed in a long line round the room. A man with filthy hands filled our hats or handkerchiefs with moldy prunes. Another thrust two lumps of bread into our hands. Supervising the distribution was a foul-mouthed Bowery tough who danced upon the table and poured forth upon us torrents of obscene, blasphemous abuse. I saw him drag one old man, a long-bearded Polish Jew, past the barrel of prunes by the hair of his face. I saw him kick another emigrant, a German, on the head with a heavy boot. [16]

A *New York Times* editorial maintained that the reporter from *The London Express* was "experienced in the observation and recording of facts and quite beyond the suspicion of exaggeration or sensationalism. Rumors about the maltreatment and robbery of immigrants arriving here," *The Times* continued, "have been numerous for some time and hidden away in Washington is a formal report which has been said with considerable authority not only to sustain every one of [the *Express*] statements, but to go far beyond them, of existing methods, conditions of management."[17]

The formal report referred to was made by an investigating committee appointed by the commissioner-general of immigration in Washington, Terence V. Powderly. The former leader of the Knights of Labor was appointed head of the Immigration Service by William McKinley, who had known Powderly for years. There was a good deal of animosity between Powderly and McSweeney over the inspection of immigrants at the Barge Office, and Powderly's investigation was roundly denounced by McSweeney as a political headhunt. The committee's 2,800-page report was a convincing indictment of McSweeney's administration, but it was not submitted to the secretary of the Treasury until a second investigation clearing McSweeney of all wrong-doing could be assembled and submitted along with the first report. No charges were brought against McSweeney, but Powderly noted with approval in his autobiography, that eleven immigration employees were eventually discharged ". . . for offenses such as overcharging for food, misleading immigrants as to destination, procuring admission of a friend or relative to see newly landed immigrants for a fee, overcharges in exchanging foreign money for American money, downright cruelty to aliens, petty thievery, and false statements as to distances to be traveled."[18]

Immigration officers in Washington and New York hoped that the battered reputation of the immigration service would somehow be redeemed once the new buildings on Ellis Island were completed and occupied. The cramped facilities at the Barge Office were seen as the major cause of the scandals and rough treatment immigrants suffered while going through their inspection.

chapter *11*

A CLEAN SWEEP

W hen it opened, the new Ellis Island reception hall was hailed as a "magnificent" structure and its facilities for inspection "admirably arranged." It was described in *The New York Times* on December 3, 1900:

Situated on one of the most prominent locations in the harbor, the new station is an imposing as well as a pleasing addition to the picturesque waterfront metropolis . . .

The main building, situated in the center of the island, is 385 feet in length and 165 feet in width. The body of the building is 62 feet high, while the four towers at each corner are 100 feet from the ground to the top of the domes. The style is a conglomeration of several styles of architecture, the predominating style being that of the French Renaissance. The material used in the construction is brick with light stone trimmings, harmonized so as to make the general effect as attractive in appearance as possible. The spires of the towers are copper-covered, and in the top of each is an observatory from which a splendid view of the harbor and city may be had. On the western and eastern sides of the building are the main entrances, massive arches which extend well into the second story. Over the arch in concrete work appears the national coat of arms, while eagles of the same material make the general effect still more attractive.

But the interior arrangements are what, after all, makes the station a model of completeness. Every detail of the exacting and confusing service to which its uses are to be dedicated were considered in perfecting the interior plans. The transportation, examining, medical, inquiry, and various quarters that, while they are practically separate in every detail, yet are so arranged as to follow one after the other according to its proper place in the department . . .

It is estimated that 5,000 persons can be thoroughly examined with perfect ease, and in an emergency 3,000 more, by the application of a little added energy on the part of the examiners. Surrounding this room from the third floor is the observation gallery, where visitors can watch

the inspectors at work. The dormitories are entered from doors on the gallery. There are two main apartments which can accommodate about 600 sleepers comfortably.

There were also two roof gardens, a restaurant, a laundry, and a bathing house with showers where two hundred immigrants could wash at a time. "We expect to wash them once a day, and they will land on American soil clean, if nothing more," said Assistant Commissioner McSweeney. The new building on Ellis Island was formally opened on December 17, 1900. The first to land were 654 steerage passengers "ranging in age from three months to three score and ten" from the *Kaiser Wilhelm,* one newspaper reported. During that first day, 2,251 immigrants were inspected on Ellis Island.

But, despite the immigration depot's change of location, corruption continued unabated. In the summer of 1901, McSweeney discovered that officers of some of the steamships had conspired with immigration inspectors to sell forged citizenship papers to immigrant passengers. These papers, which cost five dollars for a single person and six dollars for a family, allowed the immigrant to land without having to go to Ellis Island for inspection. One Treasury official said the swindle had been going on for five or six years and probably over ten thousand immigrants had been landed illegally.

This was not an isolated scandal, and soon the new Ellis Island was just as discredited as the old Barge Office. Most contemporary observers maintained that the treatment of the immigrant by the inspectors, members of the Board of Inquiry, restaurant workers, money exchangers, baggage handlers, and transportation agents was characterized by intimidation, bullying, and rough language. Ex-

Architect's rendering of main building on Ellis Island, 1898. Boring and Tilton, Architects. Library of Congress.

The federal government awarded the contract for designing and building the new immigrant landing station on Ellis Island to the New York architectural firm of Boring and Tilton. Its design was selected in a competition entered by a number of eminent firms.

Ellis Island's main building, 1905. Photograph by A. Loeffler. Library of Congress.

Immigrants were brought to Ellis Island from the Hudson River or Hoboken piers by barge or ferry. The building on the left is the bathhouse and laundry. The smokestack of the power house can be seen in the background.

tortion, bribery, cheating, and petty thievery were crimes that were committed every day against those who were in Immigration Service custody on Ellis Island.

Edward Steiner, in his book *On the Trail of the Immigrant,* said of Ellis Island during this period:

The conditions steadily grew worse; at least the complaints grew more numerous. Experiences like my own were not rare. I knew that the money changers were "crooked," so I passed a twenty mark piece to one of them for exchange, and was cheated out of nearly seventy-five percent of my money. My change was largely composed of new pennies, whose brightness was well calculated to deceive any newcomer.

At another time I was approached by an inspector who, in a very friendly way, intimated that I might have difficulty in being permitted to land, and that money judiciously placed might accomplish something.

A Bohemian girl whose acquaintance I had made on the steamer came to me with tears in her eyes and told me that one of the inspectors had promised to pass her quickly, if she would promise to meet him at a certain hotel. In heartbroken tones she asked: "Do I look like that?" The concessions were in the hands of irresponsible people and I remember the time when the restaurant was a den of thieves, in which the immigrant was robbed by the proprietor, whose employees stole from him and from the immigrants also.

My complaints when I made them were treated with the same neglect as were those of others, until with the coming in of the Roosevelt administration they had their resurrection, a change was demanded and the demand satisfied . . .[1]

Immigrants disembarking at Ellis Island, ca. 1900. National Park Service.

Victor Safford, an immigration officer, recalled in his memoirs that passengers were so poorly treated in steerage that it was "not uncommon" to find that some of them had died on the steamboats or barges on their way to Ellis Island. They were in such poor physical condition, he wrote, that "when they were run off the ship onto the wharf, the exertion incident to the transfer to the Island finished them."[4]

Theodore Roosevelt, who became president in September 1901 following the assassination of William McKinley, moved quickly to clean up the Immigration Service. In December, a headline in *The New York Times* reported, "Commissioner Fitchie May Soon Be Removed—T. R. wants all immigrants protected from harsh, cruel treatment from swindlers and extortioners."[2] Despite Fitchie's and McSweeney's protestations that "the charges affecting this department are all folderol," Roosevelt's mind was made up. In a letter to Henry Cabot Lodge, dated January 24, 1902, he wrote:

Immigrant mother and child outside building on Ellis Island, ca. 1900. National Archives.

. . . there are definite charges against McSweeney, any one of which if true would mean that he should be removed. . . . The head of the office, Fitchie, is absolutely incompetent. It is admitted by everyone that he does nothing whatever for the office, and that the office is run by McSweeney. The further fact appears that it is run very badly indeed. There are the gravest complaints made about the handling of immigrants, the giving of contracts, favoring of steamship lines, and the like. Either McSweeney is absolutely incompetent or else he is more responsible than any other one man for these evils.[3]

Roosevelt chose William Williams, a Wall Street lawyer, as the new commissioner of immigration for the port of New York. It was not a political appointment. Williams, although a Republican, was not active in politics and not beholden to either the boss-dominated Republican machine or the reform Republicans. The reformers, however, heartily endorsed Williams's appointment and looked forward

Group of immigrants from eastern Europe in front of main building on Ellis Island, ca. 1900. National Archives.

"When we landed at Ellis Island our baggage was lost. We inquired for it and they said, 'Come another time. Come another time. You'll find it. We haven't got time now.' So we left and we never saw our luggage again. We had bedding, linen, beautiful copper utensils, that sort of thing.

"From Ellis Island we went by wagon to my brother's apartment on Hester Street. Hester Street and Essex on the Lower East Side. We were all bewildered to see so many people. Remember we were from a little village. And here you had people coming and going and shouting. Peddlars, people on the street. Everything was new, you know."[5] *(Pauline Newman, from Lithuania, 1901)*

William Williams, commissioner of immigration at Ellis Island from 1902 to 1905 and, in a second term, from 1909 to 1914. William Williams Papers, Mss. & Archives Division, New York Public Library.

"Commissioner Williams," commented a New York newspaper, "is a novelty at Ellis Island—a novelty anywhere in political life. A Yale man, a Harvard Law graduate, a widely traveled student, a Wall Street lawyer. . . . A millionaire bachelor, he spends his evenings in the luxury, the comfort, the elegance of the University Club. His days, even his Sundays, he spends over at Ellis Island, with all its squalor, its filth, its sorrow."[6]

to the inevitable destruction of a machine patronage system that had pervaded immigration affairs in New York for so long.

Williams gave up a $25,000-a-year practice to become commissioner—a position that paid only $5,000 a year. He was "descended from old New England ancestry," as one newspaper put it, a graduate of Yale University and Harvard Law School, a bachelor, and quite wealthy. He became commissioner on April 28, 1902, and served until June 30, 1905. After a four-year respite, he served a second term from 1909 to 1914. He presided over the management of Ellis Island during most of the years when immigration was at its peak. Williams was, by all accounts, a brilliant administrator. He was able to impose an efficient order on the affairs of Ellis Island, despite the massive overcrowding that constantly bedeviled efforts to organize the complex job of inspecting, feeding, housing, and arranging transportation for thousands, sometimes over five thousand immigrants a day.

Williams kept two scrapbooks of newspaper and magazine clippings covering his administration of Ellis Island. These scrapbooks, which also include Williams's own comments typed and pasted in among the clippings, give a detailed view of the day-to-day routine and tumult of running one of the most controversial offices in the country. Williams took charge of what he found to be a "disorganized and demoralized office." In his first report to Washington, made only two months after he became commissioner, he described the dreadful conditions he found at Ellis Island:

. . . [Immigrants] were hustled about and addressed in rough language by many of the Government and railroad officials until they were frequently both bewildered and frightened. The fact that the quarters in which they were detained were formerly called "pens" is suggestive of the rest of the treatment they received; nor can any exception be taken to the former application of this word to these quarters, in view of their filthy condition. This was particularly the case with the dining room, the floor of which was allowed by the former privilege holder to remain covered with grease, bones, and other remnants of food for days at a time. In the first days of my administration, I witnessed with my own eyes the fact that immigrants were fed without knives, forks, or spoons, and saw them extract boiled beef from their bowls with their fingers. It would not be difficult to conceive what went on in this dining room a year ago; but we are not left to our imagination, for Dr. Stearns, a marine-hospital surgeon, stated under oath in December "The kitchen methods and methods of serving food to the immigrants are filthy and unsanitary in every way, as the restaurant employee in charge at dinner time, in each room where immigrants are fed, commonly uses his hands in assisting to serve

Interior of registry hall on the second floor of Ellis Island's main building, ca. 1905. William Williams papers, Mss. & Archives Division, The New York Public Library.

Williams rearranged the inspection floor with benches so that aliens could sit down while waiting to be interviewed by an immigration officer.

Russian woman and children in registry hall on Ellis Island, 1905. Photograph by Lewis W. Hine. New York Public Library.

Hine captioned this beautifully evocative image "Mona Lisa visits Ellis Island." The peace and calm that the photograph suggests were rare on Ellis Island during 1905, the first year that admissions to the United States broke one million.

out the portions of meat; and as the number of bowls of soup and meat are entirely insufficient in number, it is the common practice to use the same bowl over and over until all have been supplied."

I have referred only to the dining room. During this time improper practices prevailed both at the food stands and in the kitchen. At the former an employee of the privilege holder wore a cap with a gilt eagle and compelled immigrants to buy bags of food, in some cases even when they were bound for New York, Jersey City, or Brooklyn. The prices charged were in many cases exorbitant. Occasional instances of excusable error will always occur in dealing with these ignorant people, but I am compelled to believe from the evidence before me that there was formerly a

The dining hall, ca. 1900. Culver Pictures.

The food concession was a disgrace before Williams took over Ellis Island, but he succeeded in ousting the old caterer and replacing him with another. This, however, did not mean the end to the prune sandwiches that continued to be one of the restaurant's staples. Each year Ellis Island ordered twenty million prunes, which were considered a "great delicacy."

In 1905 the restaurant owners decided to serve prunes only twice a week, not because the delicacy was becoming monotonous, but because of the mess the prune pits left once thrown on the floor. One waiter said that the floor was often so slippery that it was like a skating rink.

systematic failure on the part of the authorities to secure to them fair treatment. In the kitchen immigrants were frequently compelled to perform service, sometimes receiving a bottle of beer or some such trifle in return. In one instance a sick immigrant was found peeling potatoes.[7]

It was alleged later that the concessions kept their privileges by kicking back a certain percentage of their profits to Assistant Commissioner McSweeney.

Williams also charged in his report that McSweeney's chief inspector, John Lederhilger, marked "Hold" against certain names on the ship's manifests. When the immigrants came up the line, they were taken to be personally questioned by Lederhilger. "The fact that many of those so marked," Williams wrote, ". . . were able bodied people with large amounts of money are points not without interest." Lederhilger would dispatch these people to certain boarding-houses or railroad agents in New York City and receive a kickback for his trouble.

"The boards of special inquiry," Williams continued, "failed to exclude hundreds of immigrants reported by the medical staff to be incapacitated from earning a living. . . . It goes without saying that immigrants once held for special inquiry should be thereafter sent before these boards, but it appears that some officials were in the habit of passing upon such cases themselves, bringing the immigrants out of the detention rooms, discharging them, or putting them back, according to their whims. The resulting

Immigrants detained at Ellis Island take time to be happy, 1905. Photograph by Lewis W. Hine. New York Public Library.

"In 1905 there was no organized recreation," Hine wrote, "so the immigrants supplied their own. The sign overhead reads: 'No charge for meals here.' It is written in six different languages."

Slavic woman on Ellis Island, 1905. Photograph by Lewis W. Hine. New York Public Library.

This woman's bulky sack probably contains a cherished feather bed carried all the way across Europe and the Atlantic to provide some reassuring comfort in a strange new home.

power of blackmail and of exerting other improper influences involved in this practice will be readily seen."

Williams attacked the problems of Ellis Island with the energy and zeal of a born crusader. His first step was to discipline his work force of over five hundred people. "Reform Tidal Wave Whelms Ellis Island" one newspaper headline read, "Old employees swept off their feet by set of new rules."[8] Williams put all on notice that: "Failure to report promptly for duty, to yield implicit obedience to the orders of any superior officer, or to give undivided attention to the business in hand are matters which will be taken into consideration in determining whether an official is guilty of 'dereliction of duty, delinquency, or misconduct.' "

Furthermore, there would be no more smoking, reading newspapers, writing private letters, or loitering during business hours. But *The Evening Post* reported:

Many of the employees said yesterday that they thought little notice would be taken of the new rules, asserting the Commissioner had no power to interfere with what had been the regular regime since the existence of the island.

Within two weeks Williams had occasion to prefer charges against one of his clerks who had been absent from work for four days without explanation. Williams found out that the man, who was a Civil War veteran, had been drunk during his absence. Williams recommended the man's dismissal. "This brought the G.A.R. down on me," he wrote in his scrapbook, "and it was thought that I would be reversed in Washington; but I was not, and the whole force (including the other veterans) took notice." Any delusions the workers may have entertained about the new reforms were quickly dispersed by Williams's actions and the support he received from his superiors in Washington. When Secretary of the Treasury Leslie M. Shaw appeared at Ellis Island later that month for an informal visit, he told reporters:

I am very much interested in the efforts Mr. Williams is making to systematize the work over there and to discharge all the employees who have been neglecting their duty or abusing their powers. I think Mr. Williams has accomplished a vast amount of good already and that he will soon have everything running like clock-work.

By June 1903, Williams could report to Washington that his force at Ellis Island could compare favorably with that of any other public office. He said many were "men of great intelligence, untiring energy, and scrupulous honesty." His praise, however, had to be qualified by stating the difficult circumstances surrounding immigration work:

Having in view the vastness of the work, the ignorance of the people with whom we deal, the large number of employees, and the temptations to

which they are subjected, it is inconceivable that the millennium can ever exist here, but it is quite possible, through incessant vigilance and the punishment of all wrongful or careless acts, to keep evil practices well within bounds, and bring about proper treatment of immigrants while in charge of the Government.

Williams had posted a notice around Ellis Island saying: "Immigrants must be treated with kindness and consideration." This notice was meant not just for government workers but also for employees of the various concessions. Williams barred from the island a railroad agent whose manner toward the immigrants he found "abusive." A barber was dismissed for threatening immigrants with deportation if they did not allow him to cut their hair.

Boardinghouse runners posing as missionaries were also ousted from their positions of trust. A telegraph boy who defrauded an immigrant of fifteen dollars was arrested and sent to the Ludlow Street Jail. Immigrants, too, who were overbearing and abusive were reprimanded. Jacob Riis tells of seeing Williams chastise a strapping Flemish peasant for beating a child.

Another of Williams's accomplishments was to improve the ap-

The joys and sorrows at Ellis Island, 1905. Photograph by Lewis W. Hine. New York Public Library.

pearance of the island. Before he took over as commissioner, the grounds surrounding the main building were filled with unsightly rubble and rubbish. Williams cleaned up the area, planted grass, and lined the new lawns with clipped hedges. Benches were placed along the walkways so that immigrants could sit outside to enjoy the fresh air and the view of New York harbor.

His greatest coup, however, was undoubtedly getting rid of the current privilege holders—those who held the contracts for feeding the immigrants, changing their foreign money, and delivering their baggage. These concessions were patronage plums that had belonged to New York City's Republican party since the days when Castle Garden was the immigrant landing station. The old contract expired two months after Williams took office, giving him the opportunity to award them to new bidders.

The restaurant concession was the most profitable privilege. Its costs were charged to the steamship companies, which were required by law to provide food for immigrants detained while undergoing inspection. Many times Ellis Island officials had been accused of holding up large numbers of immigrants simply to provide business for the restaurant. The contract for feeding the immigrants was held by Schwab & Co., which was owned by Charles Hess, a Republican district leader characterized by one reformer as an "unmitigated scoundrel."

The money exchange was run by Frank Scully, whose father had the exchange at Castle Garden. Scully was accused of paying less than the market rate, neglecting to give receipts to immigrants, and, in at least one case, of paying an immigrant less than half the exchange he should have been paid.

The baggage concession, too, had been accused of extortion, gross overcharging, and mismanagement. Williams estimated that with an immigration of 600,000 a year, these contracts altogether should have netted from $75,000 to $100,000 yearly in legitimate profit. But, as he observed in his scrapbook:

It was generally understood that [the concessions] brought in a great deal more. Under the methods pursued by Scully, and with immigrants presenting to him at least $5,000,000 of foreign money yearly for exchange, there is no telling what his profits were . . . there was brisk bidding for the new contracts, the old concessionaires feeling confident that with their strong political influence and being in the saddle they would *be chosen again. All had strong Republican backing.*

What I did was to make a clean sweep with resulting consternation. I had considered not only the amounts of the bids but the standing and character of the bidders. Many of the unsuccessful bidders through their political agents and personal friends made direct protest to the President . . . the President deemed it of sufficient importance to grant all the bidders a hearing at the White House (a very unusual proceeding). I was present and roundly abused but emerged triumphant, for all my recommendations were approved by the President himself, and in doing so he turned down politicians and friends alike.

One of the losers was Barney Biglin, who had held the baggage concession since Castle Garden days. One newspaper described him as "the confidential friend of President Grant, President Hayes, President Arthur, and a personal friend of President Harrison. He fought for the Republican party when a Republican had to go armed to protect himself in the East side of New York city."

Biglin wanted to appeal his case directly to Roosevelt.

"But when he called at the White House yesterday," the article continued, "and presented a card of introduction from Senator Platt, the present Republican President refused to see him."

Party regulars saw Roosevelt's backing of Williams as a serious affront to Senator Platt and the New York Republican machine. Loss of patronage always meant loss of prestige. A newspaper quoted one disgruntled Republican as saying:

Who is this fellow Williams anyway? Who ever heard of him until the President discovered he was a college man and appointed him to Commissioner Fitchie's place? Why should he snub and turn down Republicans who were fighting for the party when both the President and this dude Commissioner were in swaddling clothes? This kind of business cannot keep up too long, and the President will find that out before he gets through with politics.

The reformers, however, were jubilant. "A Political Ring Smashed" chimed *The Evening Post:*

A new era begins today at Ellis Island. Cigars no longer net 700 percent profit as in the palmy days before William Williams became commissioner and milk at two cents a glass takes the place of lacterized

water at five cents. The feeding, money changing and baggage transfer
privileges pass out of the control of a political faction and the Augean
stables of the Immigration Bureau are being laboriously swept clean of the
accumulated filth of twenty-five years."

Williams had managed to accomplish an enormous task in a relatively short period of time. One of the main villains of the former administration, however, was still employed at Ellis Island, and Williams undertook a full-scale investigation in order to have the man ousted.

"Chief Clerk Lederhilger had been the right-hand man of former Assistant Commissioner McSweeney," Williams wrote. "He was a civil servant employee, removable only upon charges. It took some time to dig out from the records the facts on which charges could be based and sustained."

Part of the work was already done. The investigation of 1899, which had been buried in Washington, was exhumed and found to contain specific accusations against McSweeney, Lederhilger, and other officials at Ellis Island. The report was a full exposé of the graft, extortion, bribery, shakedowns and kickbacks that were so common on Ellis Island that they had become accepted as business as usual. Williams conducted his own investigation, too, and preferred eighteen separate charges against Lederhilger, ranging from extortion and accepting bribes to gross dereliction of duty. Among other offenses, according to *The World,* Lederhilger tried to deport an artificial limb maker at the request of a rival manufacturer, and he received "packages containing wine and liquor from steamship lines."

Other charges said:

You have pretended to inspect, register and detain immigrants of whose
language you had no knowledge whatever.

Through your failure to properly superintend the delivery of telegrams
and money orders, numerous instances have occurred in which aliens have
actually been deported on the ground that they were apt to become public
charges, where sufficient funds have been received to entitle them to entry,
but were not delivered by you.

You further neglected to properly perform your duties, in that you
failed to report the following abuses known by you to exist at the station
in connection with the feeding of detained immigrants: the filthy condi-

tion of the dining-rooms; the fact that immigrants were compelled to eat without knives and forks; the fact that one Martin, an employee of Schwab & Co., was in the habit of compelling immigrants to purchase food against their will and in larger quantities than necessary, under the threat that they would be sent back to the detention room in case they did not comply with his demand."

Lederhilger was fired along with several other inspectors and registry clerks. In his defense, he maintained that he had often filed complaints against subordinates for dereliction of duty that were never followed up.

In trying to verify Lederhilger's assertion, Williams ordered a search of storage vaults that resulted in the discovery that hundreds of official documents were missing. Many of these documents were later found in several boxes that Edward McSweeney had marked "private" and placed in temporary storage on Ellis Island. Before McSweeney could send for them, however, Williams obtained permission from Washington to open the boxes in order to search for the missing documents. Williams found over three thousand items that pertained to the former management of Ellis Island.

McSweeney was accused of embezzling documents mainly for the purpose of concealing his own misdeeds. On October 10, 1902, Williams wrote to Secretary of Treasury Shaw:

This office is now seeking light upon several important matters, including the true facts concerning an aged Italian named Isidor Termini, who mysteriously disappeared in 1900 while under the jurisdiction of the United States, but I find only sufficient data to show that at some prior time further documents existed in this case.

Williams found many papers that McSweeney had told federal officials in 1901 were lost. These documents concerned immigrants who had been allowed to land contrary to instructions from Washington. There was also a good deal of evidence indicating that McSweeney had lent his Pennsylvania Railroad pass to friends, including Samuel Gompers.

A flurry of accusations followed Williams's discovery, but as with the Termini papers, there was not enough evidence to build a conclusive case against McSweeney. He was charged with theft of public documents, but even this was dropped since the government had

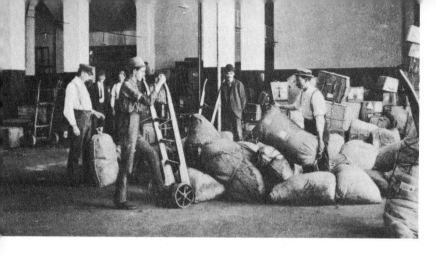

The baggage room on Ellis Island, 1902. Library of Congress.

The baggage room occupied the entire ground floor of the main building on Ellis Island. Baggage handlers in charge of shipping and local deliveries were supposed to provide their services to immigrants at a fair cost, but Williams found that sometimes they were charging twice the rate of commercial freight handlers.

recovered its property and supposedly suffered no damage.

Meanwhile, Williams was busy cleaning up other aspects of Ellis Island. Immigration officials had long allowed missionaries or representatives of welfare societies to establish offices on Ellis Island in order to aid detained immigrants in locating friends and securing employment. By 1908, forty-one of these organizations were represented on Ellis Island. Since the federal government offered no help whatsoever to the immigrants in introducing them to their

Italian immigrants at Ellis Island, 1905. Photograph by Lewis W. Hine. New York Public Library.

"Lost baggage is the cause of their worried expressions," Hine says about his subjects. With five thousand immigrants being inspected nearly every day during the peak season—spring to fall—keeping track of everyone's baggage was a major logistical problem.

Missionaries stationed on Ellis Island, May 1908. Photograph by Augustus Sherman. National Park Service.

Over forty missionaries or representatives of immigrant aid societies had access to Ellis Island. The Hebrew Immigrant Aid Society and the Society for the Protection of Italian Immigrants were two of the most important. A reporter from The Outlook *magazine who observed these social workers and the personal care they gave troubled immigrants said, "The visitor to Ellis Island would have to be of very callous heart not to be conscious of the real tenderness with which helplessness is treated."[9]*

new country, the work of the volunteer agencies was absolutely vital. But sometimes these missionaries were found to be abusing their trust. One of the first to be reprimanded and then barred from the island was the Rev. H. J. Berkemeier of the German Lutheran Immigrant Home on State Street, near Battery Park. In his letter to Berkemeier Williams said:

. . . I have conclusive proof that instead of assisting immigrants you are in the habit of actually preventing recently arrived girls from meeting their friends and compelling them to accept employment against their will with people who have previously directed you to look up servants for them at Ellis Island. Your action is the more reprehensible because you have prefixed to your name the word "pastor."

Representatives of immigrant homes in New York City, ca. 1908. Photograph by Augustus Sherman. National Park Service.

Immigrants often made arrangements while still overseas to stay at one of the immigrant homes run by religious organizations in New York. Representatives of the homes would meet these immigrants on Ellis Island and escort them to the city.

Man distributing Bibles to immigrants at Ellis Island, 1911. Library of Congress.

In 1909, the commissioner of immigration reprimanded missionaries for handing out Christian literature to recently arrived Jews on Ellis Island. "A great many of our immigrants are Hebrews," he explained, "who are on their way from persecution by one style of Christians, and when they have Christian tracts—printed in Hebrew—put in their hands, apparently with the approval of the United States Government, they wonder what is going to happen to them there."[10]

Immigrants from Prinzessen Irene going to Ellis Island, 1911. Geo. G. Bain Collection, Library of Congress.

Williams related several instances where Berkemeier coerced immigrants by threatening them with deportation. In one case he put an immigrant girl to work in a home against her will, and refused to let her communicate with her relatives who were expecting her. She was released only by legal proceedings and even then was swindled out of the pay due her.

After the Prinzessen Irene docked at a Hoboken pier, the steerage passengers were lined up for transfer to Ellis Island by barge or ferry.

Broughton Brandenburg, who sailed on the Prinzessen Irene in 1902, said that in the hustle to get the immigrants assembled and off the ship, they were often pushed, punched, or kicked by the ship's stewards. The man in front is a boarding inspector of the immigration service.

Immigrant barge on its way to Ellis Island, ca. 1900. Geo. G. Bain Collection, Library of Congress.

Barges were chartered by the steamship companies to transfer steerage passengers to Ellis Island. These barges were usually overcrowded—nine hundred crushed onto a vessel built for six hundred—with hardly any toilet arrangements or even lifesaving equipment for all the passengers. They were good enough, it seemed, for a short trip down the river, but often immigrants were imprisoned on these vessels for hours while they waited their turn to disembark at Ellis Island.

Immigrants aboard barge, ca. 1900. Brady-Handy photograph. Library of Congress.

Philip Cowen, who served on Ellis Island during the first decades of this century, recalled the busiest day the inspectors ever had was March 27, 1907, when 16,050 passengers arrived in twenty-four hours. By the end of the following day, the total number of passengers to be inspected was 21,755. Arriving immigrants had to stay on board ship for two or three days before they could be brought to Ellis Island. Even then they would have to spend hours more waiting on barges for their turn to go through inspection.

Williams closed his letter to Berkemeier saying:

Your boarding house rates range from 75 cents to $1.25 a day a person. This is business, not charity. The time has come when I propose to draw a sharp line between the true missionaries (of whom there are a number at Ellis Island) and the boarding house runners who, parading under false colors, are for that reason the most dangerous people to whom an immigrant may be turned over.

Williams also kept an eye on the activities of the railroads and the domestic steamship lines. In April 1903 he posted the following notice:

It has come to the knowledge of this office that immigrants destined to Chicago have been forwarded in some instances by the Old Dominion S.S. Co. to Norfolk, Va., thence to Newport News, and thence by rail to Chicago, such journey requiring from 52 to 78 hours; that in addition such immigrants have been compelled to spend a night at Richmond, Va., and that they have been compelled to buy baskets of food in New York City at the most exorbitant rates. The cost of such journey to Chicago is $14. The cost by the all rail route to Chicago is $15, and the journey requires less than 36 hours.

. . . immigrants shall hereafter proceed to Chicago directly from Ellis Island without passing through New York City unless they already hold tickets or orders purchased in Europe requiring them to take another route.

The general policy of this office will be to prevent immigrants destined to western points from unnecessarily spending a night in or even passing through New York City, where they fall into the hands of unscrupulous people. Any one, whether an official, privilege holder, or any other person at this station violating the terms of the foregoing, will be severely dealt with.

This would seem to indicate the railroad pool was up to the same old mischief it had engaged in since it was first set up several decades ago at Castle Garden. Unfortunately, Williams's directive had little effect on the pool's workings, and agents for the Old Dominion Steam Ship Co. would remain a thorn in the side of the commissioner of immigration for many years to come.

Williams also called the trans-Atlantic steamship companies to task for the slipshod manner in which they prepared their manifests. Each manifest was supposed to record the names of thirty immigrants and their answers to questions regarding age, birthplace, health,

Disembarking at Ellis Island, 1912. National Archives.

Immigrants, carrying their health certificates in their teeth, proceed into the main building at Ellis Island, ca. 1905. National Park Service.

*Immigrants on their way to the main
building on Ellis Island, ca. 1900. National Archives.*

*"While the statesman ponders the perils
of unrestricted immigration, and debates
with organized labor whom to shut out
and how, the procession moves serenely
on. Ellis Island is the nation's gateway to
the promised land. There is not another
such to be found anywhere. In a single
day it has handled seven thousand immigrants. 'Handled' is the word; nothing
short of it will do."[11] (Jacob Riis)*

*Immigrants at Ellis Island, ca. 1900.
Geo. G. Bain Collection, Library of Congress.*

destination, and other details. Often the manifests were incomplete, erroneous or illegible. Since each manifest had to be notarized, steamship representatives would squeeze ten to twenty extra names onto a page to save notary fees. Sometimes they would fill out the manifest without consulting the passenger.

A manifest that had many omissions or incorrect information wreaked havoc on the inspection line inside the registry hall at Ellis Island. Inspectors would have to question immigrants at length to get the information they needed. Since anywhere between two thousand and five thousand immigrants were being inspected each day, it was essential, in order to keep the lines moving, that the manifests be in proper order. By law, Williams could impose a ten-dollar fine on the steamship companies for each name not properly listed. This he did, much to the consternation of the steamship lines, since this fine had rarely been previously imposed. The improved manifests greatly aided the long and tedious job of the registry clerks.

chapter 12

A GREAT SIEVE

On a day when all was moving smoothly, an immigrant could complete the process of inspection at Ellis Island in a matter of two or three hours. Broughton Brandenburg, the journalist disguised as an immigrant, described the procedure in 1904 in his book *Imported Americans:*

Half-way up the stairs an interpreter stood telling the immigrants to get their health tickets ready. . . . The majority of the people, having their hands full of bags, boxes, bundles, and children, carried their tickets in their teeth, and just at the head of the stairs stood a young doctor in the Marine Hospital Service uniform who took them, looked at them, and stamped them with the Ellis Island stamp . . .

. . . from the head of the stairs, we turned into the south hall of the great registry floor, which is divided, like the human body, into two great parts nearly alike, so that one ship's load can be handled on one side and another ship's load on the other. In fact, as we came up, a quantity of people from the north of Europe were being examined in the north half.

Turning into a narrow railed-off lane, we encountered another doctor in uniform, who lifted hats or pushed back shawls to look for favus heads, keenly scrutinized the face and body for signs of disease or deformity, and passed us on. An old man who limped in front of me, he marked with a bit of chalk on the coat lapel. At the end of the railed lane was a third uniformed doctor, a towel hanging beside him, a small instrument over which to turn up eyelids in his hand and back of him basins of disinfectants.

As we approached he was examining a Molise woman and her two children. The youngest screamed with fear when he endeavored to touch her, but with a pat on the cheek and a kindly word the child was quieted while he examined its eyes, looking for trachoma or purulent opthalmia. The second child was so obstinate that it took some minutes to get it examined, and then, having found suspicious conditions, he marked the woman with a bit of chalk, and a uniformed official led her and the little ones to the left into the rooms for special medical examination. The old man who limped went the same way, as well as many others.[1]

Favus, a fungal disease of the scalp, and trachoma, an eye infection resembling conjunctivitis, were considered highly contagious and difficult to cure. Both diseases were common in southeast Europe,

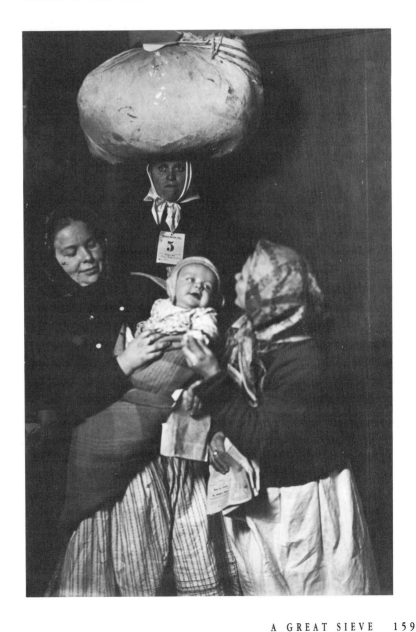

Slavic mother and child at Ellis Island, 1905. Photograph by Lewis W. Hine. New York Public Library.

The manifest tag on the woman in the background shows that her name is recorded on manifest sheet number five of the Hamburg-America line. The woman in the foreground clutches her medical certificates as the group walks into the main building for inspection.

Climbing into America, 1905. Photograph by Lewis W. Hine. New York Public Library.

The design of the main building was criticized by every commissioner of immigration starting with Thomas Fitchie. In 1903, William Williams wrote in his annual report that because the inspection room is on the second floor, "every alien, be it man or woman, encumbered with heavy and unwieldly baggage and often surrounded with clinging children, has first to mount stairs and then to descend, in undergoing the process of examination."

but relatively unknown in the United States. Trachoma, if left untreated, would eventually lead to blindness. Doctors checked for this disease by pulling the eyelids up and over a buttonhook. The so-called buttonhook exam was greatly feared because it was known to be very painful. The medical examination required that only one eye had to be checked, but after Williams became commissioner, he directed that both eyelids must be turned up. Even Brandenburg, who found little to complain about on Ellis Island, remarked that the pain of this examination was severe.

If the doctor found any indication of disease, he would mark the immigrants with a piece of chalk: X for feebleminded, C for conjunctivitis, Ct for trachoma, E for eyes, Ft for feet, G for goiter, H for heart, K for hernia, Pg for pregnancy, S for senility, etc. The marked immigrant would be taken out of the inspection line and held for further examination. This would often cause great anxiety

Registry hall on the second floor of the main building, ca. 1904. Photograph by Underwood & Underwood, Library of Congress.

for a family if a child or grandfather for example were suddenly taken out of the line while the other members were pushed brusquely forward.

This first medical examination took perhaps two to three minutes.

Immigration doctor inspecting eyes, 1913. Photograph by Underwood & Underwood, Library of Congress.

The man in line has already acquired several chalk marks on his coat. The X stands for feebleminded. He will probably be taken out of the inspection line and placed in the doctor's pen—the enmeshed area on the right of the photograph—and held for further examination. His wife will continue her inspection alone.

According to Victor Safford, the "rapid, hasty procedure" was enough to detect those who should be held for more careful examination. Safford wrote:

We used to like to have passengers while under inspection make two right angle turns. The scheme served to bring the light on both sides of a passenger's face. The turns also helped to bring out imperfections in muscular coordination and this also together with facial expression, posture and perhaps evidence of indifference to personal appearance, served to make the detection of abnormal mental conditions easier . . .[2]

Safford said that this method of observation could not be validly applied to all classes:

For instance, in standing in the foyer of an Opera House and testing out our immigration inspection mentally of the people who entered, it was apparent that if they were immigrants the inspection would result in the detention of nearly everybody for a lengthy medical examination. It is to be noted that in times of heavy immigration, 80 percent of our alien

Immigrants waiting in a "pen" to be inspected, ca. 1905. Culver Pictures.

arrivals have been between the ages of 14 and 44. Of these two-thirds have been males, and of these males about two-thirds have been accustomed to hard out-of-door labor. In spite of all the dumping of the troublesome elements of foreign countries on us a very large proportion of our immigrants have been physically healthy young males and females of the sturdy European peasant class.[3]

One of the representatives of the Hebrew Immigrant Aid Society recalled that the doctors had other tricks to help them spot suspicious cases:

. . . the doctor would have them put their hands down on the desk and if they showed pink, he passed them as not suffering from a heart condition. But when the nails were very blue we put them aside as a heart case.

When a man came in with a very thin, stringy beard, they thought there was some lack of physical development, for whatever reason.

When someone walked and hesitated and constantly looked down on the ground to see where he was, they knew that he had trouble with his eyes.

When a woman was pregnant, for some reason she always had disheveled hair. We all wore our hair neat in those days, with braids, you

The desks of the immigration inspectors, ca. 1905. Photograph by Edwin Levick. William Williams Papers, Mss & Archives Division, New York Public Library.

"There seems to be no language or dialect under the sun that does not lie handy to the tongue of these men at the desk. There were twelve of them. One would never dream there were twelve such linguists in the country till he hears them and sees them; for half their talk is done with their hands and shoulders and with the official steel pen that transfixes an object of suspicion like a merciless spear, upon the point of which it writhes in vain."[4] (Jacob Riis)

Immigrants at inspector's desk, ca. 1910.
Geo. G. Bain Collection, Library of Congress.

" 'How much you got?' shouts the inspector at the head of the long file moving up from the quay between the iron rails, and remembering, in the same breath shrieks out, 'Quanto moneta?' with a gesture that brings up from the depths of Pietro's pocket a pitiful handful of paper money. Before he has it half out, the interpreter has him by the wrist, and with a quick movement shakes the bills out upon the desk as a dice-thrower chucks the ivories.

"Ten, twenty, forty lire. He shakes his head. Not much, but—he glances at the ship's manifest—is he going to friends?

" 'Si, Si! signor,' says Pietro, eagerly; his brother has a vineyard—oh, a fine vineyard! And he holds up a bundle of grapesticks in evidence. He has brought them all the way from the village at home to set them out in his brother's field.

"Ugh, grunts the inspector as he stuffs the money back in the man's pocket, shoves him on, and yells, 'Wie viel geld?' at a hapless German next in line. 'They won't grow. They never do. Bring 'em just the same.' " [7] (Jacob Riis)

know, and very carefully done. But these little women—their hair seemed more what they look like today, cut short and very pale and very dirty. They knew there was something wrong with these women.

The tuberculars all had, not hunchbacks, but a little curvature of the spine. They showed the tuberculosis that way, and were not admitted either." [5]

After the medical inspection, Brandenburg continued, ". . . we turned to the right, [where] a stern-looking woman inspector, with the badge, stood looking at all the women who came up to select any whose moral character might be questioned, and one of her procedures was to ask each party as to the various relationships of the men and women in it. Her Italian was good." [6]

Then the immigrants were directed to sit in the waiting area just behind the registry desks. Each manifest group had its own enclosure or pen. When the registry clerk was ready, he would call up one

RAILROAD TICKETS ^{TO ALL} POINTS
EISENBAHN BUREAU BIGLIETTI FERROVIARI
JÆRNBANE BILLET KONTOR
VASUTI JEGYEK ZELESNICKI KARTI

*The railroad ticket office at Ellis Island,
ca. 1910. Brown Brothers.*

*After passing inspection, aliens were free
to exchange their money for American
dollars and purchase railroad tickets, or
if they had prepaid tickets, to get them
verified.*

group at a time to form a line. Then one by one, the immigrants
would file up to the clerk's desk for questioning. On busy days the
registry clerk, using information on the manifest as a basis for cross-
examination, had about two minutes to decide whether an immigrant was qualified to land.

One of the most difficult questions for an immigrant to answer
was: "Do you have a job?" Ever since the Alien Contract Labor Law
of 1885, immigrants had been thoroughly warned by their friends
or by representatives of the steamship lines never to admit that they
had a job waiting for them in the United States. Even if the job
was through a relative, the immigrant could be deported for violating the Alien Contract Labor law.

Fiorello H. La Guardia, who was an interpreter on Ellis Island
from 1910 to 1912, wrote that the immigrant had the difficult task
of proving he was not likely to become a public charge without
saying he was sure to get a job:

*It is a puzzling fact that one provision of the Immigration Law excludes
any immigrant who has no job and classifies him as likely to become a
public charge, while another provision excludes an immigrant if he has a
job! Common sense suggested that any immigrant who came to the United*

States in those days to settle here permanently surely came here to work. However, under the law, he could not have any more than a vague hope of a job. In answering the inspectors' questions, immigrants had to be very careful, because if their expectations were too enthusiastic, they might be held as coming in violation of the contract labor provision. Yet, if they were too indefinite, if they knew nobody, had no idea where they were going to get jobs, they might be excluded as likely to become public charges. Most of the inspectors were conscientious and fair. Sometimes, I felt, large batches of those held and deported as violating the contract labor provision were, perhaps, only borderline cases and had no more than the assurance from relatives or former townsmen of jobs on their arrival . . .[8]

When the ordeal of inspection was over, the immigrant was ushered to the other side of the registry desk to the "Stairs of Separation," so called, Brandenburg explains, because:

Group of Italians in the railroad waiting room, Ellis Island, 1905. Photograph by Lewis W. Hine. New York Public Library.

"These are some of the Italians who became the barbers, waiters, chauffeurs, and mayors of America," Hine wrote. "Some became the artists and sculptors of our national Capitol and other public buildings."

Doctors examining a group of Jewish immigrants, 1907. Photograph by Underwood & Underwood, Library of Congress.

These men, who failed to pass the line inspection, will be examined more thoroughly to determine whether they can be admitted to the United States. The man in the left background has his lapel marked with a clear chalkmark "K" indicating hernia.

Here family parties with different destinations are separated without a minute's warning, and often never see each other again. It seems heartless, but it is the only practical system, for if allowance was made for good-byes the examination and distribution process would be blocked then and there by a dreadful crush. Special officers would be necessary to tear relatives forcibly from each other's arms. The stairs to the right lead to the railroad stations for shipment to different parts of the country. The central stair leads to the detention rooms, where immigrants are held pending the arrival of friends. The left descent is for those free to go out to the ferry . . .[9]

All in all, Brandenburg was greatly impressed by the inspection routine at Ellis Island. He summarized his account by saying: "The more I saw of the inside of the great system on the Island the more I was struck with its thoroughness and the kindly, efficient manner in which the law is enforced."[10]

Ellis Island's tragic reputation as an "Isle of Tears" or a "Hell's Island" is based not so much on the experiences of the millions who

were quickly inspected, registered, and sent on their ways, but rather on the thousands of stories of aliens who were detained and then ordered deported. Immigrants who were sick, or without money, or suspected of being contract laborers, or thought to fit the "likely to become a public charge" category were held pending an investigation. Immigrants who had incurable, contagious diseases like trachoma or favus, or were "feebleminded," or had any physical defect that would make it difficult for them to earn a living would be detained and most likely deported.

A woman traveling alone was usually detained until immigration officials were sure that she would be in safe hands after she left the island. Sometimes foreign governments would request that a run-

Detained women being examined by doctors, 1911. Photograph by Underwood & Underwood, Library of Congress.

The two elderly women in this photograph are being held for a more careful examination of their eyes. If the doctors decide that they need more time to make a diagnosis, these women will be sent to the Ellis Island hospital for observation.

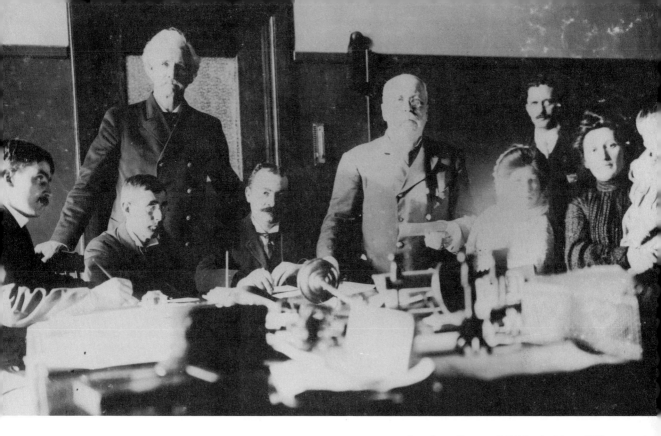

Board of Special Inquiry of Ellis Island, ca. 1910. Photograph by Augustus Sherman. National Park Service.

Immigrants who appeared before the board had to plead their cases through an interpreter who was a government employee. One interpreter was Fiorello H. La Guardia, who worked on Ellis Island from 1910 to 1912.

away criminal or runaway husband, wife, or child be held at Ellis Island.

These sundry cases were heard before a Board of Special Inquiry made up of four inspectors. Later, after the Immigration Act of 1907, boards had only three members. The boards were administrative bodies, not legal tribunals. Their sole purpose was to decide whether an alien should be admitted to the United States. The Supreme Court had ruled as early as 1893 that aliens had no right to land and therefore no right to a legal hearing to decide their eligibility to land. The boards' procedures, therefore, were uninhibited by due process. Immigrants whose cases were referred to the board were not allowed to confer with relatives or friends or a lawyer. Nor could they be represented by a lawyer at their hearing, although they could request that relatives and friends appear on their behalf. If the board rendered an unfavorable decision, the immigrant had the option of appealing his case with the help of counsel directly to the Secretary of Labor and Commerce in Washington. (In 1903 the Immigration Service was transferred from the Treasury Department to the Department of Labor and Commerce.)

Immigration officers were often chagrined at how quickly the

Detained immigrants in waiting room, 1907. Library of Congress.

"Here are the old, the stricken, waiting for friends able to keep them; the pitiful little colony of women without the shield of a man's name in the hour of their greatest need . . . and the hopelessly bewildered . . . often enough exasperated at the restraint, which they cannot understand."[11] *(Jacob Riis)*

families of new arrivals were able to enlist the help of their congressman or senator in getting an exclusion order reversed in Washington. In his memoir, Victor Safford noted especially President Theodore Roosevelt, who knew "that it was good politics to have stringent immigration laws to point to, [but soon discovered] it was poor practical politics to enforce them impartially."

Generally, 20 percent of the total arrivals were temporarily detained, of which half were held for special inquiry. About 2 percent of the total number of arrivals were eventually deported. Detainments would last from one to two days to several weeks. The fear and anxiety that the immigrant suffered while awaiting the decision of the board or of the Secretary of Labor was contagious and was felt by all who passed through Ellis Island. One woman recalled that the despair was pervasive and that "everybody was sad there."

Williams was especially strict on deportations and noted with satisfaction that the number of exclusions during his term of office was over twice as high as in the former administration's. Rarely did a month go by that there were less than 1,000 people deported. About half of this number was deported on grounds of "likely to become a public charge".

Williams was quite outspoken about the need to restrict immigration and was often quoted as saying "aliens have no inherent right to land here." In his first annual report, he wrote:

While I believe that the coming here of all desirable immigrants should be facilitated, yet I am very emphatic in the belief that rigid means should be adopted to keep away those who are undesirable. Many of the latter are unquestionably coming or attempting to come, particularly from portions of Russia, Syria, and Italy. Last year over 2,000 cases of aliens who had arrived within the past twelve months and in the meantime become destitute, were reported to the out-of-door poor department of the city of New York. People of this class are being returned to Europe almost daily, either at the expense of the line which brought them or at that of the Government. The most ardent advocate of immigration will not claim that a family of eight ignorant people from eastern Europe, composed of a broken-down father, a mother with a nursing infant and six other children, all under 11 years old and possessed of only $20, with no responsible people to go to, are a desirable addition to this country; nor that a mother of frail appearance, with three infant children and 20 lire ($4), should be admitted, yet I am constantly being compelled to send back just such people.[12]

Children standing outside hospital on Ellis Island, ca. 1910. National Archives.

Most deportation cases were not this extreme, however. Edward Corsi, commissioner of immigration in the 1930s, often referred to the old Ellis Island files in his memoir *In The Shadow of Liberty*. In

a chapter entitled "Who Shall Apologize?" he cites case after case where the decisions made by the immigration service were blindly legalistic and sometimes downright cruel. He related the following case, which occurred during Williams's first term of office:

Mrs. Schmitzky and her children arrived August 13, 1904. The 13th proved to be her unlucky day.

Frail and weak, practically a dwarf with curvature of the spine, Mrs. Schmitzky was unable to pass the medical examination.

While she was in detention, her husband, Maurice, haunted the Island, prowling distractedly about the buildings. The case was appealed to Washington and every effort was made by the Hebrew Immigration Aid Society to prevent a separation of the family for Maurice Schmitzky had been here nearly two years and had established a home for his wife on Rivington Street in New York.

When Mrs. Schmitzky had been ordered excluded and the order had been affirmed, she sat in the "excluded room," nervous, but with a brave attempt at dignity. "I look poorly now," she told one of the newspaper reporters, "because I have had such a long journey, and such a long stay here. But I am really in perfect health." She pushed her two toddlers forward. "You see," she said, "I am perfectly able to bear children."[13]

In 1903, when over 600,000 immigrants were processed at Ellis Island, Williams was quoted in the *Wall Street Journal* as describing "this alien flood" as the "poorest, the most vicious, the most wholly

Children's playground on the roof garden of the main building, ca. 1902. Photograph by Augustus Sherman. Museum of the City of New York.

The playground, equipped with a little swing, a tricycle, a hobby horse and a wagon with Uncle Sam stenciled on the side, does not seem to have cheered the enforced stay of these little children.

undesirable peoples that have ever come to American shores."

On another occasion he wrote:

It is generally conceded that immigration in the past has been an important factor in enabling this country to attain the position of eminence which it now occupies, and that it has contributed in a large degree towards the wonderful material development of the United States. . . . But such a development has been caused not by the mere fact that hundreds of thousands of foreigners have been coming here annually, but by the further fact that they have gone out into the agricultural regions and that they have come from Great Britain, Germany, and Scandanavia, countries whose inhabitants more closely resemble our people in blood, traditions and ideas of government than is the case with any of the other larger countries of Europe from which our immigrants come. It is almost certain that had our early immigration proceeded from these portions of Eastern and Southern Europe which are now sending such large numbers of illiterate aliens into our great cities, this country would not now enjoy its present civilization.[14]

Soon after the congratulations for cleaning up Ellis Island had died down, protest arose in regard to the high number of exclusions. The immigration societies were especially alarmed and vocal in their objections to Williams's policies. The Hebrew, German, Italian and Hungarian societies issued a circular accusing him of using "harsh and arbitrary" methods in ordering many of the deportations. The *New York Times* reported on January 4, 1903:

The specific charges made against the Ellis Island authorities are to the effect that immigrants are deported before their relatives know they have arrived; that since Dec. 1 immigrants have not been allowed counsel at the Board of Special Inquiry hearings, and that no bonds are accepted to guarantee that the immigrant will not become a public charge, the reason for which most of them are deported. The appeal says also that the methods of inspection are arbitrary and inhuman, that wives are separated from husbands, and mothers from children, and that the Commissioner is using his influence not alone to exclude certain cases, but to restrict immigration in abuse of the powers allowed him by Congress.

Williams was attacked by the foreign-language press, especially the *Staats-Zeitung,* which Williams himself noted "attacked me vi-

olently sometimes with vitriolic force." The *Staats-Zeitung* published
editorials under such headlines as "Hell's Island," "Tyrannical Des-
potism," "Disgrace for the Country," and "No Pity." It told sensational stories of immigrants being forced to clean spittoons in the
hospital, locked outside on balconies as punishment, herded about
like cattle, and eaten alive by vermin.

Williams suspected that the influence of the steamship companies,
not concern for the immigrant, motivated these attacks. The *Staats-
Zeitung,* like most of the foreign-language press, relied on advertising
revenue from the shipping lines. These companies were beginning
to feel the harsh financial pinch of Williams's strict policies. With
the rising number of detentions, deportations, and fines for bringing
unqualified immigrants to the United States, shipping profits diminished.

The *Staats-Zeitung* continued to run stories about abuses on Ellis
Island, and to clear the air, Williams asked President Roosevelt to
appoint a committee to investigate the paper's allegations. On September 16, 1903, Roosevelt came to inspect the island himself and
the following clipping from Williams's scrapbook describes his visit:

*President Theodore Roosevelt visits Ellis
Island, September 16, 1903.* **William
Williams Papers, Mss. & Archives Divi-
sion, New York Public Library.**

Immigrants leave main building to board ferry, 1907. Photograph by Underwood & Underwood, Library of Congress.

President Roosevelt inspected the immigrant station on Ellis Island yesterday and appointed a committee of four to follow up his personal visit by an investigation and report to him on what they find.

This committee was appointed at the personal request of Immigration Commissioner Williams of this port and Commissioner-General Sargent, who were the President's hosts yesterday.

The President's own verdict when he left Ellis Island last night after a four-hour visit was that everything about the institution and its management was admirable. He made that statement to Mr. Sargent and Mr. Williams with a good deal of enthusiasm. That also seemed to be the opinion of the four members of the new committee, all of whom were in the President's party . . .

Inspection began in the big hall of the registry department. There were 2,400 immigrants, 1,200 who had been held over from the day before and 1,200 who arrived yesterday from the steamships Lahn *and* Kaiser Wilhelm II.

A long line of men and women were waiting to tell their stories to the immigration officials when the President entered the registry department. He began to ask questions at once. Rosa Klausner and her three-year-old boy from Germany were at the desk. The President called Dr. Lee K. Frankel from his group of friends and pressed him into service as an interpreter to talk to the woman. She said her husband was a baker, earning a great deal of money in this city and that he had sent for her to come with the boy. Besides her German money, she had $15 in United States bills, which her husband had sent her. It is unusual for an immigrant to have United States money.

"That's fine, fine!" exclaimed the President. "The right sort."

The committee's report, which was issued three months after Roosevelt's visit to the island, completely vindicated Williams, who continued his work for another year. In that time he had another building constructed that housed one thousand beds for detained immigrants. He also got an appropriation from Congress to enlarge the island with landfill. A hospital for contagious diseases was eventually built on this new extension.

Williams resigned in 1905 in a dispute with Roosevelt concerning Assistant Commissioner Joseph Murray. Murray, one of Roosevelt's earliest supporters, was known as "the man who discovered Roosevelt," but Williams found Murray "ignorant, inefficient and wholly worthless as an official. He is neither industrious, energetic or in-

telligent."

In December 1904, Roosevelt wrote to a friend:

I am in a quandary about Joe Murray. Williams, who is an excellent man, but arbitrary and difficult to get along with, has got on such terms with Murray that one or the other of them will have to leave. I want to keep Williams if I can. Is there some place with a salary of at least $3,000 in which I could put Joe Murray by March fourth? Do help me out and see if you can find such a place among the Federal appointees in New York.[15]

Either Roosevelt changed his mind or else no other place could be found for Murray. He reluctantly accepted Williams's resignation on January 12, 1905:

In accepting your resignation, let me repeat to you in writing what I said

Immigrants waiting on dock at Ellis Island, 1912. Photograph by Underwood & Underwood, Library of Congress.

"The railroad ferries come and take their daily host straight from Ellis Island to the train, ticketed now with the name of the route that is to deliver them at their new homes, West and East. And the Battery boat comes every hour for its share. Then the many hued procession—the women are hooded, one and all, in their gayest shawls for the entry—is led down on a long pathway . . . On the boat they meet their friends, and the long journey is over, the new life is begun."[16] *(Jacob Riis)*

to you by word of mouth in endeavoring to get you not to insist upon it. I feel that you have rendered a service of real and high importance to the whole nation in your management of the office under you. When I asked you to take the position, I realized that I was asking you to do what meant genuine self-sacrifice on your part, and I realize that your consenting to stay in so long has meant further loss to you. But surely you must feel recompensed by the knowledge of the value of your work. You have set a standard of unceasing industry, of untiring energy, of high administrative ability and of single-minded devotion to duty which your successor will find it difficult to equal, no matter how good a man he may be.[18]

On board the ferry from Ellis Island, 1905.[17] *Photograph by Lewis W. Hine. New York Public Library.*

chapter *13*

A MAN WITH A HEART

President Roosevelt named Robert Watchorn to be the new commissioner of immigration at Ellis Island in January 1905. Watchorn, who immigrated to the United States from England during the old Castle Garden days, had worked as a coal miner in Pennsylvania when he was a young man. Later he joined the Immigration Service as an inspector at Ellis Island while Fitchie and McSweeney were in power. Before Roosevelt appointed him commissioner, Watchorn was stationed in Montreal in charge of immigration inspection along the Canadian border.

Edward Steiner, who dedicated his book *On the Trail of the Immigrant* to Watchorn, described how Roosevelt made his decision:

In looking for a successor, the President consulted the records, evidently with the purpose of discovering one thoroughly conversant with the conditions, and of experience coupled with executive ability, sufficient to further extend the needed reforms. Mr. Robert Watchorn was chosen for this important office. . . . I ventured to ask the Commissioner one day if he had been given any instructions by the President as to the course to be pursued. He replied: "Yes, the President gave me instructions very brief but very pointed. 'Mr. Watchorn, I am sending you to Ellis Island. You will find it a very difficult place to manage. I know you are familiar with the conditions. All I ask of you is that you give us an administration as clean as a hound's tooth'."[1]

When Watchorn was appointed, he immediately wrote to William Williams saying:

You have dispersed and routed the derelicts and knaves which at one time made Ellis Island a byword and a reproach . . . you have reduced to order, discipline and decency that which was chaotic and sinful, and the best thanks of the nation are due you because of your great and worthy

---

*achievement . . . all the good you have accomplished will be conserved by
the course I shall pursue. No backward steps will be taken.*[2]

Watchorn brought to the office of commissioner a humanity and
kindness that complemented his predecessor's sweeping reforms.
One story that typified the new commissioner's character involved
a young Jewish orphan who had to be deported from Ellis Island
when no relative appeared to assume custody. Within an hour after
the child's ship had left dock, his brother arrived at Ellis Island.
Watchorn, himself, quickly boarded a tug, overtook the ship and
brought the boy back in his arms to be united with his brother.
Watchorn's sympathy with the new arrivals was praised by the
immigration societies, which were gratified that the new commissioner was a man with a heart.[3]

The restrictionists, in the meantime, were greatly chagrined by
Watchorn's more lenient application of the law; there were fewer
deportations. Watchorn's attitude was also at odds with that of
Commissioner-General Frank P. Sargent, his immediate superior in
Washington. Shortly after Watchorn's appointment, *The New York
Times* published a lengthy interview with Sargent during which he
expressed his ideas on immigration policy:

*. . . the time has come when every American citizen who is ambitious for
the national future must regard with grave misgiving the mighty tide of
immigration that, unless something is done, will soon poison or at least
pollute the very fountainhead of American life and progress. Big as we
are and blessed with an iron constitution, we cannot safely swallow such
an endless-course dinner, so to say, without getting indigestion and perhaps national appendicitis . . .*

*During the present month all records for deportation have been broken,
over a thousand immigrants having been ineligible for admission into the
country. What is the principal reason for their ineligibility? Disease and
destitution. Since the outbreak of the Russo-Japanese war thousands and
thousands of Russian Jews are fleeing here to escape conscription. Poor
fellows, most of them are hardly more than food for powder, having been
ill-fed, ill-housed, and ill-clad all their lives, and the impromptu accommodations here on the island are amazing luxuries to them. Others
who are being deported today are contract laborers and decrepit men and
women inveigled by steamship agents who have willfully disregarded the
law . . .*

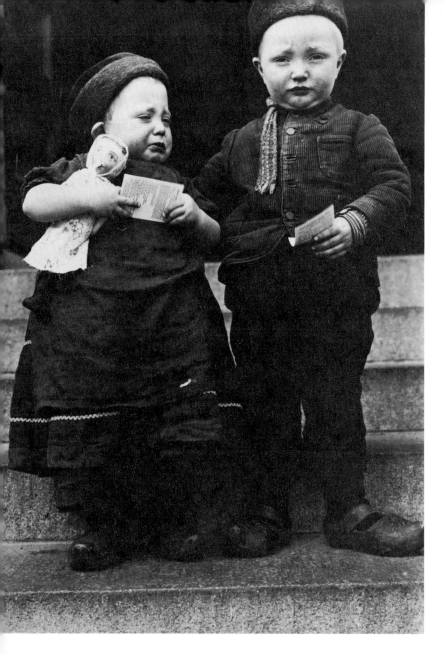

Augustus F. Sherman, ca. 1915. National Park Service.

Sherman, who was a clerk—later chief clerk—at Ellis Island from 1892 to 1925, made over 135 photographs of immigrants as they arrived at America's threshold. His collection provides an extraordinary record of the years when immigration was at its highest. All of the following photographs—from the Augustus F. Sherman Collection of the National Park Service—are at the American museum of Immigration on Liberty Island and the manuscript and Archives Division of the New York Public Library.

> *During the past year there has been a notable increase in the number of criminals coming over here, some of them being the worst criminals of Europe. There is no question about it, for we have positive evidence of the fact. In short, the time has come for the country to demand to know the character of immigrants that Europe is shedding or trying to shed.*[4]

Immigration records were broken once again in 1905, with 1,026,499 coming to the United States. In June 1905, an article

Two Dutch children with doll and landing cards. WWP.

Russian Giant. NPS.

"Simon Sing Foo from Burma weighs 20 lbs, 34" tall, 1905." NPS.

In both photographs Commissioner Robert Watchorn stands on the right. The other man is probably Joseph Murray, the assistant commissioner. The Russian and Burmese gentlemen could well be performers, many of whom came to the United States each year for the circus season.

Slovak girl with children. WWP.

Russian Cossack. WWP.

in *Harper's* reported that the powers in Washington were "much concerned at the number and quality of the immigrants now coming into the United States."

The President had an efficient live check to undesirable immigration in the person of Mr. Williams, late Commissioner of Immigration at Ellis Island. Without reflecting at all on the zeal or capacity of the present commissioner, Mr. Watchorn, it is possible to regret that an officer of such exceptional fitness for the job of sifting immigrants as Mr. Williams was allowed to retire from the public service. Our present immigration laws are more, or less, effective according to the way they are enforced. A good deal is left to the discretion of the commissioner at Ellis Island, and it seems a matter for regret that the unprecedented flood of

African group. NPS.

Cossack group. WWP.

immigration that is now rolling in should not be confronted by a commissioner whose personal qualifications were made more valuable by several years of active and successful experience. To any sign of weakness at Ellis Island there is an immediate response in the shape of increased pressure from Europe."[5]

And Broughton Brandenburg, now a government investigator of immigration, was quoted as saying:

On all hands in the foreign quarters . . . one can hear rejoicing over the fact that it is much easier to get relatives of doubtful perquisites through Ellis Island in the grand rush than it was under Williams.[6]

Watchorn's supporters maintained that the inspection at Ellis Island was as careful and discriminating as it had been under Williams. It was true that the "likely to become a public charge" clause of the immigration law was not invoked as often as it had been previously, but medical examinations were rigorously enforced as was the Contract Labor Law.

Syrian family. NPS.

Swedish woman. WWP.

Eight Russian-Jewish children who arrived aboard the SS Caronia, May 8, 1908. NPS.

The mothers of these children who were gathered from all over Russia, were killed during the brutal pogroms which ravaged the country from 1903 to 1907. Their passage, paid for by a Jewish philanthropy, reunited them with their fathers in America.

Scottish children. NPS.

Steiner, in *On the Trail of the Immigrant,* takes pains to point out that Watchorn was a vigilant guardian of America's gateway. He describes his friend in terms that evoke an image of St. Peter standing at the gates of Paradise.

Let no one believe that landing on the shores of "The land of the free, and the home of the brave" is a pleasant experience. It is a hard, harsh fact, surrounded by the grinding machinery of the law, which sifts, picks, and chooses; admitting the fit and excluding the weak and helpless.[7]

Steiner had no patience for those social workers who insisted that

Albanian soldiers. NPS.

English family, arrived aboard the S.S. Adriatic, *April 17, 1908. NPS.*

Guadaloupe women (French West Indies) arrived aboard S.S. Korona, *April 6, 1911. NPS.*

Albanian. WWP.

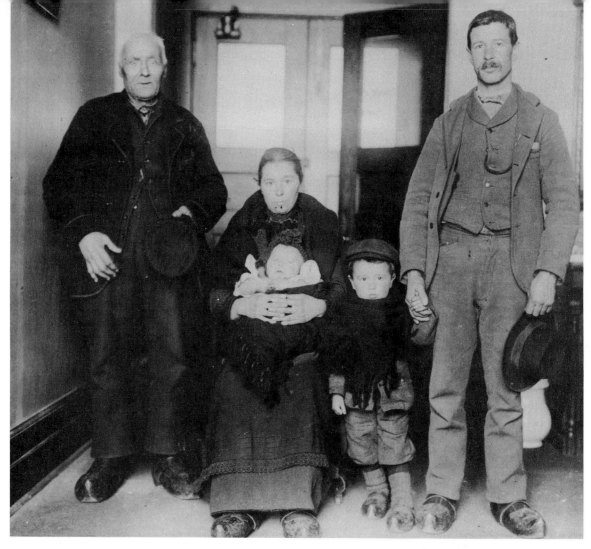

Dutch family. NPS.

Dutch girl. WWP.

indigent immigrants were crowding the charity asylums of the United States and wreaking havoc in the slums of America. He maintained that the southern Europeans, Italians, Jews, Slovaks, Bohemians, and Syrians who were so often maligned by the restrictionists would be assimilated with the same ease as were the much-praised "old immigrants" from northern Europe.

Much ignorance needs to be dispelled regarding these [new] immigrants. It was my privilege recently, as a member of the National Conference on Immigration, to be among the guests of the commissioner of the Port of New York, and one of the spectacles which we witnessed was the landing of a ship-load of immigrants. We stood in the visitor's gallery and . . . many of the visitors were beginning to hold their noses in anticipation of

North African. WWP.

the stenches which would come with these foreigners, and were ready to be shocked by the horrors of the steerage.

Slowly the bewildered mass came into view; but strange to relate, those who led the mass appeared like ladies and gentlemen.

The women wore modern, half acre hats a little the worse for wear, but bought in the city of Prague a few months before . . . the men carried band-boxes, silk umbrellas and walking canes, the remnants of past glories . . .

After them came Slavic women with no finery except their homespun, rough, tough and clean; carrying upon their backs piles of feather-beds and household utensils. Strong limbed men followed them in the picturesque garb of their native villages; Slovaks, Poles, Roumanians, Ruthenians, Italians, and finally, Russian Jews; but lo, and behold! no smells ascended to our nostrils, and no horrors were disclosed . . .

The first time I entered New York was at Castle Garden, from the steamer Fulda, *twenty years ago; and having watched the tide of immigration ever since, I can say that I never have seen, at any time, a shipload of better human beings disembark than those which came from the steamer* Wilhelm II *on December 7, 1905.*[8]

Immigrants excluded by the Board of Special Inquiry could have their cases reviewed by the commissioner. If they still did not get a favorable ruling, they could appeal to Washington. Most immigrants, however, did not have the means to appeal, and the commissioner's hearing was their last hope. Steiner describes one such session that Watchorn presided over shortly after he took office:

Two undersized old people stand before him. They are Hungarian Jews whose children have preceded them here, and who, being fairly comfortable, have sent for their parents that they may spend the rest of their lives together. The questions, asked through an interpreter, are pertinent and much the same as those already asked by the court which has decided upon their deportation. The commissioner rules that the children be put under a sufficient bond to guarantee that this aged couple shall not become a burden to the public, and consequently they will be admitted.[9]

The next case is that of an elderly, emaciated Russian Jewish man and his "stalwart son, neatly attired in the uniform of a Russian college student."

"Ask them why they came," the commissioner says rather abruptly. The answer is: "We had to." "What was his business in Russia?" "A tailor." "How much did he earn a week?" "Ten to twelve rubles." "What did the son do?" "He went to school." "Who supported him?" "The father." "What do they expect to do in America?" "Work." "Have they any relatives?" "Yes, a son and brother." "What does he do?" "He is a tailor." "How much does he earn?" "Twelve dollars a week." "Has he a family?" "Wife and four children." "Ask them whether they are willing to be separated; the father to go back and the son to remain here?" They look at each other; no emotion as yet visible. The question came too suddenly. Then something in the background of their feelings moves, and the father, used to self-denial through his life, says quietly, without pathos and yet tragically, "Of course." And the son says, after casting his eyes to the ground, ashamed to look his father in the face, "Of course."

The next case is that of an Englishman fifty-four years of age to whom the court of inquiry has refused admission. He is a medium-sized man, who betrays the Englishman as he stands before the commissioner, and in a strong, cockney dialect begins the conversation in which he is immediately checked by the somewhat brusque question: "What did you do in England?" "I was an insurance agent." "How much did you earn?" "Four pounds a week." "Why do you come to America?" "Because I want a change." "How much change, that is, how much money have you?" "Forty dollars." "What do you expect to do here?" "Work at anything." "At insurance?" "Yes." "The decision of the court is con-

Johanna Dÿkhoff, forty years old, from Holland with her eleven children. Arrived aboard the Noordan, *May 12, 1908. NPS.*

The family stands outside the wooden barracks built by William Williams for detained immigrants. Watchorn, who wanted the building torn down, described it in a letter to the commissioner-general in Washington: "This is a wooden structure, one story in height, in which 700 aliens may sleep, and in order to prevent their escape, all the doors and windows are necessarily barred, and I need only to leave it to the imagination of the Bureau as to what would occur if the place should ever unfortunately take fire."[10]

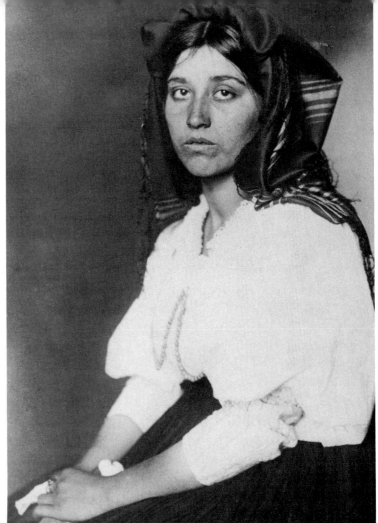

Unidentified woman. NPS.

Women from Holland. NPS.

firmed; deported, because likely to become a public charge." Evidently in- surance agents are not regarded as desirable immigrants.

It is all done quickly, firmly and decisively as a physician, conscious of his skill, might sever a limb; but it is done without prejudice.

He knows no nationality nor race, his business is to guard the interests of his country, guarding at the same time the rights of the stranger.

Watchorn's administration often came under fire. Roosevelt first ordered an investigation in 1906 when there were hints that the commissioner was too friendly with the steamship lines and certain privilege holders. Watchorn was also accused of conniving to take over Commissioner-General Frank Sargent's job in Washington. Sargent's friends said that Watchorn "tried to secure the creation of a Commissioner-General of Labor for the Panama Canal Zone in

the hope that Mr. Sargent would be appointed so that he (Watchorn) might succeed Sargent at Washington."

In 1906, Roosevelt appointed Oscar Straus secretary of commerce and labor. Straus investigated the allegations against Watchorn but found them groundless, and he supported Watchorn's humane consideration of those immigrants who previously would have been deported as "paupers." Straus was much more in sympathy with Watchorn's view of immigration than he was with Sargent's.

Watchorn ran into trouble again in 1908 when New York City Police Commissioner Theodore A. Bingham accused him of not deporting alien criminals. Organized crime, according to Bingham, was flooding New York because of the lax application of the immigration laws. The newspapers were filled with stories about the "Black Hand," violence, extortion, and murder. One Italian immigrant said that his house was dynamited because he refused to pay a gangster seven thousand dollars for "protection." There was also a sensational gang-style murder in Brooklyn.

Watchorn denied that criminals were being allowed in through Ellis Island and said that they came into the country through Quebec or small ports in the South. Watchorn cooperated closely with the police department's "Italian squad" headed by Joe Petrosino to stop

"John D. Third and family, natives of Scotland, ex S.S. Caledonia, *September 17, 1905. Went to friend, John Fleming, Anniston, Alabama. NPS.*

The Third family arrived in Alabama at a time when the Charleston News and Courier *was forcefully urging that more immigrants be encouraged to move south. "If more {textile} mills are to be built in the south," it said, "the people to run them must be brought here, not by twos and threes . . . but by the hundreds and thousands continually."*[11]

Unidentified woman. WWP.

Man from Serbia. NPS.

the flow of foreign criminals to New York. But when Petrosino was assassinated the following year in Sicily, there was another outcry against Watchorn's open-door immigration policy.

Before he left office in 1909, Theodore Roosevelt recommended Watchorn for reappointment. But before Congress could act, bidders for the Ellis Island food contract charged Watchorn with favoritism and unfair practices. Their allegations obliged President William Howard Taft's secretary of commerce and labor, Charles Nagel, to open yet another investigation. Shortly thereafter, Watchorn resigned saying that he was forced out by "political exigency." Taft denied this, and appointed William Williams once again to the job.

chapter *14*

Williams resumed office with the same attack he displayed at the beginning of his first term in 1902. One journalist said he resembled a "human bull terrier," explaining that the bull terriers don't growl, "they just grab a leg and hang on."

"I took hold on May 28, 1909," Williams wrote, "and before the day was over observed that the service had retrograded substantially since my departure in 1905, though not quite to the low point at which I had found it in 1902. For four years Oscar Straus had been Secretary of Commerce and Labor. He stood for a lax application of the law and the Commissioner under him readily adapted himself to the views of his superior officer. Straus claimed that he was "humanizing" the law, but in fact he was largely disregarding it, with the result that the asylums and the charitable institutions of the State were being filled to capacity. The steamship companies at once sensed the change that came about when Straus took office in 1905, and had things more or less their own way from that time till the Taft administration was able to familiarize itself with the situation, which it lost no time in doing. Not only had the inspection standards been lowered but corruption was again rampant.[1]

Williams accepted his reappointment on condition that Joseph Murray, the assistant commissioner, resign. Murray's place was filled by Chief Clerk Byron Uhl, who had had many years experience at Ellis Island.

Williams lost no time in re-establishing his regime. His first morning he wrote to Fritz Brodt, who had the restaurant concession:

Pending the adoption of more definite regulations, you will forthwith cease selling to an immigrant travelling alone any package of food for which he is charged more than fifty cents, excepting that an immigrant travelling to a point as distant as Chicago may purchase a dollar-bag of

William Williams, ca. 1910. William Williams Papers, Mss. & Archives Division, New York Public Library.

Italian family at Ellis Island, ca. 1910. Joseph Kossuth Dixon Collection, Library of Congress.

food, provided he ask leave to do this of his own motion. You will report to me daily how many bags of each class you have sold.

The slightest coercion on the part of any of your employees in compelling an immigrant to buy even a fifty-cent bag of food will be punished with dismissal from the island.

For your information I will state that I was dissatisfied with the manner in which food was being sold at the only one of your stands which I have thus far had time to inspect, and a radical change must occur in these matters.

Williams dismissed a keeper of a food stand for taking five dollars from an immigrant in payment for a dollar bag of food and then giving no change. To the keeper's protest that he had made a mistake, Williams countered that Ellis Island could not afford to have people around who were too stupid to distinguish between a five-dollar bill and a one-dollar bill.

Williams wanted to get rid of Brodt and award the food contract once again to Hudgins and Dumas, who had been in charge of the commissary during Williams's first term. The contract with Brodt, however, was scheduled to run for some time before its expiration, and to have it annulled, Williams had to furnish proof that Brodt was not living up to its specifications. In August, Williams sent to Washington his case against Brodt. In its report *The World* said:

It is alleged in the data now in the hands of the Department of Commerce and Labor, that Commissary Contractor Felix Brodt reaped a profit of over $17,000 in the six months beginning last November through the substitution of inferior sausage in the luncheon boxes provided for the immigrants passing through the immigration station bound for distant interior points . . .

Over a quarter of a million pounds of this inferior grade of sausage were delivered at Ellis Island through the substitution engineered by Brodt so it is alleged in evidence. The actual difference in the cost per pound averaged nearly 7 cents. His deliveries in November, 1908 were 30,000 pounds; in December, 1908, 34,000 pounds; in January, 52,000 pounds; in February 52,000 pounds; in March, 54,000, and in April 50,000 pounds.

Williams thought the substitution netted Brodt an excessive profit. There had been other substitutions as well, Williams maintained, that made the box lunches unappetizing. The so-called Sausage-War was settled after a four month investigation by the Department of Commerce and Labor. Williams was the victor; Brodt's contract was canceled, and the food privilege was awarded to Hudgins and Dumas.

Next, Williams concentrated on weeding out bogus missionary societies. Williams barred representatives of St. Joseph's Home for the Protection of Polish Immigrants. In his letter to the trustees of that home he practically declared that immigrants had been beaten with rubber hoses and forced to pay exorbitant sums of money despite

Immigrants waiting outside main building, ca. 1907. Photograph by Burt G. Phillips. Museum of the City of New York.

the home's assertion that meals were furnished free; that the home has been used as an employment agency for profit; and that employees of the home had taken money from immigrants for safe-keeping and then refused to give it back.

The agent for the Swedish Immigrant Home was also banished from Ellis Island. Williams accused Andrew Dahlberg of giving the Immigration Bureau false addresses for over half the single immigrant women who had been entrusted to his care. In case after case, a government investigator found that the women who were being traced did not go to the address that Dahlberg had furnished as their final destination. Where the girls went remained a mystery.

The fear was that they had fallen into the hands of "white slavers."

"Mr. Williams makes no secret," said a reporter, "that many young girls have been lured from these [homes] to disreputable resorts under the promise of receiving honorable employment."

The Austrian Society was likewise barred as was a local Armenian representative for having induced an immigrant who wanted to deposit three hundred dollars in a savings bank to lend the money instead to one of the agent's friends.

Williams also made the steamship companies toe the line on regulations governing their conduct. One responsibility the companies wanted to avoid was paying for the hospital care of immigrants too sick to be inspected at once. In December 1909, they made it known that they would no longer pay these costs, which, they maintained, were amply provided for by the four-dollar head tax

collected by the government for each landed immigrant. Williams was not one to let such a bald challenge to his authority go unanswered. "I brought the companies to terms, by exercising the statutory option of conducting medical examinations on board, and leaving sick immigrants there." The medical examination thus carried out aboard ship created chaos among the sixteen hundred steerage passengers of the *Kaiserin Augusta Victoria*. The *Daily Mail* reported:

One of the "1000 Marriageable Girls" from the Baltic, *September 27, 1907. Geo. G. Bain Collection, Library of Congress.*

Part of the "1000 Marriageable Girls" in front of main building on Ellis Island, September 27, 1907. Geo. G. Bain Collection, Library of Congress.

When news spread around Europe that there was a shortage of wives in the United States, over one thousand women independently decided to book passage on the White Star liner Baltic, *which sailed out of Liverpool with a stop at Queenstown, Ireland. "You ought to have seen them come up the side of the ship," the purser said. "They did it just as if they expected to find husbands awaiting them on the steerage deck."*

Their arrival caused quite a stir and even prompted a committee of Michigan farmers to come to New York to persuade the young women that their state was the best place in the country to live. The women had their own ideas, however. Some already had fiancés awaiting them. "Others," reported The New York Times *on September 28, 1907, "want to be wives of railroad engineers, and some decided, after they arrived in the lower bay, that the only men who could win their hands were the ones who built the skyscrapers. One little blue-eyed girl from Liverpool showed that she was strictly up to date by declaring that 'it's a Pittsburgh millionaire for me.' "*

When the physicians began examining the passengers there was a great uproar. Children were parted from their parents and wives from their husbands. Women rushed about crying for their children and men pushed through crowds or ran about the decks in an effort to find their families. It was more than an hour before quiet was resumed and the examination could proceed in an orderly manner.

The shipping lines quickly yielded. The next day they sent Williams formal notice that they would pay the hospital charges for detained immigrants. In return, Williams gave permission to transfer to Ellis Island hospital the few ill steerage passengers who had been left aboard the *Kaiserin Augusta Victoria* the day before.

The most explosive issue of Williams's second term was provoked by his notice to steamship companies that each immigrant should have at least twenty-five dollars when he landed at Ellis Island, plus a railroad ticket to his destination. He admitted that this was not a statutory provision but a "rule of thumb" to help immigration inspectors decide whether an immigrant was "likely to become a public charge."

Williams applied his new rule immediately, even to those who had left Europe before the rule was made public. The protest was immediate. Many of those affected were Russian Jews coming to join friends and family in New York. When 247 deportations were ordered in one day, with over half due to the new rule, the Jewish

community of Brownsville in Brooklyn held a mass protest meeting. They wanted to remind President Taft that when he spoke in Brownsville before his election, he had promised he "would do all in his power to see that the immigration laws were liberally interpreted."

An editorial in one of the Jewish morning newspapers began by referring to the current Fourth of July celebrations:

But while our children listen to-day to this inspiring story of American revolt against tyranny they are aware that behind the bars at Ellis Island hundreds of their poor relatives and brethren are kept confined like prisoners in a Russian dungeon.

After declaring that the detention and treatment of immigrants "shakes every fibre of justice and humanity in our hearts so that we cannot allow ourselves to think of anything else," the editorial continues:

Taft and Williams bar the gate at Ellis Island, July 1909. YIVO Institute for Jewish Research.

Williams tells Christopher Columbus that he cannot enter America unless he has twenty-five dollars. This cartoon, translated into German and Italian, was published in other foreign newspapers as well.

"Mauretania Apr. 30-09.
Wealthy Dane in search of pleasure."

"*Peter Meyer—57, Denmark,*" 1909.
Photograph by Augustus Sherman. National Park Service.

Among the passengers disembarked from the Mauretania *on April 30, 1909 was Peter Meyer, who—perhaps based on his own explanations—was referred to by his photographer as a "wealthy Dane in search of pleasure." It seems fitting that such a man had arrived on the* Mauretania, *renowned as "the fastest steamship in the world" and one that provoked headlines about gamblers and card sharps being on board, fleecing unsuspecting passengers.*

On Meyer's crossing, for example, The Times *reported that gamblers cleaned up about $2,000. "About all the playing," it said, "was done at a table placed directly under a special notice warning passengers that there were card sharps on board."*

Our new Commissioner of Immigration at Ellis Island, Mr. William Williams, issued a ukase that every immigrant who is unable to show $25 in cash on landing is to be deported; furthermore, that none of those detained at the port of deportation be allowed to telegraph or write relatives or friends. The immigrants whose only sin is not having a certain arbitrary sum of money are thus treated more cruelly than a criminal.

In eleven days, from June 26 to July 8, 668 persons were denied admission at Ellis Island and sent back. Many more were held in detention pending decisions from the Board of Special Inquiry. The people who were held at Ellis Island, caught in Williams's show of power to the steamship companies, were distraught and angry. A letter published in the *Jewish Daily Forward* from a St. Petersburg student described their circumstances:

People of all nationalities are here; most of them, however, are Russian Jews. Many cannot return to Russia for political reasons. There are many families who have sold all they possessed in the old country in order to buy passage to the United States, expecting by the aid of their relatives and friends to start life anew in this "country of opportunity."

None know better than the Russian Jew how much suffering an immigrant must undergo before he can reach this country in safety. First he must, at the risk of his liberty and with a great deal of bribing, manage his way across the Russian border. Then a few days of misery in a harbor town before going aboard ship. The suffering on shipboard as a penniless steerage passenger is too well known to need any comment. And on landing in this country we are met by an expected (sic) order: "$25 in cash or go back to whence you came." Had we known that, we should have managed in some way or another to scrape together the required $25.

A reporter for *The Evening World* who interviewed Williams at this time wrote that "he looks like a man whose emotions are conducted by a card system. If the Commissioner . . . even at night is haunted by the misery of uncertainty that surrounds him by day, he does not show it."

Williams's actions seemed arbitrary and cruel to representatives of immigrant welfare societies. The head of the Alliance for Roumanian Jews spoke for many when he said: "If Oscar Straus were Secretary of the Department of Commerce and Labor, this rule would

Servian Gypsies.

not have been tolerated. Mr. Straus knows that to send a Jew back to the old country after he has once left it, makes him a target of official tyranny, worse than before he went away."

To test the rule, lawyers from the Hebrew Immigrant Aid Society obtained a writ of habeas corpus from Judge Learned Hand on behalf of four Russian Jews who had been excluded as "likely to become a public charge," but Hand never had to rule on the case because the four Russian men were granted a new hearing by the Board of Special Inquiry and new evidence was introduced that admitted them.

Later that month, Williams's twenty-five dollar rule was upheld by Secretary Charles Nagel. *The Commercial Advertiser* reported:

Secretary Nagel said he was entirely satisfied with the way Commissioner Williams was running things at the island. The commissioner had done much to keep out undesirables. The secretary said he had received bushels

Servian Gypsies. National Park Service.

Williams pasted this photograph in his scrapbook and under it an article about how twenty-four Roumanian gypsies were ordered to be deported. "They learned the other day that they were to be sent back," The Sun reported on July 21, 1909, "and they began cutting up in pantomime. Every uniformed inspector who came near them received a villainous glare from fierce eyes, and six forefingers were passed under six swarthy throats."

Immigrants leaving Ellis Island. National Park Service.

of communications from Jewish societies and Jewish people who were not in favor of the restrictions at this port; on the other hand, he had received as many letters and protests from labor organizations, Jewish and otherwise, approving the course of Commissioner Williams. Organizations in the tailors' trade, including those of women, wrote that they did not want any more tailors in New York as there was hardly enough work for those already here.

The high rate of deportations lessened gradually as steamship agents refused to sell tickets to immigrants who could not show the required sum of money. Once again deportations totaled up to 3 percent of the number of immigrants landed at Ellis Island. Williams commented with some satisfaction that this was at least double the percentage ordered by Watchorn.

One of the many deportation cases that made the headlines in New York newspapers was that of a Welsh miner who happened to be detained at Ellis Island during a visit by President Taft. Williams invited the president to conduct an "appeals" session where ten cases referred from the Board of Special Inquiry were heard. A report of the session appeared in *The World:*

Mr. Taft was particularly interested in George Thornton, a Welsh miner, and his seven motherless children, oldest nineteen, youngest two. Thornton's health was not quite up to the standard the immigration law sets, but he was not actually sick nor weak and his children seemed as healthy as could be.

The President questioned Thornton:

"What have you with which to start life here?"

"One hundred and sixty-five dollars and these two hands, sir" answered the miner, who did not recognize Mr. Taft. Thornton added he had a sister in Pittsburgh who would care for his children until he and the older of them found work.

"Do you know who is President of the United States?" Commissioner Williams asked.

"William H. Taft," answered Thornton promptly.

"Would it surprise you to know that I am the President?" asked Mr. Taft with that smile of his.

"So you are, sir," said Thornton after studying him a moment. "I have seen your picture often, sir."

Thornton and his family came in. But soon Williams got letters from Wales; Thornton had left debts there. It was said he was not getting along here. The president was informed, and Thornton was asked to explain. He wrote a "hard luck" letter to the immigration commissioner and was deported at his own request.

President Taft visits Ellis Island, October 18, 1910. William Williams Papers, Mss. & Archives Division, New York Public Library.

"President Taft, standing on Ellis Island, the gateway to American citizenship, gazed thoughtfully today into the faces of two thousand aliens who are awaiting a chance to enter the New World," The New York Globe reported. "The immigrants, who had been told by the interpreters that the President was the ruler of the republic, stared wonderingly, even reverently, at him." In this photograph the president is flanked by Secretary of Commerce and Labor Charles Nagel (left) and William Williams (right).

Seven children at Ellis Island hospital, n.d. National Archives.

The president's experience seemed to justify Williams's strict policies. But liberals pointed out that since immigrants could be deported within the period of three years at the steamship companies' expense, why not, in doubtful cases, give them a chance to prove themselves instead of excluding them out of hand. *The World* lamented:

The immigration laws are to be enforced even more strictly at New York. Not more harshly, but without the beneficence and hopefulness with which President Taft, a merciful judge, interpreted one of them.

About the same time Secretary Nagel was quoted as saying:

You couldn't let personal feelings enter this matter of immigration . . . and you cannot make a hard and fast rule for individual cases. . . . Every case has its individual conditions, and of course, as in a court, every case appeals first to discretion, then sympathy and individual feelings.

In July 1911, several German immigration societies joined to request that Williams's administration be investigated. They charged that the buildings on Ellis Island were filthy and filled with vermin;

"DEVIL'S ISLE."

THE AMERICAN IMMIGRANTS' INQUISITION SCANDAL.

Map-makers write it down Ellis Island, but immigrants to New York call it "Devil's Isle" —appropriately, as I can testify, writes an *Answers* reader. For, having to visit the States at a time when practically every berth in every Transatlantic liner was taken, I was forced to travel as an immigrant.

I trust that I shall never again have to submit to such indignities as I was subjected to on my arrival across the "Pond."

Before being officially received on American soil, immigrants to New York are taken over by steam-packet to Ellis Island. When this vessel arrives alongside the liner, loud orders are given to the immigrants: "All form in line for the shore! Close up! Step this way, with your green health-card handy! Bring all your hand-baggage with you!" Each immigrant has been given a green health-card by the ship's doctor, after examination. These cards have now to be pinned on a conspicuous part of the person.

Once disembarked on Ellis Isle, we move along in single file till we pass through the portals of an immense hall, divided by stout wire netting into alleyways and pens like a cattleyard. This intricate maze we traverse several times, getting shuffled up with the passengers of French and German boats.

Suddenly, there is a cry of "Halt!" and then a specialist examines us for tracoma, folding back each eyelid in a very rough manner. Next, proceeding in single file, we are individually chalked. My brand is a capital "S," which, I suppose, stands for "senile." "P" means "pulmonary"; "Ex" means "eczema." A man chalked "Face" had a large wart thereon. "Gait" is lame; "Vision" wears an eyeglass.

The rams are now separated from the ewes, the men filing to the right, the women to the left.

What happens to the ladies, I do not not know; but it is not pleasant, to judge by the squealing, crying, and protesting we can hear.

I find myself one of fifty white, black, red, and yellow immigrants. "Strip!" comes the order. "Take everything off, and line up as you were born!" I protest. I am a Britisher. "No matter!" comes the answer. "Line up naked, like the rest!" We strip, and, one by one, pass up for inspection. I am tested, and told to "Cough! Cough again!" And then, as something is written on my paper, to "Pass along and dress! Take this report with you!"

The ladies join us, and we kick our heels for a space. Then our papers are taken from us, and copied in a letter-press, the originals being filed for further inspection. Next, a strip of paper, with the word "Certificate," is pinned on our shoulders. Some have already passed along; but just as my turn arrives the officials tell us that they are going to knock off one hour for lunch, and walk through the folding glass doors marked "No admittance!" puffing their cigarettes.

I begin to light up. "No smoking allowed!" snaps an attendant. I ask for a drink. "First to the right, first to the left!" I follow these directions, and find an iron pipe without a nozzle. There is no glass. The water flows, and you just put your mouth to the pipe.

When the hour has expired the officiating medico resumes his chair. I am asked, "Are you married? Where is your wife? What have you come to America for? What do you intend to do now you're here?" etc. Then the certificate is torn from my shoulder, and I march along to the last pen, cheerfully marked, "Hospital Cases." Here I remain for another hour and a half.

Altogether, I spent four and a half hours on Ellis Island. Once outside the "Hall of Torture," I inquired for my cabin-trunk. I was told to go to the nether regions; so, mentally consigning the said trunk to that warm place, I went across myself to South Ferry, New York.

---

that there were not enough beds for the great numbers of detained immigrants and that many had to sleep on the floor; that the food was inedible; that immigrants were subjected to barbarous and brutal treatment; and that too many were being deported as a result of Williams's "severe and even cruel" application of the immigration laws.

The House Rules Committee ordered a full investigation, which was held during the summer of 1911. In his testimony Williams answered the accusations point by point. He told the committee

Clipping from William Williams's scrapbook, 1910. William Williams Papers, Mss & Archives Division, New York Public Library.

English newspapers were almost always outraged by the way British subjects were treated on Ellis Island. Despite some exaggeration, their view of conditions on the island was probably much closer to the truth than that of immigration officials.

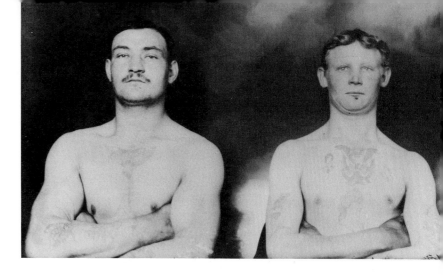

Tattooed German stowaways deported May 1911. Photograph by Augustus Sherman. National Park Service.

The same month these men were deported, The New York Times *said that less than half of the known stowaways discovered in New York were actually sent back. "In New York alone," it said, "out of 113 stowaways reported by the steamship companies, only fifty-five were sent back. . . . But not all stowaways are reported, and those who are not reported are likely to be even more undesirable than those who are."*

that his notice that "Immigrants shall be treated with kindness and civility by everyone at Ellis Island" was posted in large type in twelve or fourteen places on the premises and was not violated; that immigrants bring in vermin but that the detention rooms were cleaned and scrubbed several times a day; that the food, though plain, was healthful and plentiful; but it was true that there were not enough beds. He added:

That is not my fault. We do not always have beds enough for the immigrants . . . there are not 2,000 beds on Ellis Island, and we sometimes have to detain 2,000 . . . under the circumstances those that do not

Steerage deck of Frederick der Grosse: *Italian men being deported, n.d. Geo. G. Bain Collection, Library of Congress.*

have beds, say 200, will have to sleep on benches. I can not admit ineligible immigrants just because they have not comfortable beds to sleep in. I want them to be as comfortable as possible, but I think the execution of the law is paramount to their sleeping in the most comfortable kind of quarters, especially as Congress, with knowledge of the facts, does not provide them.

The real concern of the investigation was the number of deportations and their circumstances. Williams blamed the steamship companies for stirring up and then taking advantage of the sympathy elicited by these sad stories. He went through, one by one, the cases his accusers brought as evidence of his harsh application of the law, correcting details and filling in other information. Williams spoke dispassionately, but the stories he told were nonetheless heartrending. He made it clear that he was simply executing the law; if the consequences were tragic, that was not his fault but rather the fault of the legislators.

The first case Williams described was that of a young Jewish woman who was deported with her two sons and a daughter.

Slavic Immigrant at Ellis Island, 1905. Photograph by Lewis W. Hine. New York Public Library.

According to Williams's own testimony, it was not unusual to have over two thousand detained aliens on the island overnight. Since there were only eighteen hundred beds, two hundred immigrants had nowhere to sleep except on wooden benches.

Now, the facts in that case are these: It is perfectly true she was deported with her three children. How did she secure entry! Through stating she was going to her husband. That at the time was true, but within a month the husband deserted her in Philadelphia, and she was unable ever thereafter to locate him. That fact was concealed from the committee. A second very relevant fact which also was concealed is this, that owing to the pressure under which we have to do our work at Ellis Island, in this case (as in some others, undoubtedly), one of the children was passed as being healthy. Yet when she applied, as she did, to the juvenile court of New York, to get her children committed after the desertion of her husband, we then learned for the first time that one of them was an imbecile, and had no business to be in the country. The mere fact that we had not detected this child's imbecility at the time of the landing did not bar us from putting him out of the country at the time we did detect it, because we detected it within three years, and this 3-year law about which you will hear a great deal later, is precisely to meet such cases . . .

Maryan Willner arrived May 28, 1910, by the steamer Amerika, *Hamburg-American Line, with five young children, all under 10. They were going to the husband and father. . . . Now the child Juda turned out to be an imbecile. She was inadmissible and the mother was excluded*

Liberty, the Statue that Guards our Harbor, 1910. New York Public Library.

A political cartoon in an unidentified newspaper gives timely advice to immigrants who will have to pass through the inspection mill on Ellis Island.

under section 11 of the law to accompany her back to Russia.

Exclusion of the four remaining children properly occurred, because the father, particularly in the absence of the mother, was in no position to look after or provide for them. He was a peddler. Though he had been here four years he had only $80 saved, and the evidence showed him to be in no position to support a family.

Fiorello La Guardia remembered from his days as an interpreter on Ellis Island that he always suffered greatly when he was assigned to interpret for mental cases. He said in his *Autobiography of an Insurgent:*

I felt then, and I feel the same today, that over fifty per cent of the deportations for alleged mental disease were unjustified. Many of those classified as mental cases were so classified because of ignorance on the part of the immigrants or the doctors and the inability of the doctors to understand the particular immigrant's norm or standard.

One case haunted me for years. A young girl in her teens from the mountains of northern Italy turned up at Ellis Island. No one understood her particular dialect very well, and because of her hesitancy in replying to questions she did not understand, she was sent to the hospital for observation. I could imagine the effect on this girl who had always been carefully sheltered and never permitted to be in the company of a man alone, when a doctor suddenly rapped her on the knees, looked into her eyes, turned her on her back and tickled her spine to ascertain her reflexes. The child rebelled—and how! It was the cruelest case I ever witnessed on the island. In two weeks' time that child was a raving maniac, although she had been sound and normal when she arrived at Ellis Island.[2]

Williams was unmoved by hard-luck cases. If anything, these were the ones he especially wanted to keep out. Some reformers, who looked upon international relationships as opportunities for mutual service, thought that deportations were callous evasions of moral responsibility. But this was not Williams's viewpoint, nor was it a view shared by most Americans. At this time, the prevailing sentiment in the country seemed to be shifting away from an open-door policy to one that strictly limited immigration.

Senator William P. Dillingham had just released his commission's forty-two volume report on immigration, which had taken over three years to prepare. It covered every aspect of the subject: "immigrants as charity-seekers," "immigration and crime," "immigration and insanity," "changes in bodily form of descendants of immigrants," etc. The heart of the report was an analysis of the "old" immigrants from northern Europe and the "new" immigrants from eastern and southern Europe who started coming to the United States after 1880. The evidence slanted to show that new immigrants were inferior to and less desirable than the old immigrants. The commission strongly recommended that immigration from eastern and southern Europe be restricted. Williams had been saying much the same thing since he was first appointed in 1902. In the absence of new restrictionist legislation, Williams stretched the present law to the limit to warrant as many exclusions as possible. "Likely to become a public charge," "feeblemindedness," "senility," and other rubber-band categories were used to prevent borderline cases from landing.

An order to deport nearly always caused extreme distress. To be sent back to their port of embarkation, sometimes with no money to travel overland to their country of origin, meant disgrace, financial ruin, or political harassment for many immigrants. It was a harsh fate that many could not face. Throughout Ellis Island's history, over three thousand immigrants committed suicide while awaiting deportation or final decisions on their admission to the United States.

Board of Special Inquiry, ca. 1911. William Williams Papers, Mss & Archives Division, New York Public Library.

On the right side of the photograph stands the immigrant whose case is being decided, an interpreter, and perhaps a friend who acts as a character witness. In 1911, the special inquiry rooms were fixed up to give the board's procedures a more judicial setting.

The boards were often criticized for being too legalistic, and 50 percent of their decisions were overturned on appeal to Washington. Secretary Nagel admitted that the boards had to be improved, but as late as 1927, here is how one reporter described them for The Forum: *"To those who may have the slightest technical shortcomings in their visas, the boards show no mercy of any quality. A reentry permit minus one of its rubber-stamp signatures, obviously due to official neglect, earns weeks of detention on Ellis Island, for the Boards cut no Gordian knots with the swords of common sense.*[3]

In calling for new legislation to end this cruel state of affairs, Marcus Braun, a Republican leader inveighed against "suave" congressmen who "could not possibly be brought to a vote in the open on any definite proposal about immigration:"

And that is why the law is so non-committal and vague. It needs frank, blunt action. I do not want to say they should let in more or let in less people, but those they do let in, they should handle with humanity. I know hundreds of cases in which poor fellows have sold all they had on the other side, broken up their established homes, and came to this country, only to commit suicide on steamers on which they were sent back, rather than return where all the bridges had been burned behind them.[4]

Children being treated for trachoma at Ellis Island hospital, n.d. National Archives.

Immigration doctors believed that cases of trachoma were usually incurable, and most immigrants suffering from this contagious disease were quickly deported. A doctor's decision on such cases was legally binding, and there was no appeal. While waiting three or four days for their ship to leave, trachoma patients stayed at the hospital.

A plan for inspecting immigrants in their own countries at American consulates had been recommended as early as the 1890s, but was opposed by liberals who thought that it would give foreign governments too much control over who was allowed to leave their country. "Consular inspection," wrote John B. Weber in 1892, "will prevent the emigration, from every country in Europe, except

Great Britain, of men within the military age, the most active and productive period of life, and send to us the quite young and the old."[5]

A decade later, Edward Steiner wrote that foreign countries would probably object to the United States setting up a system of overseas inspection that would select the "best material and leave the worst."[6] Steiner also said that the proposed plan would give "foreign governments a very fine opportunity to detain those who emigrate for political reasons or those who desire to avoid service in the army."

As the immigration laws stood, the United States depended on the steamship companies to carry out the overseas inspection. The steamship companies, however, found it more profitable to save on inspection costs by doing spot checks and risked the expense of taking a few excluded aliens back to their ports of embarkation.

So long as the policy of the immigration officials was lenient, current immigration laws worked in the immigrants' favor. Inspectors would rather give borderline cases the benefit of the doubt instead of ordering them deported. But when the laws and restrictions were stringently enforced, as they were under Williams, they caused enormous hardship. When the number of deportations started to rise in 1902, one newspaper observed of the excluded aliens:

Not all of them are objectionable characters and it is a terrible thing to turn some of these people back again at the moment when they behold the goal of all their ambition, the haven of that refuge for which they have yearned and craved probably for years, to turn them back alone, shelterless, without means and homeless . . . surely this is unworthy of this the greatest Republic on earth, this glorious land free and independent by the Grace of God, the place of refuge of all oppressed.[7]

By 1911, when Williams's administration was under investigation, it was evident that overseas inspection was the only intelligent and kind way to enforce a more stringent interpretation of who belonged and who didn't belong to the immigration law's many excluded classes. Yet Congress did not legislate a new system of inspection until 1924. In the meantime, except during World War I, Ellis Island was packed every night with detained aliens waiting either for permission to land or to be deported.

One inspector who had worked at Ellis Island during Williams's administration recalled that in "those days we averaged about two

Ellis Island Hospital, n.d. National Archives.

The Ellis Island hospital was completed in 1902, but the contagious disease hospital in the background was not completed until 1909, and because of a lack of funds, not opened until 1911.

While Robert Watchorn was commissioner, he requested temporary quarters on the island for children suffering from contagious diseases. "At the present time," he wrote to Commissioner-General Frank Sargent, "we are compelled to send all cases of measles, diphtheria, or scarlet fever to outside hospitals. . . . This involves a long, tedious haul, and the exposure incident thereto produces a rate of mortality that is well-nigh appalling."[9]

thousand [detained every night]. In the detention room there were never less than nine hundred. It was an endless affair, like filling a trough at one end and emptying it at the other."[8]

An enforced stay on Ellis Island was at best unpleasant and often turned out to be tragic. One case that caused an uproar in the press was that of a woman who arrived in December 1910 with her three children. She and her family were on their way to meet the father in Chicago. But doctors discovered that two of the children had ringworm of the scalp and so the family was detained. While at Ellis Island, one of the children contracted measles and diphtheria and was sent to the Quarantine station on Staten Island, where it died three weeks later. The second child came down with scarlet fever, measles, diphtheria, and bronchopneumonia and was also sent to Quarantine, where it died within a week.

All this time the mother and the third child stayed on Ellis Island. Since this child had ringworm, he was under orders to be deported. His mother, of course, would have to accompany him. This was a case that moved even Commissioner Williams's heart, and he arranged to have the child treated until the end of March when he would be transferred to a hospital near Chicago. The mother, meanwhile, was sent ahead to meet her husband.

In his book, *Immigration Problems,* Victor Safford stated that the mortality rate for measles at Ellis Island was 30 percent. This was due, he said, to the long trip by ferry and ambulance to a New York City municipal hospital. Eventually, an isolation hospital

building on Ellis Island was opened as a "measles ward" to which persons sick with that disease could be transferred directly from the ship, and the mortality from measles dropped to almost nothing. Williams had requested an appropriation to build a contagious disease hospital separate from the main hospital in 1903 during his first term of office. The new isolation hospital building was finally completed in 1909, but because there was no money for its operation, the building was not opened until 1911.

In 1912, Taft was defeated in his presidential campaign by Woodrow Wilson, and Williams submitted his resignation. Williams wrote:

Prior to the expiration of my term of office (which was for four years from May 28, 1909) I sent in my resignation to President Wilson, to take effect June 1, 1913. He requested me to withdraw it, but this I stated I would be unable to do, whereupon he requested me as a convenience to him to serve till the end of the fiscal year (June 30) and accept my resignation as of that date. He did not fill my place for nearly a year, the office in the meantime being conducted by the excellent Assistant Commissioner, Byron H. Uhl, an appointee of mine.[10]

Immigrant children on Ellis Island, 1913. William Williams Papers, Mss & Archives Division, New York Public Library.

William Williams, President-elect Woodrow Wilson and Mrs. Wilson on Ellis Island, 1913. New York Public Library.

When Wilson visited Ellis Island on January 25, 1913, he watched the line inspection, saw the dining room, the hospital, special inquiry rooms, and other departments. He did not, however, offer any comment on what he thought of Ellis Island. "I came for information," he told the press, "and not for thought."

Williams's resignation marked the end of an era at Ellis Island. Despite his want of sympathy for the millions of people who poured through his jurisdiction, he was undoubtedly the most competent of all the commissioners of immigration at Ellis Island. His genius for running that vast landing depot with its complex amalgam of trials, heartbreaking ordeals, and endless problems was astounding. It was probably his ability to do so much with so little that kept Congress from appropriating money for a truly humane immigrant station. Williams's organizational talents would be sorely missed when a new rush of immigration descended on Ellis Island following World War I. For the time being, however, the war would cause a sharp fall-off in immigration and present Ellis Island with a radically different, though no less critical, set of problems.

chapter *15*

BUREAUCRATS DECLARE WAR

Byron Uhl, the assistant commissioner, presided over the last great surge of immigration to New York—878,052 for the fiscal year 1913–1914—before the outbreak of World War I. By the following year, immigration had declined to a fraction of what it had been in previous years. In 1915, arrivals at Ellis Island totaled 178,416, and by 1916, only 28,867.

In the summer of 1914, Wilson asked his friend Frederic C. Howe, a former law professor, writer, and director of the People's Institute in New York, to be the next commissioner. Howe accepted and took office in August.

"Ellis Island," Howe wrote in his autobiography *Confessions of a Reformer*, "was an opportunity to ameliorate the lot of several thousand human beings. It was also an opportunity to do the work I liked to do."[1]

Howe could not have been more different from his predecessor. Williams's main concentration was on efficiently processing thousands of aliens day in and day out, determined to weed out the 2 percent who did not measure up to immigration law standards. Howe's aim, on the other hand, was to humanize the island, to make it a less frightening, more comfortable place for those who were unlucky enough to be detained. He also wanted to provide services for those immigrants who were admitted to ease the often traumatic process of assimilation. In October 1914, *The Outlook* Magazine quoted Howe:

I believe it would be feasible to devise a plan whereby each immigrant could be brought into touch with the school, industrial, police, and health authorities of the place of his destination; so that, if he has children, a school board will see that they are sent to school, a market will be found for his labor, and the police of the town will hear of him, and the health authorities will be able to look after him. After all, we have

Frederic C. Howe, commissioner of immigration, 1914–1919. Geo. G. Bain Collection, Library of Congress.

Arriving at Ellis Island, ca. 1910. Geo. G. Bain Collection, Library of Congress.

been so intent on eliminating two per cent of undesirables that we have lost sight of the ninety-eight per cent whom we have invited to our shores.[2]

Nineteen fourteen was a year of high unemployment. There were thousands of men in New York who had no work and no place to live. Many of them were recent immigrants. Howe opened two buildings on Ellis Island to the city's unemployed, buildings once used as detention quarters but now not needed because of the drop in immigration. He told a reporter from the *The Immigrants in America Review:*

. . . seven hundred and fifty men, who, largely due to no fault of their own, were reduced to a state of abject misery through lack of food and shelter, had at least a roof over their heads at night for several months during the severe cold weather. The government ferry took them over at night and returned them the next morning, so that they could look for work. . . . There was no confusion or disorder among the unemployed thus cared for, and the men were wholesome, self-respecting workmen, a large part of whom were foreign born. The expense to the Government was practically nothing.[3]

For those immigrants who were detained, Howe tried to make their stay as pleasant as possible. In another interview he said that when he first came to Ellis Island, he found three hundred detained

immigrants with nothing to do except sit hour after hour on hard benches in a crowded room. Most detentions were over in a matter of one or two days, but some lasted weeks. In detention, men were separated from the women and children, and fathers could not see their families except at mealtime. Howe told the reporter:

The first thing we did was to turn the lawns about this building into playgrounds for the mothers and babies. Some of these peasants had been away from the soil, shut up indoors, for months. It meant a lot to them to get out into the sunlight and feel the grass under their feet again.

The next step was to find a common hall, that families might be together every day. As long as the warm weather lasts the enclosed porch overlooking the city makes a capital social room. . . . Now we wanted to take down the wire netting from around the examination rooms, which makes them feel like animals in a cage, and then we'll hang maps and pictures on the walls. The only thing that is lacking over here is imagination. No one ever seemed to try to imagine what a detained immigrant must be feeling.[4]

Howe also set up a little school with a kindergarten teacher for the detained children and a workroom where men could learn weaving and rug-making. The YMCA sent teachers to help detained women do needlework.

"You believe then that Ellis Island should be a concrete impression

Dutch family on Ellis Island, ca. 1910. Geo. G. Bain Collection, Library of Congress.

of the best of America?" another reporter asked the new commissioner. "I certainly do," Howe replied. ". . . it is my hope that every man and woman who passes through this port may be in some degree impressed with America's spirit of democracy—the chance to work and be happy."[5]

Howe did not accomplish all these changes without ruffling the feathers of his staff. Many of the clerks and inspectors had worked on Ellis Island for decades. They were resistant to Howe's touches of humanity and especially horrified when he allowed immigrants to walk on Commissioner Williams's carefully maintained lawns. Immigration officials in Washington were uncooperative as well. Howe says in his autobiography:

During the next few years, I learned how we were governed by petty clerks, mostly Republicans. . . . In a generation's time, largely through the Civil Service reform movement, America has created an official bureaucracy moved largely by fear, hating initiative, and organized as a solid block to protect itself and its petty, unimaginative, salary-hunting instincts.[6]

Howe believed in the wisdom of the changes he was making and, at least for his first year in office, was able to realize many reforms

Immigrants leaving Ellis Island, ca. 1910. National Archives.

By the end of the fiscal year 1914, over 800,000 immigrants came to Ellis Island, but the following year, the British blockade of German ports cut the flow to under 200,000. By 1918, less than 30,000 people came through Ellis Island.

and improvements. Because of the war, Howe's task was much different from that of previous commissioners. After the *Lusitania* was torpedoed off the coast of Ireland in May 1915, President Wilson halted deportations of excluded aliens. Ellis Island gradually filled up with detained immigrants who could not be admitted or deported. Following America's entry into the war, eighteen hundred German merchant seamen were taken off German ships seized at various ports in the United States and brought to Ellis Island. As the war progressed, aliens suspected of sympathizing with the enemy, alleged agents-provocateurs, anarchists, and radicals were added to the island's population.

"I became a jailer," Howe wrote, "instead of a commissioner of immigration; a jailer not of convicted offenders but of suspected persons who had been arrested and railroaded to Ellis Island as the most available dumping-ground under the successive waves of hysteria which swept the country." Howe had to fight his staff constantly to make sure these aliens were treated decently and not as

Ukrainian concert in registry hall, Sunday, June 4, 1916. Photograph by Augustus Sherman. National Park Service.

Immigration had fallen off so drastically that concerts could be held every Sunday. This would have been impossible during the high tide of immigration before World War I when Sunday was as busy for the inspectors as any other day in the week. Notice that the wire mesh pens are gone and that pictures have been hung on pillars and walls.

hardened criminals. "Within a short time," he lamented, "I was branded as pro-German."

But the first wave of hysteria Howe had to contend with concerned not enemy aliens but recent immigrants who were allegedly involved in white-slave traffic. Aliens accused of taking part in what was thought to be a highly organized and financially powerful business were arrested under the 1910 Mann Act, which forbade transporting women over state lines for immoral purposes. These immigrants were eventually brought to Ellis Island where they stayed because there was no way to deport them.

"Of the thousands of arrests made," Howe wrote, "the number of men and women who might be classed as white-slavers or procurers was very small. Many of them were held on slight evidence of guilt. . . . Trials had often been without witnesses for the accused, without attorneys, without the aid of friends, and in many cases the aliens knew very little as to what it was all about."

Howe invited a group of women from New York, including Mary Simkhovitch and Lillian Wald, to review the cases of some of the detained women. Some frankly admitted to being prostitutes; the great majority, however, were casual offenders whose "misfortunes were the result of ignorance, almost always of poverty."

Howe proposed to the secretary of labor that ". . . casual offenders whose offense did not involve the commission of a crime should be paroled. Responsible persons or organizations would report on their conduct until they could be deported at the close of the war. The plan was approved, partly because it was becoming impossible to carry on the work of the island in its crowded condition. Hundreds of men and women were paroled."

Apart from his struggles with the bureaucracy and government agents, Howe also had to battle the steamship companies, local businesses, and the concession-holders. The first of these controversies was over the landing of second-class passengers at the Hoboken piers in New Jersey. Many immigrants at that time were willing to spend an extra forty dollars to avoid steerage and enjoy the relative comfort of second class. Since such passengers were inspected on board ship, they did not have to go to Ellis Island.

Shortly after he took office, Howe learned that as many as seventy thousand second-class passengers were landed in Hoboken each year. There they were systematically fleeced by railroad agents, baggage handlers, and Hoboken businessmen. "I urged," Howe said, "that

these passengers be landed on the island directly from the steamships, where abuses could be stopped."

When the commissioner-general called a hearing on the proposal at Ellis Island, the place was swamped with a ". . . hungry crowd protesting against the proposal," Howe wrote. "Powerful interests had been enlisted; there were railway and steamship agents, hotelkeepers, expressmen, representatives of the New York Chamber of Commerce. Hundreds of people were angrily aroused at the suggestion that they should be deprived of their prey. Representatives of the Hoboken Chamber of Commerce said it would cost Hoboken at least five hundred thousand dollars a year. Hotel and express men claimed almost equal losses. They looked upon the money which they took from the alien as a vested interest. . . . The order for the change was never made."

Howe's proposal was probably not favored by the immigrants either, who would much rather face the businessmen of Hoboken than the inspectors on Ellis Island.

School on Ellis Island, n.d. National Archives.

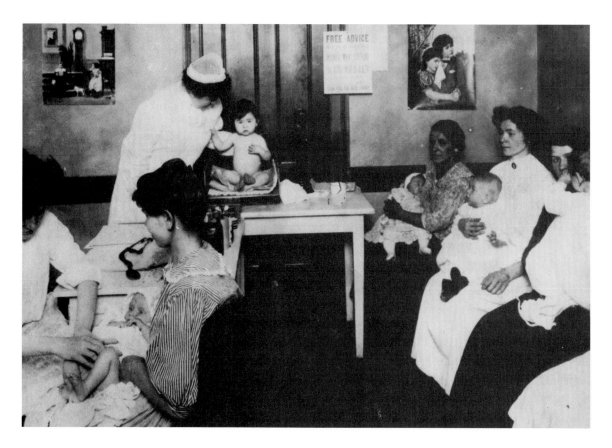

Nursery on Ellis Island, n.d. National
Archives.

"Commissioner Howe has two advantages
over previous commissioners at Ellis Island," Survey reported, "In the first
place, the great falling off of immigration since the war began, has given him
time for experiments and a small group
with which to experiment. All former
commissioners have been so buried under
the administrative detail of dealing with
a million immigrants a year that they
had no imagination for additional
work."[7]
    Howe set a good precedent and commis-
sioners who came after him tried to have
schools, nurseries, and playgrounds whenever funds and space allowed.

A more furious tempest ensued when Howe withdrew the food
concession from Hudgins and Dumas. Howe felt that the food served
at Ellis Island would never be any good so long as the contractor
profited by pushing the sale of box lunches and by scrimping on
the quality of the meals served in the restaurant. Since the government was already in charge of feeding the patients in the Ellis Island
hospital, Howe suggested that the government take over the Ellis
Island restaurant as well. The secretary of labor approved the idea,
and Congress authorized it in an amendment to an appropriation
bill in June 1916.

During the bill's debate, however, Howe was lambasted on the
House floor as a "half-baked radical who has free-love ideas." His
attacker was William S. Bennet, a representative from New York
City who had formerly been counsel for Hudgins and Dumas.

"By proposing to have the government sell food to the immigrants
on the island," Bennet charged, "in place of granting a restaurant
concession to contractors, he was committing the government to a

socialistic practice."[8]

Bennet's other accusations (that Howe admitted immoral women to the United States, failed to keep detained men and women separate, and allowed gambling) created an image of Ellis Island as an immoral playground for undesirable aliens. Bennet's slurs were unfounded, and most of the press rallied to Howe's support. *Survey* wrote:

That he is fostering immorality, Mr. Howe vigorously denies. But that he is admitting both men and women to the outdoor recreation ground, and that he is trying to make detention easier and perhaps even productive of good for the women held on charges of having lived immoral lives, he not only admits but is proud of.[9]

Perhaps the worst scare at Ellis Island occurred at about the same time as the Bennet controversy. On July 30, 1916, at about 2 A.M., fourteen barges on the Black Tom River in New Jersey, close by Ellis Island, began to explode. Each barge was packed with munitions and dynamite that had been destined for Russia for use in World War I. The explosions were set off by an undercover German agent. One of the inspectors recalled the panic:

The tide was coming in, and a west wind carried the fire toward the barges moored at Black Tom wharves. Suddenly, I saw that the barges, which had been moored by the usual hemp rope, had caught fire and were exploding as they drifted toward Ellis Island. Already the Ellis Island windows had been broken, the doors had jammed inward, and parts of the roof collapsed.[10]

Two barges floated up against the island but were quickly towed away by tugboats belonging to the Lehigh Valley Railroad. Three hundred and fifty-three immigrants were on the island that night and twenty-five employees, yet no one was killed or seriously injured. A report in *Survey* described the scene:

Visiting the little islands of the immigrant station group a day after the explosion, one feels that he is treading ground where surely a miracle has been wrought. For shrapnel and bullets rained down upon buildings and grounds; windows were blown out; locks and hinges were wrenched away; tiles loosened in patches upon the roofs; window panes and transoms were

either pulverized, bitten into, or jarred into patterns like all-over lace—
yet of the more than 500 persons on the island, not one was seriously
injured. There were a few cuts from broken glass; several bumps for those
who standing, were thrown to the ground . . . but that was all.[11]

Since immigration was so diminished during the war years, Ellis Island was gradually taken over by the War Department. The Army used the hospital for treating war casualties, and the Navy billeted sailors in the main building's detention dormitories while they awaited ship assignments. The Navy also set up a temporary hospital in the great two-story registry room. The military shared the premises with a number of enemy aliens who, following their arrests, were deposited at Ellis Island before being shipped to internment camps in Hot Springs, North Carolina, or Fort Oglethorpe, Georgia. Immigration officers, meanwhile, carried out their inspection routines either aboard ship or on the pier.

The war in Europe, which heightened America's aversion to troublesome aliens, finally gave restrictionists in Congress enough strength to enact a literacy test for immigrants. The Immigration Act of 1917, which passed over President Wilson's veto with only seven dissenting votes, replaced all previous immigration laws. It was in many respects, Wilson admitted, an admirable and well-conceived law, but he objected strongly to the literacy test and to the bill's extension of the definition of anarchist. Wilson said in his message to Congress:

In two particulars of vital consequence this bill embodies a radical depar-
ture from the traditional and long-established policy of this country. . . .
It seeks to all but close entirely the gates of asylum which have always
been open to those who could find nowhere else the right and opportunity
of constitutional agitation for what they conceived to be the natural and
inalienable rights of men; it excludes those to whom the opportunities of
elementary education have been denied, without regard to their character,
their purposes, or their natural capacity.[12]

The bill proscribed not only anarchists and those who advocated the overthrow of the government, but also "those affiliated with any organization teaching the foregoing views." Now "guilt by association" would play a determining role in an alien's hearing. Aliens who had been in the United States less than five years could

Remember Your First Thrill of
AMERICAN LIBERTY

YOUR DUTY-*Buy*
United States Government *Bonds*
2ⁿᵈ Liberty Loan of 1917

FOOD WILL WIN THE WAR

You came here seeking Freedom
You must now help to preserve it

WHEAT is needed for the allies
Waste nothing

Liberty Loan posters from World War I, 1917–18. National Park Service.

It was not until World War I that Liberty became a national symbol of America and the struggle to make the world "safe for democracy". In 1917, the United States started the Liberty Loan drives to raise money for weapons, ammunition, uniforms, and medical supplies. From millions of posters distributed across the nation, Liberty pleaded with Americans to contribute to the war effort.

Some of the posters appealed directly to immigrants in America, urging them to remember their first thrill of Liberty and warning that now they must help to preserve it. The immigrants dutifully supported the war effort, bought war bonds, and volunteered for service. Even so, World War I crystalized America's anti-alien sentiments. During this time, the Literacy Act was passed by an overwhelming margin in Congress; alleged enemy aliens with German names were rounded up and arrested; and after the war, hundreds of recent immigrants were branded socialists or communists and ordered deported.

be deported; later, the Immigration Law of 1918 authorized deportations regardless of when an alien had entered the country. The anarchist exclusion clauses of the law had a much more immediate impact on immigration policy than the literacy test.

After World War I, American antipathy toward alien Reds, labor unions, radicals, and Bolshevik agents became rampant.

During the war, the unions, thought to be hot beds of radicalism, had for the most part refrained from striking. But now that peace had come, unionized workers wanted higher wages and shorter hours. A general strike in Seattle called by the Industrial Workers of the World (I.W.W.) in February 1919 was the first of hundreds of union demonstrations carried out in cities all over the United States. For American business, a united coalition of militant workers raised a frightening threat of a Bolshevik revolution—not to mention severely reduced profits. Government agents took full advantage of America's exaggerated fears to deport as many "Reds" as they could find. Howe wrote in his autobiography:

This movement against alien labor leaders had the support of the Department of Justice. Private detective agencies and strike-breakers acted with assurance that in any outrages they would be supported by the government itself. The press joined in the cry of "Red-revolution," and frightened the country with scare head-lines of an army of organized terrorists who were determined to usher in revolution by force. The government borrowed the agent provocateur from old Russia; it turned loose innumerable private spies. For two years we were in a panic of fear over the Red revolutionists, anarchists, and enemies of the Republic who were said to be ready to overthrow the government. [13]

Aliens, allegedly anarchists, were arrested and put on board the "Red Special," a train that started its cross-country journey in Seattle. Along its way the train stopped at several points to pick up more aliens slated for deportation. By the time it arrived in New York, fifty-four were on board, mostly members of the I.W.W.

The following month, the New York City Bomb Squad raided the headquarters of the Union of Peasant Workers of America and arrested 164 men. Under the headline "Seized Bolsheviki Sworn to Violence," an article in *The Times* on March 14 said:

The presence in various cities of the United States, with headquarters and 600 members in New York City, of at least 6,000 Russian workmen closely banded together and solemnly pledged to the destruction of all government, was revealed, according to the authorities, as a result of Wednesday night's raid.

Criminal charges were lodged against only four of the 164 people arrested. But, *The Times* said, some of those who were released could

A selection of political cartoons published in American newspapers during the "Red Scare" of 1919.

The Red, Fight and Spew

BLACK AGAINST THE SKY; A CHALLENGE TO THE NATION.
—*Dayton (Ohio) News.*

WHY NOT USE THE OTHER EAR, MR. CITIZEN!
—*Cleveland Plain Dealer.*

DO YOUR CHRISTMAS SHIPPING EARLY.
—*Providence Journal.*

THE QUICKER AND HARDER THE BETTER.
—*St. Louis Republic.*

SHIP THEM HOME!
—*New Orleans Times-Picayune.*

The Red—LET'S GO TO THE BOTTOM FIRST.
—*Brooklyn Eagle.*

well be seized again if the courts decided that the mere possession of the "Little Red Book" was sufficient grounds for deportation of an alien.

Arrested aliens had little legal recourse. Often they were held incommunicado and denied counsel. Before being shipped to Ellis Island, Howe reported, they had been given a drumhead trial:

"In these proceedings," Howe wrote, "the inspector who made the arrest was prosecutor, witness, judge, jailer, and executioner. He was clerk and interpreter as well. This was all the trial the alien could demand under the law . . .

I was advised by the Commissioner-General to mind my own business and carry out orders, no matter what they might be. Yet such obvious injustice was being done that I could not sit quiet. . . . I took the position from which I would not be driven, that the alien should not be held incommunicado, and should enjoy the right of a writ of habeas corpus in the United States courts, which was the only semblance of legal proceedings open to him under the law.

In maintaining this position I had to quarrel with my superiors and the official force at the island. I faced a continuous barrage from members of Congress, from the press, from business organizations, and prosecuting attorneys. Yet day by day aliens, many of whom had been held in prison for months, came before the court; and the judge, after examining the testimony, unwillingly informed the immigration authorities that there was not a scintilla of evidence to support the arrest. For in deportation cases it is not necessary to provide a preponderance of testimony, or to convince the court of the justice of the charge; all that the government needs to support its case is a "scintilla" of evidence, which may be any kind of evidence at all. If there is a bit of evidence, no matter how negligible it may be, the order of deportation must be affirmed.[14]

Most of the men were released either on parole granted by the Labor Department in Washington or on one-thousand-dollar bail furnished by their lawyers.

In April, some radicals who were never apprehended sent mail bombs to a number of government officials. The Post Office intercepted all but one, which exploded in the hands of a servant of an intended victim. Then in June a bomb was set off in front of the Washington home of Attorney General A. Mitchell Palmer. These incidents of violence provoked renewed demands to rid the country of subversive foreigners. Members of Congress asked plaintively why radical aliens who were supposed to have been deported were instead set free. Howe's energetic defense of the aliens' rights was attracting more and more congressional criticism. The freshman congressman from New York, Fiorello H. La Guardia, suggested that Howe's salary be chopped from $6,500 to $2,500, since the commissioner "is very rarely at his station, unless he goes there for the purpose of defending a detained anarchist."[15]

Howe was severely rebuked, too, for presiding over a "Justice to Russia" rally at Madison Square Garden where Wilson was booed, and Lenin and Trotsky were cheered. The rally denounced the food blockade of Russia and the intervention of Allied troops on Russian soil. Howe denied that the rally was pro-Bolshevik: "There was no demand that the Soviet government be recognized. . . . The meeting was called to urge that Russia be permitted to buy food." He said, "200,000 people per month are dying of starvation. . . . The Bolshevik color of the meeting consisted in demonstrations made by the audience."[16]

The Times, however, was not convinced. Howe's presence at the rally was just one more manifestation, it charged in an editorial, of the man's true sympathies:

It is impossible to resist the impression, made not by the cheers, but by the speeches at the Madison Square Garden meeting, that it was an assemblage of people in sympathy not only with Russian Bolshevism, but with the overthrow of the present economic system everywhere. Least of all people should a Commissioner of Immigration have been found in that gallery.

Of Mr. Howe's attitude toward the I.W.W., that dangerous and destructive accomplice and ally of Bolshevism in the United States, testimony has been given by a distinguished witness, quoted in an article on Bolshevism in yesterday's World. *The witness is Max Eastman, who says in attacking the idea that the bombs deposited in the Post Office were sent by radicals: "One (bomb) was addressed for instance, to the Immigration Commissioner, Frederic C. Howe, obviously in revenge of the deportation of I.W.W.s, but everybody even remotely in touch with the matter knows that Frederic C. Howe did everything in his power short of resigning his office to prevent these deportations." So fond a friend of the I.W.W., so sympathetic a president of a Bolshevist meeting, so liberal a thinker, so singular a Commissioner of Immigration."[17]*

Howe did not even have the support of Commissioner-General Andrew Caminetti, who was in full sympathy with the Justice Department and its efforts to deport illegal aliens. In the summer of 1919, when Howe returned to Ellis Island from attending the Paris Peace Conference, he discovered that orders he had left had been countermanded in Washington by Caminetti.

On the way to my office one of the matrons stopped me. "Mr. Commissioner," she said, "they deported the little Armenian girl last night; the one that got away from the Turks and came as a stowaway. She can only be landed in Turkey and she will probably be killed. And I've been put on the night shift because I brought some fresh eggs over to that mother with a sick baby." At my office I was confronted with an angry group from New York, one of them an attorney. "The three East Indians have been ordered deported," said the attorney. "You promised us that we would be notified of the hearing. They are being sent back to India at the demand of the British Government and they will certainly be shot."

I had given the promise, on assurances from Washington. I had an understanding with the department that aliens should enjoy the right of counsel. I had protested against deporting aliens to devastated areas or countries in revolution. But orders of the Secretary of Labor and agreements which I had with him were ignored by bureau officials.

The next morning I was at the Department of Labor. I went first to the Commissioner-General. I was both angry and profane, for discussion with him was of no value. The action of the bureau was a "damned outrage,' I said. It was ordering cruel and inhuman things done; pledges which I had given were overruled. For once the Commissioner-General sat quiet. I had adopted methods which he could understand. Then to the Secretary of Labor with the whole story of secret deportations, of pledges double-crossed. I suspected that the secretary had been double-crossed, himself. I could not recall the deported girls, but the East Indians should have a trial and be represented by their attorneys. Their order of deportation was stayed. They were not sent back to India.

But I was through. [18]

Howe resigned in September 1919. With the commissioner-general of immigration and the attorney general preoccupied by the perils of the "Red" threat, Howe saw that he would be constantly obligated to do things that he thought were unjust and totally repugnant.

Their first Christmas in America, Ellis Island, December 1918. Photograph by Paul Thompson. Library of Congress.

After his resignation, a congressional committee held hearings on the affairs of Ellis Island. As Washington observers predicted, Howe "came in for severe criticism." *The Literary Digest* reported on December 13, 1919:

"It was asserted at the Congressional committee's hearings at Ellis Island that ex-Commissioner Frederic C. Howe had allowed immorality and gambling to exist on the island during his administration, and that he was responsible for delaying deportation and for releasing a remarkably large number of Reds on parole. Mr. Howe's successor, in fact, declared that during the Howe regime, the island was tending to become a "forum for the preaching of Bolshevism." Letters to Mr. Howe from Emma Goldman and Elizabeth Gorley Flynn were read, containing friendly and confident requests for aid for arrested radicals. . . .

Why, the committee wanted to know, had so few of the aliens sent to Ellis Island for deportation been deported? When Howe went to Ellis Island to defend himself, he was ejected from the hearing room by the sergeant-at-arms. He later told a reporter from *The World* that there was no mystery about the cases sent to Ellis Island for deportation:

From the armistice to the time I resigned, there were about 100, possibly 150 aliens sent to Ellis Island for deportation. . . . The reasons why only a few were deported was that the evidence did not warrant it, that there were no facilities for deportation and that there were no funds available to pay for deportation. Congress reduced the appropriation of the bureau by about $500,000 this year.

Until last June the navy was using most of the island, and we had to confine all aliens in one room. Conditions were so congested that the bureau in Washington decided it was better to release many rather than hold them for deportation when they couldn't be deported. [19]

Newspaper editorials roundly condemned Howe for being radical, red, inefficient, and immoral. They also criticized Woodrow Wilson for appointing a man whose radical sympathies were so well-known. A typical comment was that of *The Minneapolis Tribune* which said:

"Perhaps nothing has revolted popular sentiment against the present [Wilson] Administration more than its habitual leniency, not to say sympathy, toward the whole trend of radical revolutionary sentiment and activity so prevalent in these days."

Throughout the fall of 1919 and into the spring of the following year, special agents and local police carried out a new series of roundups, arresting three thousand aliens, many of whom were sent to Ellis Island. Attorney General A. Mitchell Palmer, his eager assistant J. Edgar Hoover, and the Justice Department organized the raids, gathered evidence, made the arrests, and then handed over the cases to the Department of Labor for final decision.

The arrests were often violent. When the People's House (run by the Union of Russian Workers) in New York City was raided on November 7, 1919, aliens were driven down a flight of stairs through a gauntlet of men wielding blackjacks and clubs. An affidavit signed by the arresting officer was in some cases the only evidence submitted at the alien's hearing. Slightly more substantial evidence consisted of membership cards, tickets to meetings or social gatherings sponsored by a radical organization, subscription lists containing names of those who had given money to help the wives of men arrested or photographs showing the aliens carrying a radical newspaper.

In his study *The Deportation Cases of 1919–1920,* Constantine Panunzio, an active social reformer, reported that many of the arrested had lived in the United States with their families for over five years. Some had applied for citizenship, had substantial bank accounts, and had purchased Liberty Bonds during the war. Several men had served in the United States Army and fought during World War I. Their reasons for joining socialist or communist organizations often had nothing to do with the revolutionary character of that organization. They joined to attend classes or social functions, to enjoy the companionship of their countrymen. One woman stated that she did not know that the Communist Party, to which she belonged, was a proscribed organization. "Had I known that," she said, "I would not belong to them."

By December 1919, over two hundred aliens were detained on Ellis Island. Howe had resigned the previous September, and Byron Uhl was filling in for a second time as acting commissioner. During Uhl's term of office, most of those detained were held incommunicado, often not even receiving their mail. One typical case of abused rights was that of Joseph Polulech who had been arrested during the November 7 raid on People's House in New York. At his hearing on Ellis Island, Polulech strenuously denied that he belonged to any subversive party.

"I am not an anarchist," he stated, "I do not belong to anything but the church."[20] The only evidence submitted against Polulech was a carbon copy of some pages extracted from a membership book of the Union of Russian Workers. Panunzio tells the rest of Polulech's story:

The pastor [of his church] and other friends of Mr. Polulech were astounded at his being arrested, but were unable to come to his rescue. It seems that he wrote daily letters from Ellis Island to his friends and especially to his pastor. Some of these letters were not received and likewise it appears that some of the letters that his pastor and friends wrote him were not received by him . . .

Before he could establish connections with friends who would gladly have helped him, Polulech was deported on December 21, 1919, after having been held in custody and "incommunicado" for six weeks.

Polulech was one of 249 alleged radicals deported to Russia on board an Army transport, the *S.S. Buford,* popularly known as the "Soviet Ark." Also on board was Emma Goldman, an avowed anarchist, who had just recently been released from prison, and her former lover, Alexander Berkman, who was famous for having attempted to assassinate Henry Clay Frick during the Homestead steel strike in 1892.

In an interview with Edward Corsi, Goldman described her last night on Ellis Island:

An official said: "Get your things together—you're being taken to the deportation boat!"

Those who were sleeping were pulled from their beds. We were marched between two long lines of soldiers with loaded guns to the cutter. We had to stand in the freezing cold. When two hours had elapsed we reached the Buford. *Two hours later we were heading out to sea, and none of us knew where we were being taken.*[21]

Aboard the *Buford,* the aliens were ill-fed, crowded into poorly ventilated compartments, and kept under constant guard. A soldier stood outside Goldman's cabin at all times.

One day I pushed a camp stool out to him. "Why don't you sit down?" I asked.

"Why should you give me a camp stool?" he returned.

I explained to him my feelings. Something about it must have gone the rounds of the other seventy soldiers, for one of them came to Alexander Berkman on Christmas Eve and said: "This thing is getting on our nerves—it doesn't seem right. Say the words and we'll throw the damn Captain and Colonel overboard. You'll be in charge of the ship, we'll go wherever you want to go."

Berkman explained that he was not a navigator and that ended what might otherwise have been a mutiny.

We reached Finland without knowing where we were, having crossed the Baltic Sea, which was still underlain with German mines. We were placed in sealed cars on a Finnish train, each door manned by a guard, just as Trotsky went through Germany . . .

Alexander Berkman, 1919. Geo. G. Bain Collection, Library of Congress.

This photograph was taken just before Berkman was deported on the S.S. Buford.

We were received in Russia with military honors. It was a grand ovation. None of us knew for sure that we were nearing Russian soil until we were so informed. The Russians in our party fell down to the ground and kissed the snow. The band played. We were cheered. It was magnificent.

The wives and children of the men deported on the *Buford* were left behind to endure the mental anguish and severe economic hardship caused by the sudden removal of the sole provider of the family. These women were not even notified of the *Buford's* departure.

The "Red Scare" did not run its course until the end of 1920. Finally, Assistant Secretary of Labor Louis Post put a stop to the Immigration Bureau's collaboration with Attorney General Palmer's secret agents. But long-term scars were needlessly and brutally inflicted on thousands of innocent people. The incomprehensible hostility hurled at aliens by the government agents amounted to outright persecution. This is how one Polish immigrant expressed his bitterness:

When I came to this country, and saw the Statue of Liberty, I tipped my hat to it and I was happy. During my stay in this country, I could not find any understanding from the American people towards myself, and have been frowned upon all the time as a "Polack" in public places. When my wife came here, both of us went to work, and my wife also came to the conclusion that Americans did not treat her as they treated one another, but always called her "Polack." The final result is that the wife is in the hospital and I am arrested by the government which I tried to understand and obey.[22]

Emma Goldman, 1919. Photograph and caption by Augustus Sherman. National Park Service.

chapter *16*

*E*llis Island's wartime interlude ended in 1920. As soon as Atlantic ports and shipping lanes were reopened to nonmilitary vessels, refugees from the war-stricken areas of Europe sailed for the United States. "The New Pilgrims," an article in *The Survey* of October 30, 1920, reported that ten to thirteen thousand immigrants were arriving each week at Ellis Island. The magazine added:

All have participated in the Great War—and whether actively or passively, spiritually or materially, all have suffered. If their home was in the zone of fighting, they were forced to hide in ditches and trenches, with disease as a possible companion. Where bombs and bullets missed them, hunger found them, and persecution sought them out. With their homes in ruins, their near ones overtaken by death, their spirit remained unbroken, and their faith in the future unshaken. As soon as war conditions permitted, these dauntless creatures with their babies in their arms and their household goods on their backs, began their march to the cities and ports where passports and visas could be procured. Warsaw, Trieste and Danzig, Rotterdam, Antwerp and Paris felt the pressure of the multitude as they poured into these centers. There were some among them who had tramped their way across the continent from Warsaw to Paris in an effort to start life anew.[1]

Survey went on to describe what one sixteen-year-old Galician girl had to do to obtain all the visas and other necessary papers to emigrate from war-torn Europe:

After three weeks' waiting at a hotel, she succeeded in obtaining [her passport], paying the usual fee of course. Then she went to the American consul for a visa. This did not take as long as the passport, but she spent another two weeks at the hotel while she applied for the rest of the neces-

sary visas. From the American consul she went to the Dutch consul; from the Dutch consul to the German consul; from the German consul to the French consul; then finally back to the Polish officials. More fees and more hotel bills. Began the waiting at Rotterdam for passage. So depleted was her fund when she finally arrived in New York City that the money which awaited her from her western relatives proved a dire necessity.

The war had delayed the reunion of families for six years. Fathers who had come to America before the war were now desperately trying to arrange transportation for their wives and children, some of whom were holding steamer tickets purchased in 1914. *The Survey* article continued:

An excited father burst in one day to show a cablegram he had just received. He had sent passage money to his fifteen-year-old daughter for herself and her two little brothers, and the cablegram read that the children (whose mother had died during the war) were stranded in a port, their money having apparently been taken from them.

Two women, one with a daughter of ten, the other with two younger children, had escaped from Ukraine into Constantinople. There they were forced to wait for over six months until their husbands in America succeeded in getting money to them and they could finally procure passage . . .

And measles, and scarlet fever and diphtheria and all the other child-loving ills have added to the cost of the journey, both in anguish and in money. It is not an unusual occurrence to learn that an entire family is held up for months because of the illness of one of the children, with the anxious father in America sending money and cablegrams to the equally anxious and frequently destitute mother in Europe.

Yet behold the miracle! "How could you stand it?" I asked a girl who had told a tale of war; of bombs dropping about them; of starvation; of the horrors of pogroms. "We had hope," she said simply. "Without hope we would have died. . . . And see—we are here, my sister and I in America. Now we are with our father, we can begin again." "We can speak a little English," she added proudly; "we studied for three months in Warsaw and in Paris while we were waiting for our passports and the steamer."

One immigrant from Kiev who had endured the war and the Russian Revolution recalled that she and her brother had only $3.20 in their pockets by the time they finally arrived at Ellis Island.

At Ellis Island, clerks started to ask our names and put our papers in front of the commissioner [immigration inspector]. . . . He looked at our papers and greeted us very nicely. He said, "Well, you won't have to stay on Ellis Island. I see you are going to your brother in Buffalo. While your papers are in order and things are right, you know the rules of the United States are that each of you has to have $25. Everybody has to show it."

But the commissioner didn't ask us to show it, so we didn't have to answer. He was so delighted with our papers, our diplomas, everything. He said, "I'm sure that you both will succeed in this country." He shook our hands and said, "Such immigrants we greet, and we are happy to admit them into the United States." He was very nice.[2]

The postwar rush to America overwhelmed Ellis Island. The Immigration Act of 1917 required a more thorough medical examination and a literacy test. These two additions to the inspection routine meant that only two thousand immigrants could be processed each day. This is less than half the number that could be inspected

War refugees waiting outside the American consulate in Warsaw, 1920. YIVO Institute for Jewish Research.

each day during Commissioner Williams's term. There was soon an enormous backlog of immigrants waiting to be admitted.

In another *The Survey* article, a college professor who had to travel steerage because of the scarcity of upper-class cabins, reported that immigrants were sometimes kept waiting as long as three days before they could be transferred to Ellis Island. Then even the short voyage from their Hudson River pier to Ellis Island, he said, was "a perfect miracle of slowness, the venerable ark in which the immigrants were towed by a wheezy old tug being contemptuously passed by every ferry boat in sight."[3]

Once on the island, however, the professor noted the "friendliness with which the over-worked officials greeted new arrivals. . . . The atmosphere which Commissioner Howe did so much to create seems to pervade the place. . . . After the long and weary detention on the steamer, the relative ease and rapidity with which we were passed through the island was to all a very pleasant surprise." The writer admitted that he probably received special treatment because Oberlin College had alerted immigration officials to his arrival.

An immigrant from Russia who came to Ellis Island with her mother, brother, and sisters remembered the inspection in greater detail:

. . . they put all the women in a room. My sister and I were with my mother; the boys were in a separate room. They took off all our clothes and deloused them, and they gave us showers to take with certain medication, I guess a disinfectant or something.

Then we went before the inspectors—you could not get off without the doctor's examination. The only thing is that my mother had trouble with her eyes. You see, my sister took sick on the way—she had some kind of childhood sickness, measles or something. My mother was very concerned and here we were on the boat. She said, "I left Europe with five children, I promised your father five children, and I am going to bring him five children!" She was only worried that my sister would die. You know, you get into such a depressive mood. She was very worried, so every night she would sit and cry. My sister got better on the boat, but when we got off, my mother's eyes were very red from crying. So when she got to the doctor at Ellis Island, he wouldn't pass her. They thought she had some trouble with the eyes. . . . that is what kept us three more days . . .[4]

For those who were caught in the web of immigration restrictions, Ellis Island was, as it always had been, a dismal and frightening place, only worse than before the war. The hospitals, the main reception building, and the detention dormitories had all received hard use by the Army and Navy. The buildings were old, inadequate, and in dire need of a paint job, a thorough cleaning and extensive repairs.

In a third *The Survey* article, "The Jaws of the Machine," Ellis Island is given a thorough drubbing:

The detention room is built to accommodate four hundred people at the most, but its quota of sitters-upon-benches is frequently above a thousand, and their stay anywhere from one day to much over two weeks. The cases for special inquiry are sometimes at the Island for as many months. The sleeping quarters, adequate for fifteen hundred, have been at times in demand for more than three thousand immigrants who sometimes sleep standing up before being put to bed on the floor. The dining-rooms, with facilities for taking care of eight hundred people, often have to feed three thousand at one meal. When the crowd is too great to be taken care of, the people are not even taken off the barges but are fed coffee and sandwiches there. The antediluvian toilet rooms, the missing laundry facilities (the women wash their babies' clothes in a wash basin with sample sizes of government soap and then hang them on their beds to dry), the stinted, cramping detention quarters are things that God in His mercy and an appropriating Congress will have to care for. The long, long delays in procedure, with results sometimes no more important than a complete loss of morale to the waiting immigrant, and sometimes materially tragic loss of wages and suffering and sickness, will be taken care of by the same dispensations when a not more competent force but a more elastic one shall be put at the disposal of the commissioner through the medium of an improved Civil Service.[5]

Other newspapers charged that walls in the main building were covered with vermin, that many washbasins had no water supply, and that lavatories were a menace to health.

The man who had to contend with these problems was the newly appointed commissioner, Frederick Wallis, a former deputy police commissioner. Wallis, who began his term of office on June 1, 1920, tried to carry on Howe's efforts to humanize Ellis Island. Most of his plans had to be laid aside because of the tremendous

Colonel Helen R. Bastedo and Osman Louis, 13, 1921. Photograph by Augustus Sherman. National Park Service.

Colonel Bastedo was the director of the Committee of Visitation, a federally-appointed body that took over much of the social work on Ellis Island once done by the missionaries. Members of the committee, including Bastedo, worked as interpreters and tried to unravel the problems of the new, often penniless arrivals. "In addition to this," said an article in The Survey, *"she meets deputations of well wishers and turns them into well-doers. Ladies with hands full of Americanization tracts are sent home to make diapers. Societies with funds for printing the American Constitution are urged to buy shoes against the winter. . . . She has organized a shoe committee upon which every shoe manufacturer in the city of New York will serve."*[6]

crush of immigrants arriving day after day. Wallis had not nearly enough staff to carry out even the basic inspection let alone make the sweeping improvements that were so desperately needed. Nor did Wallis have any money for renovating the buildings.

One big change that Wallis did make was to move inspection to the ground floor so that immigrants laden with babies and heavy luggage no longer had to climb the stairs to the main hall. Also a playground that was closed after Howe's resignation was reopened for the children of detained immigrants.

Wallis was quite overwhelmed by the terrible conditions on the island. When newspapers and magazines attacked the administration of Ellis Island, he emphatically agreed with them, but he laid the blame on Congress and the immigration laws.

"We have managed to pass laws bearing no relationship to our needs," he said, "such as the literacy test and then to make matters still worse, their application is as inhumane and cruel as it is possible to imagine."[7]

As a means of restricting immigration, the literacy test was a failure. By the time Congress passed the law, free access to education in Europe had all but eradicated illiteracy, even in the poorer classes. The older immigrants bore the brunt of the new law. But there were ways to get around the literacy test. A man who as a boy of thirteen came through Ellis Island with his mother recalled that the inspectors asked her to read a passage from a *seder*, a Hebrew prayer book:

Well, they opened up a seder. There was a certain passage there they had you read. I looked at it, and seen right away what it was. I quietly

Frederick Wallis, commissioner of immigration from 1920–1921. Geo. G. Bain Collection, Library of Congress.

Despite the post-war deluge of immigration, the newly-appointed commissioner tried to preserve the reforms made by his predecessor, Frederic C. Howe.

studied it—I knew the whole paragraph. Then I got underneath the two of them there—I was very small—and I told her the words in Yiddish very softly. I had memorized the lines, and I said them quietly and she said them louder so the commissioner could hear it. And that served the purpose. She looked at it and it sounded as if she was reading it, but I was doing the talking underneath. I was Charlie McCarthy.[8]

David Brownstone, in his book *Island of Hope, Island of Tears*, interviewed an Armenian family who told him how their mother, who could not read, was fortunate enough to encounter a kind-hearted inspector:

When the inspector asked her to read from an Armenian book, she put her finger on the page and recited the Lord's Prayer. He asked her to read again. And again, she recited, "Our Father who art in heaven . . ." in Armenian. Finally, he looked at the family and said "Bono," and let them pass.[9]

Washington, meanwhile, was watching with increasing alarm as growing numbers of refugees were rushing to America's shores. It was estimated that between two million and eight million persons in Germany alone wanted to come to the United States.

The restrictionists in the House of Representatives wanted to call a halt to immigration until a radically new policy on admitting immigrants to the United States could be formulated. The Senate came up with an alternative to the House's drastic proposal. This was the First Quota Act, a stopgap measure that would give Congress the time it needed to compose a permanent law to restrict immigration. The First Quota Act, which passed both the House and the Senate by overwhelming majorities, was signed by President Warren G. Harding on May 19, 1921. This law marked the end of America's open-door policy. It cut down sharply on immigration from southern and eastern Europe by limiting the admission of each European nationality to 3 percent of its representation in the United States Census of 1910. This meant that the annual quota for countries from southern and eastern Europe would be 155,000. Previously, the number of immigrants from these areas had averaged 738,000 a year. Not more than 20 percent of each quota would be admitted per month.

Before the new immigration restrictions could be imposed, steam-

"Immigrant fleet" at anchor in Quarantine, New York harbor, photograph by Underwood & Underwood, ca. 1921. The Bettman Archive.

According to the undated press release which accompanies this photograph, twenty liners had rushed across the Atlantic to land their passengers on the first of the month. But, because of fog, only ten arrived outside New York in time for the midnight race into the harbor across the imaginary line between Fort Wadsworth and Fort Hamilton. The ten ships carried 13,000 immigrants.

ship companies made a frantic rush to land their passengers in the United States. Edward Corsi wrote in his memoirs:

Imagine the ships, bulging with human cargo, racing through the Narrows and into New York harbor, actually colliding with one another in their hurry to be at Ellis Island before the last minute.

The Saxonia of the Cunard Line was one of the last of the immigrant ships to get under the wire. But there was no more room at Ellis Island. Guarded by Customs officials and Cunard Line detectives, her eight hundred human souls were landed at Pier 53, North River, at the foot of West Thirteenth Street, where they camped on the floor for four days. [10]

The Quota Act went into effect June 3, 1921. That day three steamships arrived with a total of 3,391 Italian immigrants, while

Italian family aboard S.S. Madonna, *photograph by Underwood & Underwood, ca. 1921. The Bettmann Archive.*

This group of women and girls wait to disembark from their ship which was fortunate to finish second in the race into New York Bay, just 30 seconds behind the first ship.

Emigrants leaving for America from Antwerp, Belgium, September 18, 1922. Library of Congress.

the quota for Italy was only 2,500. On June 10, Commissioner-General W. W. Husband told the House Immigration Committee that "there were already 10,302 immigrants in excess of the June quota on their way to this country." Six countries had already exceeded their quotas—Albania, Italy, Yugoslavia, Poland, Roumania, and Portugal.

Congress finally passed a bill allowing entry of those immigrants who had sailed on or before June 8. Their numbers would be charged against the annual quota. Meanwhile, thousands of people were stranded at European ports where they had expected to disembark for the United States. In Antwerp alone there were three thousand prospective immigrants who had to be left behind because their nationality's quota had already been filled. A *Times* editorial observed that the latest immigration muddle was due to Congress' failure to provide means for "ascertaining how many of the various nationalities were embarking from other ports . . . the seriousness of the situation lies in its revelation of a lack of forethought."[11]

The First Quota Act turned out to be one of the most cruel and inept immigration laws ever passed; and though it was supposed to run only one year, it was renewed twice, remaining in effect for three years. On the night before the first of every month, sometimes as many as twenty ships just outside New York Bay, loaded with thousands of immigrants, waited for the stroke of midnight to rush into the harbor. Immigration officers stationed at Fort Wadsworth and Fort Hamilton on either side of the Verrazano Narrows judged the winners whose passengers would be counted first in the new

Polish family of ten at Ellis Island,
1923. Photograph by Augustus Sherman.
National Park Service.

In March 1923, both the Polish and Roumanian quotas were exhausted early in
the month, and 330 Jewish immigrants
from these countries were ordered deported. A lawyer for the immigrants had
tried to persuade authorities to solve the
matter by allotting the Polish Jews to
the Eastern Galicia quota and the Roumanian Jews to that of Bessarabia. The
authorities however, were unwilling to
establish such a precedent. The photographer, Augustus Sherman, does not tell
us whether this Polish family succeeded
in staying in America or was deported.

monthly quota. The passengers on the losing ships, if their quotas
were filled, would be deported.

In the meantime, conditions on Ellis Island were becoming chaotic. Bewildered relatives asked in vain for immigrants long since
deported; letters and money sent to immigrants was sometimes lost,
and records were not kept up to date. In July 1921, an investigation
by the Department of Labor uncovered a scheme on the part of at
least five Ellis Island officers to extort bribes from immigrants for
supposed favors. Many of the immigration inspectors were accused
of being surly and discourteous. An Armenian woman who was
detained on Ellis Island for a week at about this time recalled bitterly
that the inspectors were heartless and ignorant:

*They were very crude. Many were foreigners, who delighted in the fact
that they could lord over the new entries, the new immigrants. They had
accents as thick as molasses, every kind of accent, but they acted the way*

small people become when they have a little power. They pushed everybody around, actually, literally pushed.[12]

Wallis resigned as commissioner in October 1921 and was succeeded by Robert Tod, a Harding appointee. With the appointment of each new commissioner came new hope that perhaps now the mess at Ellis Island would be cleaned up. Such was the case with Robert Tod, who was praised by *The Survey* as being an able administrator. "He knows the life of the island domain by day and by night. His orders are issued with precision, born doubtless of his naval experience, and they result in action."[13]

But under Harding's plan to reduce government expenses, Tod's staff at Ellis Island was cut from seven hundred to five hundred. And even though Congress had appropriated $100,000 for improving the physical conditions at Ellis Island, the money was not being used. *The Survey*, in the same article, reported that the use of the funds was planned in great detail by an advisory commission. These plans required the railroad ticket agents and certain concessionaires to give up space so that a larger, more comfortable detention room could be provided for the immigrants. The magazine reported:

Great hope was pinned to these plans and their immediate initiation. . . . July brought 25,822 immigrants, August 24,469, and September over 30,000—but the situation at Ellis Island as regards physical conditions is unchanged in spite of the solicitude of Congress.

On September 24, the number of detained aliens was 1800. Those held for more serious charges were sitting despondently in the old "S. I." room, described as the "black hole of Calcutta" because of its lack of ventilation and its overcrowding. Those immigrants who were held temporarily were wandering restlessly up and down the old "T. D." (temporarily detained) room, a gloomy shut-in court, as their only opportunity for airing in the sultry September weather. Meanwhile the ticket agents of the railroad companies and the representatives of the steamship companies continued to occupy their spacious quarters which boast as many windows and access to the lawn. The plans of the commission for shifts in detention whereby larger and more airy quarters would be available for the detained immigrants are still ignored.

Immigrants, meanwhile, were registering their complaints with representatives of their native countries. British subjects were especially vocal about the poor treatment they received; their plight was so well publicized in England that it became a subject of debate in the House of Commons.

In December 1922, Secretary of Labor James Davis, invited British Ambassador Sir Aukland Geddes to visit Ellis Island himself. Geddes accepted the invitation and afterward wrote a report of his visit that he sent to his superiors in London. The report was not made public until eight months after Geddes's visit, and by that time American officials maintained it was long out of date. Perhaps some details that were criticized by Geddes had been improved, but as an overall view, the vivid account he gives of what it was like to experience Ellis Island was most likely true. He is careful, however, to place most of the blame on the immigrants themselves rather than on the staff at Ellis Island.

Geddes's report began with a generous commendation of Tod and his staff:

Mr. Tod is a gentleman of independent means, who, some fourteen months ago, accepted office as Commissioner of Immigration at the Port of New York. He is a sympathetic, kindly, energetic and efficient man who holds office for patriotic reasons. Any country might be proud to point to him as one of its officials. Mr. Tod has spared neither time, thought nor pocket in his efforts to make Ellis Island humanely efficient.

I met several members of the immigration staff. They seemed to me to be suitable and efficient . . .

I was not favorably impressed by the plan of the buildings of the immigration station. . . . While it is obviously necessary that the drifting crowd of immigrants who have to be handled in the building be prevented from straying and getting lost, I can quite understand that persons of some refinement and intelligence sent to Ellis Island resent the locked doors and wire cages. These are much in evidence, and inevitably suggest imprisonment. I am satisfied, though, that the work of the immigration station could not be done without them. To unlock the doors and leave them open and to remove the "cages" would produce chaos. [14]

The report also took note of the "unsuitable" and "inadequate" medical rooms, the obvious need for painting and repairs, the lack of space in all the buildings, the presence of filth and dirt, and the cramped sleeping quarters.

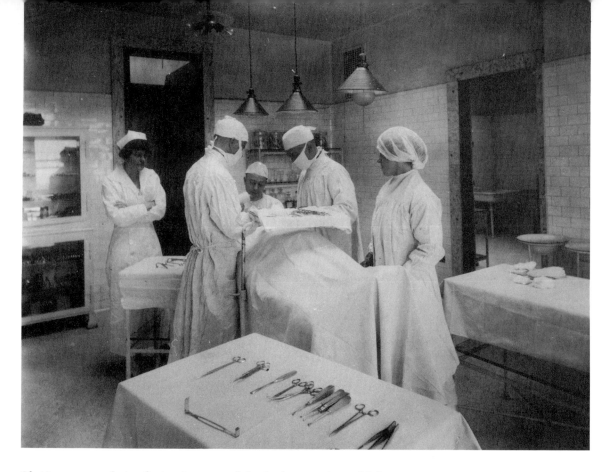

Sleeping accommodation for immigrants and detained persons is provided chiefly in two-tiered bunks. These, in most of the sleeping rooms, are arranged in wire cages, the alley-ways being roofed over with stout wire net.

I am sure that it is necessary to encage the bunks to prevent thefts and even more unpleasant outrages. Yet I can understand a certain reaction of annoyed surprise on the part of those whose early experiences were of decent surroundings on being told to go to bed in a cage, even though the cage is necessary and provided for their protection.

The actual surface upon which the immigrant reclines is either woven wire or canvas, supported on metal laths.

But, the heart of Ellis Island's tragedy, Geddes maintained, was the anguish of uncertainty suffered by the detained immigrant:

I feel profoundly sorry for some of the temporarily detained, a mother waiting for a delayed child, or a father with his children anxiously watching for his wife to come to him. . . . It is no one's fault and

Operating room in Ellis Island hospital, ca. 1920. National Archives.

The hospital, Geddes reported, ". . . has to deal with every sort of disorder, ranging from slight injury to obscure tropical diseases. It is at once a maternity home and an insane asylum. . . . On the whole, I thought the hospital arrangements were good."[15]

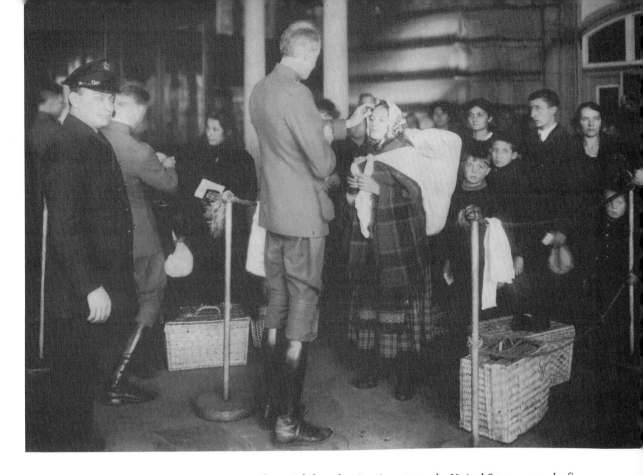

Doctor examining eyes, n.d. National Archives.

The line inspection now starts on the ground floor where immigrants are quickly scrutinized for signs of infectious disease. "If a child has developed measles," Geddes wrote, "he is picked out for treatment in the isolation hospital. The mother passes on with the crowd. Her feelings can be imagined."

cannot be avoided, unless immigrants to the United States are to be finally approved for admission to their own land before they set out upon their journey.

Large numbers of the immigrant have to go before a board to determine whether or not they may be admitted. I saw five or six of these boards at work. The proceedings were decorous and seemly; the arrangements for witnesses who come to speak for or against the admission of an immigrant are good. Every immigrant rejected by a board is told of his right to appeal to the Secretary of Labour in Washington.

This arrangement, the theory of which is probably right, is in practice nothing short of diabolic. For days some wretched creature is kept in suspense. The appeal board at Washington, which advises the Secretary of Labour, works on paper records, tempered, I have heard it said, by political pressure. The Secretary of Labour may be busy, overwhelmed, perhaps, with work in connection with some labour dispute, or anything. Days slip by, into weeks sometimes, before a decision is reached. When the doubt affects one member of a family, perhaps a child, the mental anguish must be excruciating. The system is to blame. In my judgment

there can be no question that power to decide should be delegated by law to someone on the spot with the facts and the people before him. If the United States Government will expedite the decision of appeals so that the results can be announced within twenty-four hours of the completed collection of the facts, the anguish of Ellis Island will be appreciably reduced.

Geddes concluded his report by saying that he thought it was "impossible to administer any immigration station under existing United States laws without hardship and tragedy. If a system could be devised which would prohibit persons desiring to come to the United States from sailing from Europe or elsewhere without the certainty of admission to the United States, the problem would be almost entirely solved."

Tod resigned in 1923 in apparent disgust over the pressure brought to bear on his office to admit "mental defectives, undesirables, and people afflicted with loathsome disease." Henry H. Curran, a New York City Republican politician, was appointed by Harding to take his place. *Pillar to Post*, Curran's high-spirited memoir of his life in politics, includes chapters on Ellis Island that describe among other

Immigration doctors examine men and boys, ca. 1920. National Archives.

things, how he coped with the First Quota Act. On his first day in office, two thousand men, women and children arrived who were "excess quota." Curran wrote:

Women doctors examine immigrant women, n.d. National Archives.

The Immigration Act of 1917 required more thorough medical examination. Both men and women had to strip to the waist. Men were also checked for venereal disease. In 1922, Ambassador Geddes commented, "no recruiting medical board that I saw was quite so badly accommodated as the medical inspection board I saw at work on Ellis Island."

Here by our country's permission, the two thousand would now be turned back, at the very gate, by our country's mandate.

In a week or two they all went back. I was powerless. I could only watch them go. Day by day the barges took them from Ellis Island back to the ships again, back to the ocean, back to—what? As they trooped aboard the big barges under my window, carrying their heavy bundles, some in their quaint, colorful native costumes worn to celebrate their first glad day in free America, some carrying little American flags, most of them quietly weeping, they twisted something in my heart that hurts to this day.

The hardest quota cases were those which separated families. When part of the family had been born in a country with a quota still open, while the other part had been born in a country whose quota was exhausted, the law let in the first part and deported the other part. Mothers were torn from children, husbands from wives. The law came down like a sword between them, the wide ocean suddenly separated them. And there were other foot trips in the quota law, to work unexpected and exquisite cruelty on these innocent wayfarers. When the cases were reported in the papers there were waves of public rage that fairly lapped the shores of the little island. I could do nothing about the separated unfortunates, save plead with Washington to "find a way."

Once, in desperation, I found a way myself. The Polish wife of a Pennsylvania coal miner—both good Poles, admitted a year before—had gone back suddenly to Poland to visit her old father and mother who had taken sick and might soon die. The visit over, she returned quickly to America. She would be admitted at once, for little visits do not count against quotas. . . . On the day before the ship made port, out on the high seas, a baby Pole had been born to the returning mother. The expected had happened, "mother and child both doing well" in the Ellis

An immigrant woman taking a mental test, ca. 1920. Brown Brothers.

Philip Cowen, who was a Special Inquiry board member for many years, remembers when the Binet-Simon tests and jigsaw puzzles were introduced on Ellis Island to test an immigrant's intelligence: "I had taken home with me a set of some of the mental and other tests one day to give them careful study. My daughter chanced to have at dinner a group of friends, nearly all school teachers, and as a game to while away an hour we submitted to the group these tests for immigrants, and they stumped most of them. One day a member of the medical staff . . . said; 'You ought to see the new jig-saw puzzle they have downstairs; it beat me all right.' But the poor greenhorns . . . were expected to solve the puzzle!"[16]

The Ellis Island dining room, ca. 1920.
The Bettmann Archive.

The British ambassador to the United
States, Sir Auckland Geddes had some
rare praise for the Ellis Island dining
room. "The food is of good quality and
well cooked," he wrote in his 1922 report.
"The dining room is the cleanest room in
the building . . . tables are covered for
each meal with clean paper 'cloths' . . . I
personally saw the dinner served. It was
excellent."[17]

Island hospital, everybody delighted, until—the inspector admitted the
mother but excluded the baby Pole.

"Why?" asked the father, trembling.

"Polish quota exhausted," pronounced the helpless inspector.

"The baby was not born in Poland," I ruled, "but on a British ship.
She is chargeable to the British quota . . ."

"British quota exhausted yesterday," replied the inspector.

"Come to think of it, the Lapland hails from Antwerp." I remarked.
"That's Belgium. Any ship out of Belgium is merely a peripatetic extension of Belgian soil. The baby is a Belgian. Use the Belgian quota."

"Belgian quota ran out a week ago." Thus the inspector. I was
stumped.

"Oh, look here," I began again, wildly. "I've got it! How could I
have forgotten my law so soon? You see, with children it's the way it is
with wills. We follow the intention. Now it is clear enough that the
mother was hurrying back so the baby would be born here and be a na-
tive-born American citizen, no immigrant business at all. And the baby
had the same intention, only the ship was a day late and that upset
everything. But—under the law, mind you, under the law—the baby,
by intention, was born in America. It is an American baby—no Pole

baby at all—no British, no Belgian—just good American. That's the way I rule—run up the flag!"[18]

Curran, a lawyer and former judge, admitted others by stretching the quota law's exemption for artists. A young Hungarian woman who was over her quota was allowed to land because she knew how to play the violin. A Dane, adept at riding a "high bike," demonstrated his skill to inspectors by doing a few turns around the waiting room. "The inspectors were convinced," Curran wrote. "It takes an artist to do that." The Dane was admitted.

Tragic cases of exclusion and deportations were greatly lessened by the National Origins Act of 1924. Curran called this new law, which replaced the First Quota Act, the "law with a heart." It required that prospective immigrants apply for special visas from United States consulates before they sail.

Immigrants had to submit medical records showing they were in good health and answer a list of questions that determined eligibility for admission. Only 10 percent of a country's quota of visas would be issued in any one month. Once an immigrant had obtained his visa, he was assured of his right to land in the United States, provided he could pass inspection on Ellis Island. Under this new law, the quota system was made even more restrictive than under the First Quota Act. The new law stipulated that only 2 percent of each nationality as represented in the 1890 census would be admitted annually. This further reduced the number of immigrants from Italy, Russia, Poland, and other countries in south and eastern Europe and the Middle East.

Congress passed the National Origins Act by a majority of 308 to 58 in the House and 69 to 9 in the Senate. President Calvin Coolidge signed it into law on July 1, 1924. Later that month *The Times* covered a visit made to Ellis Island by the Secretary of Labor:

Secretary of Labor James J. Davis . . . spent a good part of yesterday inspecting Ellis Island and came away pleased and boasting over the fact that it looked like a "deserted village." Secretary Davis explained the reason for his gratification was that while at this time last year Ellis Island was choked with immigrants who could not be handled, the new law in operation July 1 had proved all that was expected in relieving congestion. Immigrants must now be examined on the other side of the water and their detention on landing here is only brief . . .

Entrance to Ellis Island, 1926. Photograph by Lewis W. Hine. New York Public Library.

Hine shot two series of photographs on Ellis Island, one in 1905 and the second in 1926 when the bustling days of unrestricted immigration were over. By then, only those who were not examined at overseas American consulates had to come to Ellis Island.

"The new selective law is just beginning to function", Davis said. "It is more pleasant now for the immigrants. There is no pulling and hauling. It is more pleasant for the mother or her child and for the brother and sister. Fathers do not greet me now as they did under the old law. The hangman's job used to be a pleasant one compared to mine . . ."[19]

Now that Ellis Island was no longer crowded with people waiting either for permission to land or for deportation, Curran was able to carry out many plans to improve the facilities on the island. He set up recreation areas, a nursery, a library, and more semiprivate rooms. He also got rid of the three-tiered and two-tiered beds in small wire cages. Curran said that these were contraptions that would make a sardine sick. "I have seen many jails," he wrote, "some pretty bad, but I never saw a jail as bad as the dormitories at Ellis Island, where nine out of ten of the immigrants had never committed any crime at all."[20]

Gradually, public health officers were assigned to American consulates to give the medical examination. Inspection overseas became so thorough that immigrants no longer had to go to Ellis Island.

Third-class passengers (by this time steerage was nearly nonexistent) would have their papers checked by immigration officers while still aboard ship. After passing through customs, they were allowed to land directly from the pier.

By 1927, the only aliens at Ellis Island were those who had not been given a medical exam at an American consulate, or had some other problem with their entry papers, or those who were awaiting deportation.

An article in *The Forum* magazine, March 1927, asked:

Is it time to scrap this Ellis Island, to make the hard benches of the United States Immigration Station gruesome relics of an Inquisition—its dens of detention as obsolete as the oubliette of old?

Our immigration laws are in a state of transition, as numerous experiments in the methods of grading and rejecting arriving aliens are being tried. What better time for doing something![21]

German family and Ellis Island officer, 1926. Photograph by Lewis W. Hine. New York Public Library.

This attentive family group watches quietly as an officer attaches tags bearing the number of the railroad line they are to travel to their final destination. The photograph shows that a calm and orderliness have replaced the frenzied confusion which prevailed before passage of the 1924 National Origins Act.

The writer draws a portrait of Ellis Island that, despite the physical improvements and lack of crowding, seems very much the same as

Armenian Jew on Ellis Island, 1926. Photograph by Lewis W. Hine. New York Public Library.

Hine's portrait of a bearded man, neatly attired in a western style hat, coat, and tie, has become one of the most evocative images of the great migration. This young Armenian is one of thousands who fled to the United States to escape Turkish persecution following World War I.

earlier descriptions. Waiting for word from Washington was still the most cruel ordeal:

Frantic, too frightened to grasp what is afoot, the captives vainly batter the hard walls of officialdom. Social agencies give them tatting to do, or tracts; but the only thing to be said is: "I am quite sure this will come out all right. I should not worry, if I were you!" Under lock and key, these aliens wait. They may send telegrams to relatives, but not use a telephone. They are here as the nation's unbidden hostages.

The process of appealing an unfavorable decision by the Board of Special Inquiry was as frustrating as ever: "When days and weeks pass and appeals lag, many abandon both appeal and hope. Outward bound, such as these cast their dossiers into the bay and clench their fists as they are borne past Liberty's hollow shell." Nearly thirty more years would pass before Congress would take action to end detention, really imprisonment, pending appeal to Washington.

Curran, who had resigned by the time the *Forum* article was published, complained to Washington vociferously and often about the lack of urgency surrounding the handling of appeals cases. Delays sometimes stretched into months. Curran cited one case where a husband and wife had been detained for over five months. In a letter to the commissioner-general in Washington, he wrote that the couple had "become so indigenous to the soil of Ellis Island that Mr. Einsiedler has mastered the American game of basketball and is now the leader in alien outdoor sports here. Mrs. Einsiedler has been occupied having a baby at Ellis Island. I do not know what will happen next. But I do know that this case could have been decided before this time."[22]

The depression brought a turnaround on the immigration scene. Nineteen thirty-two was the first year in more than a hundred years that more people left than arrived at our shores. Only 35,576 immigrated to the United States in 1932, and the following year the figure had declined still lower to 23,068.

Edward Corsi, who became commissioner in November 1931, recalled that deportations—not admissions—were the main business at Ellis Island in those days. Mass deportations were, as a matter of fact, a clearly defined policy of Secretary of Labor William N. Doak. Corsi wrote:

*He had publicly announced that he intended to rid the country of unde-
sirable foreigners. In some instances, he employed the "anarchist" or radical clause of the law, but he also made a drive against vagrants and the
unemployed, as well as those here illegally.*

*Early in my regime at the Island, New York's Alien Squadron of the
Police Department accompanied by ambitious Immigration Inspectors detailed by Secretary Doak to Ellis Island for the grand clean-up, entered
a Finnish dance hall in Harlem and locked the door behind them. The
celebrating Finns were lined up against the walls, searched, and sur-
prised by star-chamber proceedings, and all who could not convince the
excited officers that they were in the country legally were arrested.*

*A repetition of the performance occurred at the Seaman's Home on
South Street. Seamen, many of whom were later released, were jerked
from their beds and taken to Ellis Island.*

*It was my duty under my oath of office to enforce the law. The depor-
tation of admitted and proven anarchists and those here illegally was
mandatory and I had no power of discretion in these matters.*[23]

The month after he took office, Corsi had occasion to be moved
by the bitterness of his responsibilities. He had to host a Christmas
concert at Ellis Island that was going to be broadcast by NBC radio.
The guest artists from the Metropolitan Opera Company dedicated
their performance, according to a printed program, to "those Immigrants who wait at our Gates."

Just before the concert, a friend of Corsi's pointed out this dedication to him with "evident astonishment."[24]

"What is the matter with that?" I asked.

*"Simply this," he whispered. "I've just come from a look-in on the
Deportation Division. There are only three immigrants on the Island—
but I have just seen the guards march nearly two hundred deportees into
the concern room."*

*For a moment I was perplexed as to what I should say to him, but
finally the words came to me. "It's Christmas, after all," I countered.
". . . Do you think it will hurt them any to hear the songs of their
native lands? Why, it may even do something for them—it may make
their going easier and happier."*

"I hadn't thought about it that way," was my friend's reply.

*But when I faced that audience and the microphone, when I was tell-
ing the unseen audience in foreign lands how their countries had contrib-*

Handwork under the auspices of the D.A.R., 1926. Photograph by Lewis W. Hine. New York Public Library.

"Men as well as women," Hine wrote, "were given instruction in making pillow cases, shirts and hand embroidery. Some of the more skillful of the men were able to complete whole suits of clothing during their detention on the Island." Edward Corsi recalled that one Irish communist detained on Ellis Island made a red flag during his sewing session with the D.A.R.

uted to the upbuilding of America, I must confess that I felt a tinge of shame. And over and over the words dinned in my ears, "What a Christmas present! Deportation!"

Now that I am no longer at the Island and can speak more freely, I must confess that the duties of deportation were never very pleasant to me and often very bitter. Our deportation laws are inexorable and in many cases inhuman, particularly as they apply to men and women of honest behavior whose only crime is that they dared enter the promised land without conforming to the law. I have seen hundreds of such persons forced back to the countries they came from, penniless, and at times without coats on their backs. I have seen families separated, never to be reunited—mothers torn from their children, husbands from their wives, and no one in the United States, not even the President himself, able to prevent it.

Corsi made as many improvements as were in his power. He placed a mailbox in the detention rooms so aliens could write to him directly about any complaints they might have. He would also talk to them personally if they wished.

In my own mind Ellis Island was not a prison, not even a prison for the deportees, who had served their prison terms and presumably paid their penalties to society. Accordingly it was wrong to treat them as prisoners.

It was obvious that one of the things they most wanted was more freedom. Another was the right to receive visitors. Previously they had been allowed to have their friends and relatives only on Tuesdays and Thursdays. This regulation was at the discretion of the Commissioner. I rescinded the old ruling and issued an order that friends and relatives might come to the Island any day in the week or every day if they chose.

Another drastic ruling was the ban on the use of the telephone. Detained immigrants were allowed to write letters and to telegraph. It was foolish to forbid their telephoning. We discussed the matter at a staff meeting and I subsequently had telephones installed in the detention rooms. All guards were instructed to act as interpreters and to assist the aliens in obtaining their desired numbers.

At that time the aliens spent but an hour or two a day outdoors. The reason for this limitation was the lack of sufficient guards. A request to Washington soon produced the necessary number of officers, and the immigrants, weather permitting, now spent most of the day playing games or walking in the sunshine. [25]

Corsi set up meetings with reporters and told them that they would have complete access to the island. He also invited Secretary Doak, who came on several occasions. "He watched the games of the aliens," Corsi said, "mingled with them and gradually changed his attitude."

Such wholesale raids as that of the Finnish dance hall were stopped. The Washington special agents, untrained and overly ambitious, were gradually cleared from the Island. Raids were canceled; arrests were made in orderly fashion and on warrants as provided by law; third-degree methods were strictly prohibited; agents abusing aliens, severely punished; hearings on warrants of deportation were orderly, fair and strictly in accordance with law. All this was in direct contrast to conditions which the public had protested vigorously. [26]

Corsi remained commissioner when Franklin D. Roosevelt became president. Secretary of Labor Frances Perkins ordered a complete study of Ellis Island, and over one million dollars was appropriated to improve conditions there. The study noted that only 4,488 aliens came to Ellis Island during the past fiscal year. Most were detained for only one or two days. For the same period, however, there were 7,037 aliens brought to the island under orders of deportation. Many of them had to stay weeks or months waiting for passports and other papers. The Labor Department's study recommended that another building be erected for the detained immigrants to separate them from the deportees who were often of the criminal class.

Corsi, in the meantime, continued with other improvements. He cleaned up and painted the buildings, made repairs, tore down the dilapidated marquee in front of the main building, built a beautiful plaza, and planted more flowers. After a while, said Corsi, the routine of the island became so well established that "there was little need for me to do more than sign my name to letters and documents. Aside from overseeing the functioning of the job, my daily duties were practically nil. My work there was finished."

Corsi resigned in January 1934, and immigration continued to fall off until Ellis Island was nearly deserted.

During World War II, the government considered immigration primarily as a security problem. In 1940, therefore, the Immigration Service was transferred from the Department of Labor to the Department of Justice. As in World War I, Ellis Island was used once again to detain enemy aliens and their families and seamen from enemy ships that had been sequestered at American ports. The Coast Guard also took up residence in several buildings.

After the war, the island returned to its usual routine of sorting out the papers of misprocessed aliens, examining immigrants suspected of having a contagious disease, and deporting illegal aliens. The average daily population numbered around six hundred. Passage of the Internal Security Act of 1950 at the beginning of the Korean War brought Ellis Island its last glimmer of notoriety. The new law banned entry to the country of anyone who had ever been a member of a totalitarian organization, either Fascist or Communist. Fifteen hundred suspicious aliens were rounded up in various raids and temporarily detained at Ellis Island.

By the following year, there were only eight to ten security cases on Ellis Island. The case of George Voskovec, a playwright and actor from Czechoslovakia, was reported in the *New Yorker* in a lengthy article that gave a chilling account of an enforced stay of ten months on Ellis Island in a political limbo.

Voskovec had been taken to the island two hours after his arrival from Paris—with a valid entry permit—at LaGuardia Field last May 16. Two days later, he had been taken to the office of a representative of the Immigration and Naturalization Service, which is a division of the Department of Justice, where he had been put through a series of questions that seemed to indicate that he was suspected of having Communist affiliations.[27]

During an interview with the *New Yorker*, Voskovec described his daily routine on Ellis Island:

At the ringing of a bell at seven o'clock every morning, I roll out of a neither comfortable nor notably uncomfortable bed in my dormitory, where there are about fifty beds, all of them usually occupied. I line up for the adjacent bathrooms and showers, dress, gather up my books and papers and a portable typewriter I've borrowed from an American friend—whatever I intend to use during the day—and am downstairs in Passenger Hall before eight o'clock, when the dormitory doors are locked. At eight, another bell rings, and my fellow-passengers and I file down to a cafeteria on the ground floor. Except for lunch (twelve to twelve-thirty) and supper (five-thirty to six), I am in Passenger Hall. At nine P.M., a guard blows a whistle, and I go upstairs to my dormitory, put my belongings under my bed—the only place for them—and usually do my laundry. Lights are snapped out at ten-thirty . . .

As you are probably aware, the Russians have long made heavy propaganda use of Ellis Island. They call it a concentration camp, which, of course, is outrageous. No one mistreats us here. Our jailers—nearly all of them, anyway—are very kindly people, who go to extraordinary lengths, within the system, for which they don't pretend to be responsible, to make our stay here as little like a nightmare as they can. There is a movie every Tuesday and Thursday night; the children get milk six times a day and go to school three hours a day. We are kept warm and fed generously—nothing like the Colony, I assure you, but more than enough. And, as people are always pointing out to us, it doesn't cost us anything . . . but I will tell you . . . it is hard not to be depressed at the realization that within the American government, which has rightly been honored so long as the guardian of individual freedom and human dignity, and which before this has always been so good to me, there is one small agency that can seize a man and bring him to his place, where every day of his life he can look on the mocking face of the Statue of

Opposite.
Ellis Island's Passenger Hall, formerly Registry Hall, ca. 1940. The Bettmann Archive.

The great two-story hall is no longer used for registering immigrants but rather as a waiting room for detainees whose papers are not in order. As in Ellis Island's early history, most detentions lasted only one or two days. But, quite lengthy stays, often over four months, were not unusual. The record was held by a German who arrived at Ellis Island following World War II and stayed for four years. He finally gave up hope of being admitted to the United States and returned to Germany with his American wife and their two children. Ilona Bartok, who came to America from Hungary in 1951, recalled that through a mix-up of entry visas she and her father also "ended up on Ellis Island." She was only thirteen at the time. "What frightened me most there," she said, "was a Yugoslavian who had a kind of cigarette stand; and he had been there on Ellis Island for two and a half years. I had visions of us staying there two and a half years. After all these dreams of freedom and seeing the Statue of Liberty from the boat and watching people disembark, I had to remain."[28] *Her stay, however, was mercifully brief.*

Liberty and where—almost as if this were that other kind of world, behind the Curtain—he is walled in by silence. He isn't told the particulars of his offense, his accusers are nameless, and the weeks and months pass, as if human beings were no more to be considered than ciphers in a manila folder . . .

Seven months after Voskovec was brought to Ellis Island, the Board of Inquiry voted to exclude him. Voskovec's lawyer appealed that decision to immigration officials in Washington. After many weeks the officials ruled that the appeal should be sustained. Thus, Voskovec was finally allowed to land after ten months of virtual imprisonment. He found out later that the board's exclusion decision was based on the testimony of one minor Czech politician whom Voskovec had never met.

Ellis Island's days as an immigration station, however, were close to an end. By 1950, the hospitals had to be shut down because the Public Health Service did not have any money for maintenance expenses. The buildings on island No. 2 (the main hospital complex) were used for a while by the Coast Guard, but over all Ellis Island was becoming a financial problem.

"This detention station," the 1950 Annual Report of the commissioner of immigration said, "with its great wide halls and corridors, high ceilings, unusable spaces and outmoded utilities, will always present the dual problem of how to utilize it with economy and yet make it serve our purposes efficiently."[29] By 1953, there were about 230 residents on Ellis Island while the staff numbered 250. Clearly the cost of maintaining immigration facilities there had become prohibitive and the Department of Immigration finally made plans to move its operations from Ellis Island to a government building in Manhattan.

At a mass citizenship ceremony in New York City on November 12, 1954, Attorney General Herbert Brownell announced that Ellis Island would be closed:

In all but a few cases, these aliens whose admissability or deportation is under study will no longer be detained. Only those deemed likely to abscond or those whose freedom of movement could be adverse to the national security of the public safety will be detained . . .

The new detention policy is so far-reaching in scope and effect that the Department of Justice is discontinuing its six seaport facilities at New York, Boston, Seattle, San Francisco, San Pedro, and Honolulu.[30]

On the day Ellis Island closed, there was only one detained alien on its premises. His name was Arne Peterson, a seaman who had overstayed his shore leave. Peterson spent three days on Ellis Island before he was paroled by the new regulations announced by Brownell.

It is said that today the descendants of the men, women, and children who passed through Ellis Island's portals make up nearly half the population of the United States. Thus, that vast deserted immigration station, which once aroused so much fear, now suggests the fulfillment of millions of dreams. Despite the hardships the immigrants suffered, they were able to realize many of their ambitions—if not for themselves, then for their children—and in the process, they made remarkable cultural contributions to their new homeland. As a *New York Times* editorial stated on the day Ellis Island closed:

They made their way into the texture of our national life . . . They gave us scientists, artists, writers, actors, philosophers, teachers. They produced great men of affairs. Their descendants sit in Congress. They make part of what is now the American temperament—a livelier and richer national personality than could have existed without them. Perhaps some day a monument to them will go up on Ellis Island. The memory of this episode in our national history should never be allowed to fade.[31]

NOTES

Introduction

1. "But your sonnet": J. R. Lowell to E. Lazarus, December 17, 1883, *Letters to Emma Lazarus*, ed. Ralph L. Rusk (New York: Columbia University Press, 1939), p. 74.
2. "They brought to us strength": *New York Herald Tribune*, October 29, 1936.

Chapter 1 Liberty Enlightening the World

1. "The Frenchmen who fought": F. A. Bartholdi, *The Statue of Liberty Enlightening the World described by the Sculptor Bartholdi*, ed. A. T. Rice (New York, 1885), pp. 13–14.
2. "We cannot bear to be deprived": A. de Toqueville to Nassau Senior, December 23, 1851, *Memoirs, Letters, and Remains of Alexis de Toqueville* (Boston: Ticknor & Fields, 1862), p. 192.
3. "I hope to get in touch": F. A. Bartholdi to E. de Laboulaye, May 8, 1871, quoted by Andre de Laboulaye, "La Statue de la Liberte, 1886–1936," *Franco-American Review*, 1938, p. 246.
4. "His pen and his influence": John Bigelow, *Some Recollections of the Late Edouard Laboulaye* (New York, 1888), pp. 4–17.
5. "Thanks to your letters": F. A. Bartholdi to E. de Laboulaye, July 15, 1871, quoted by A. de Laboulaye, op. cit., p. 246.
6. "Mr. Longfellow": F. A. Bartholdi to E. de Laboulaye, April 30, 1872, ibid., p. 248.
7. "a missionary's pilgrimage": F. A. Bartholdi to E. de Laboulaye, April 30, 1872, ibid., p. 248.
8. "to elevate in commemoration": Union Franco-Americaine, *Subscription for the Building of a Commemorative Monument of the Centennial Anniversary of United States Independence*, 1875.
9. "Everyone has seen the models": quoted by Andre Gschaedler, *True Light on the Statue of Liberty and Its Creator* (Narbeth, Pa.: Livingston, 1966), p. 15.

Chapter 2 Liberty Rising

1. "The workshop was built": quoted by Hertha Pauli and E. B. Ashton, *I Lift My Lamp: The Way of a Symbol* (New York: Appleton Century Crofts, 1948), p. 193.
2. "The effect was imposing": quoted by Jacques Betz, *Bartholdi* (Paris, 1954), p. 143.
3. "A feature of": Rudyard Kipling, *Souvenirs of France* (London: Macmillan and Co., 1933), p. 6.

1. James Pinchot wrote to Richard Butler on January 10, 1881: "My dear Butler, At a breakfast given by the Franco-American Union in July last . . . an address was signed, noting that the necessary funds to complete the Statue of Liberty have been provided. This address sent directly to Mr. Evarts by the American Minister Paul Noyes. The letter explanatory of the address was sent to you as Secretary to be forwarded to Mr. Evarts. No acknowledgment has been received to either . . ." On April 5, Pincchot wrote another letter to Butler indicating that the address sent to Evarts the previous July had, for some reason, not been received and so a second one was quickly dispatched. American Committee of the Statue of Liberty Papers, Manuscript and Archives Division, New York Public Library (hereafter cited as ACSLP).
2. Richard Butler to Levi Morton, November 18, 1881, Levi P. Morton Papers, ACSLP.
3. "Not only individual": The American Committee of the Statue of Liberty, *An Appeal to the People of the United States in Behalf of the Great Statue, Liberty Enlightening the World*, (New York, 1882).
4. "I shall have to go": Joseph W. Drexel to his wife, October 4, 1883, ASCLP.
   Contributions were recorded by A. S. Sullivan, member of the American Committee, in a *Pedestal Fund* booklet, now part of the Statue of Liberty collection at the New-York Historical Society.
5. "the statue , the noble gift": *The World*, May 14, 1883.
6. "If agreeable": F. A. Bartholdi to R. Butler, August 3, 1883, ACSLP.
7. "Let us hope": F. A. Bartholdi to R. Butler, February 1, 1884, ACSLP.
8. "I have recently written": F. A. Bartholdi to R. Butler, February 1, 1884, ACSLP.
9. "The biggest statue in creation": *The Morning News*, July 5, 1884, clipping in scrapbook, Levi Morton Papers, ACSLP.
10. Liberty nears completion: In a letter to R. Butler dated August 3, 1883, Bartholdi mentions that his workers are in the process of "Putting up the head but do not urge on the work, having ample time before us." By February 1, 1884 he could write "our statue is completed, the interior staircase and all small accessory work is being finished. We will have it on exhibition for the public for three months more and in the course of the summer we will send it over to you." ACSLP.
11. "This work, Mr. Minister": quoted by Bartholdi, op. cit., p. 59.
12. "Yes, this beautiful work": Victor Hugo contemplating the Statue of Liberty in Paris, November 29, 1884, quoted by A. Gschaedler, op. cit., p. v.
13. "Form to the sculptor": quoted by Bartholdi, op. cit., p. 5.

Chapter 4 Pulitzer's Campaign

1. "monopoly soup": *The World*, October 30, 1884, p. 1.
2. "Let the party": ibid., p. 4.
3. "The *Isere*, surrounded": *Frank Leslie's Illustrated Newspaper*, June 27, 1885.
4. "You were too mean": excerpt from U.S. House of Representatives debate, quoted by Pauli and Ashton, op. cit., p. 296.

Chapter 5 The Unveiling

1. "Many anxious glances": Liberty's unveiling was reported extensively in all the New York City newspapers. The excerpts quoted here are from a scrapbook of clippings in the Statue of Liberty collection at the New-York Historical Society.
2. "Liberty it is": quoted by Jose de Onis, "Jose Marti 1853–1895", *Abroad in America: Visitors to the New Nations 1776–1914*, ed. Marc Pachter (National Portrait Gallery, Smithsonian Institution and Addison-Wesley Publishing Co., 1976), p. 224.
3. "Instead of grasping": American Committee of the French-American Union, *Inauguration of the Statue of Liberty Enlightening the World by the President of the United States* (New York, 1887), p. 32.
4. "In erecting a statue": "Women suffragettes think the ceremonies an empty farce," *The New York Times*, October 29, 1886.
5. "a curious festival": *Times* of London quoted by *The World*, October 28, 1886.

Chapter 6 The Great Migration

1. "The parents of some": Fiorello H. LaGuardia, *The Making of an Insurgent: An Autobiography, 1882–1919* (Philadelphia: Lippincott, 1948), p. 68.
2. "I inform you": all three letters quoted by William I. Thomas and Florian Znaniecki, *The Polish Peasant in Europe and America* (New York: Knopf, 1927), pp. 1505–1507.
3. "I am living": quoted by Phillip Taylor, *The Distant Magnet: European Emigration to the USA* (New York: Harper Torch Books, 1972), p. 88.
4. "Here at home": Bertalan Nemenya, a Hungarian sociologist, quoted by Juliana Pushkas, *From Hungary to the United States* (Budapest, 1982), p. 79.
5. "There is scarcely": *Scribner's Monthly*, September 1877, p. 577.
6. "To see a Norwegian peasant": quoted by Sigmund Skard, "Bjornstjerne Bjornson 1832–1910," *Abroad in America: Visitors to the New Nation 1776–1914*, ed. Marc Pachter (National Portrait Gallery, Smithsonian Institution and Addison-Wesley Publishing Co., 1976), p. 195.

Chapter 7 The Journey

1. "you can hear the rattle": R. L. Stevenson, op. cit., p. 4.
2. "These were all the arrangements": Friedrich Kapp, Immigration and the Commissioners of Emigration of the State of New York (New York, 1870), p. 25.
3. "To give an adequate idea": ibid., p. 190.
4. "beaten about the head": letter quoted by Theodore C. Blegen, *Land of Their Choice: The Immigrants Write Home* (The University of Minnesota Press, 1955), p. 107.
5. "To descend on an empty stomach": Robert Louis Stevenson, *The Amateur Emigrant* (New York: Charles Scribner's Sons, 1925), pp. 46f.

6. "the cabin passengers": Edward Steiner, *On the Trail of the Immigrant* (New York: Fleming H. Revell Co., 1906), p. 41.

7. "It was just a gleaming day": quoted by Maldwyn A. Jones, *Destination America* (New York: Holt, Rinehart and Winston, 1976), p. 40.

8. "With the gradual supplanting": Report to the Secretary of the Treasury by John M. Woodworth, Supervising Surgeon, United States Marine Hospital Service, quoted by Edith Abbott, *Immigration: Select Documents and Case Records* (Chicago: The University of Chicago Press, 1924), p. 48.

9. "the profit of the immigrant traffic": 1873 report to the Secretary of the Treasury by special investigators, quoted by E. Abbott, ibid., p. 52.

Chapter 8 Passage by Steam

1. "They come here and buy": excerpt from debate in Congress, April 18, 1882 on "Bill to Regulate the Carriage of Passengers by Sea," *Congressional Record*, 47th Congress, 1st session, quoted by E. Abbott, op. cit., pp. 55–56.

2. "I remember the day": quoted by Joan Morrison and Charlotte Fox Zabusky, *American Mosaic* (New York: Meridian, 1982), p. 6.

3. "The day I left": ibid., p. 68.

4. "At the Hotel Cunard": "Emigration conditions in Europe," *Reports of the U.S. Immigration Commission*, IV (1911), quoted by E. Abbott, ibid., p. 76.

5. "Well, we're off": Sholom Aleichem, "Off to America," *The World*, 1916, quoted by Irving Howe and Kenneth Libo, *How We Lived* (New York: R. Marek Publishers, 1979), p. 20.

6. "The plight of the bewildered": Mary Antin, *The Promised Land* (Boston: Houghton Mifflin Co., 1912), pp. 174–178.

7. "Waiting for the ship": ibid., p. 21.

8. "Steerage bunks": Steiner, op. cit., p. 46.

9. "But when the sun": ibid., p. 40.

10. "All the steerage berths": "Steerage Conditions," *Reports of the U.S. Immigration Commission, XXXVII* (1911), quoted by E. Abbott, op. cit., pp. 82ff.

11. "For sixteen days": M. Antin, op. cit., p. 178.

12. "Clean they are": E. Steiner, op. cit., pp. 35ff.

13. "We had chosen": Broughton Brandenburg, *Imported Americans* (New York: F. A. Stokes Co., 1904), p. 189.

14. "the steerage cooks": ibid., p. 184.

15. "The third-class": "Steerage Conditions," *Reports of the United States Immigration Commission, XXXVII* (1911), quoted by E. Abbott, op. cit., pp. 90ff.

16. "A sudden, great excitement": quoted by I. Howe and K. Libo, op. cit., p. 22.

Chapter 9 Castle Garden

1. "One of the common frauds": "1847 Report of the New York State Legislature's Committee of Investigation," quoted by F. Kapp, op. cit., p. 65.

2. "run the O.P. line": ibid., p. 80.

3. "The steamer Holland": "A Day in Castle Garden," *Harper's New Monthly Magazine*, March 1871, pp. 547–556.

4. "enjoy themselves": "Report of the Grand Jury on the Mode of Doing Business at Castle Garden," (Grand Jury Room, September 9, 1856), quoted by F. Kapp, ibid., p. 197.

5. "Her brother-in-law": *The World*, August 25, 1887.

6. "A place of unlawful": ibid., August 23, 1887.

7. "During the fiscal year": "Report of the Select Committee to inquire into the Importation of Contract Laborers, Convicts, Paupers, etc., January, 1889," 50th Congress, 2d session, *House Report No. 3792*, quoted by E. Abbott, op. cit., p. 183.

8. "Liberty Island is": *The World*, March 7, 1890.

9. "The Goddess Frowns": *The World*, March 2, 4, 7, 1890.

10. "I have been glad": F. A. Bartholdi to R. Butler, April 2, 1890, ACSLP.

Chapter 10 Ellis Island

1. "It looks like": Julian Ralph, "Landing the Immigrant," *Harper's Weekly*, October 24, 1891, p. 821.

2. "He was in yisterdah": Finley Peter Dunne, *Observations by Mr. Dooley* (New York: R. H. Russell, 1906), pp. 51–52.

3. "When a stranger": Henry Hood, *The Forum*, September 1892, p. 114.

4. "during the ten years": "Report of the Immigration Investigating Committee to the Honorable Secretary of Treasury," (Washington, 1895), p. 53.

5. "the general character": John B. Weber, "Our National Dumping Ground: A Study of Immigration," *North American Review*, April 1892, pp. 424–431.

6. "On Sunday": *New York Daily Tribune*, April 16, 1896.

7. "A forlorn-looking lot": ibid., April 20, 1896.

8. "The entrance into our": Francis Walker, "Restriction of Immigration," *Atlantic Monthly*, June 1896, pp. 822–829.

9. "The danger has begun": Senator Henry Cabot Lodge, *Congressional Record* (March 16, 1896), 54th Congress, 1st session, quoted by E. Abbott, op. cit., p. 198.

10. "a radical departure": President Grover Cleveand, U.S. 54th Congress, 2nd session, *Senate Doc. No. 185*, quoted by E. Abbott, ibid., p. 198.

11. "Within five minutes": *The Sun*, June 15, 1897.

12. "Ever since I have": *New York Daily Tribune*, June 16, 1897.

13. "stuffy and ill-smelling shed": *Harper's Weekly*, January 19, 1901.

14. "It was evidently a suicide": Victor Safford, *Immigration Problems: Personal Experiences of an Official* (New York: Dodd, Mead & Co., 1925), p. 208.

15. "Why do they": *The New York Times*, June 3, 1900.

16. "We passed in a": *The Express* quoted in *The New York Times*, July 29, 1900.

17. "Editorial on *The Express*: *The New York Times*, August 20, 1900.

18. "for offenses": Terence V. Powderly, *The Path I Trod: The Autobiography of Terence V. Powderly* (New York: Columbia University Press, 1940), p. 299.

Chapter 11 A Clean Sweep

1. "The conditions": Steiner, op. cit., p. 81.
2. "Commissioner Fitchie": *The New York Times*, December 21 and 22, 1901.
3. "There are definite": *The Letters of Theodore Roosevelt*, ed. Elting E. Morison (8 vols., Cambridge: Harvard University Press, 1952–1954), 3:221.
4. "when they were run off": V. Safford, op. cit., p. 77.
5. "When we landed": quoted by J. Morrison and C. F. Zabusky, op. cit., p. 9.
6. "Commissioner Williams": William Williams's scrapbook no. 1 and correspondence folder, William Williams Papers, Manuscript and Archives Division, New York Public Library (hereafter cited as WWP).
7. "(Immigrants) were hustled": William Williams, *Annual Report of the Commissioner of Immigration for the Port of New York*, September 24, 1902.
8. "Reform Tidal Wave" and following excerpts: W. Williams's scrapbook no. 1, WWP.
9. "The visitor to": Erneste H. Abbott, "America's Welcome to the Immigrant," *The Outlook*, October 4, 1902, pp. 256–264.
10. "A great many": quoted by Thomas M. Pitkin, *Keepers of the Gate* (New York: New York University Press, 1975), p. 80.
11. "While the statesman": Jacob Riis, "In the Gateway of Nations," *The Century Magazine*, March 1903, p. 675.

Chapter 12 A Great Sieve

1. "Halfway up the": B. Brandenburg, op. cit., pp. 216ff.
2. "We used to like": V. Safford, op. cit., pp. 249ff.
3. "For instance": ibid., p. 250.
4. "There seems to be": J. Riis, op. cit., p. 676.
5. "the doctor would have": quoted by David M. Brownstone, Irene M. Franck, Douglass L. Brownstone, *Island of Hope, Island of Tears* (New York: Rawson, Wade Publishers, Inc., 1979), p. 175.
6. "We turned to the right": B. Brandenburg, op. cit., p. 218.
7. "How much you got": ibid., p. 675.
8. "It is a puzzling fact": Fiorello H. La Guardia, *The Making of an Insurgent: An Autobiography 1882–1919* (Philadelphia: Lippincott, 1948), p. 66.
9. "Here family parties": B. Brandenburg, op. cit., p. 220.
10. "The more I saw": ibid., p. 222.
11. "Here are the old": ibid., p. 678.
12. "While I believe": *Annual Report of the Commissioner of Immigration for the Port of New York*, September 24, 1902.
13. "Mrs. Schmitzky": Edward Corsi, *In the Shadow of Liberty: The Chronicle of Ellis Island* (New York: The Macmillan Co., 1935), p. 104.
14. "It is generally conceded": Address to the Federation of Churches and Christian Organizations, W. Williams's scrapbook no. 1, WWP.
15. "I am in a quandary": T. Roosevelt to N. N. Stranahan, December 24, 1904, Morison, ed., op. cit., 4:1077.

16. "The railroad ferries": ibid., p. 681.
17. "On board the ferry from Ellis Island": Hine actually captioned this photograph "the ferry to Ellis Island," but since the passengers shown are not wearing their manifest tags they must have already concluded their inspection and been on their way from the island.
18. "In accepting your": W. Williams's scrapbook no. 1, WWP.

Chapter 13 *A Man With a Heart*

1. "In looking for": E. Steiner, op. cit., pp. 81f.
2. "You have dispersed": R. Watchorn to W. Williams, January 19, 1905, WWP.
3. "Watchorn and orphan": obituary for Robert Watchorn, *The New York Times*, April 15, 1944.
4. ". . . the time has come": *The New York Times*, January 29, 1905.
5. "The President had": newspaper clipping in W. Williams's scrapbook no. 2, WWP.
6. "On all hands": ibid.
7. "Let no one believe": E. Steiner, op. cit., p. 72.
8. "Much ignorance": ibid., pp. 72ff.
9. "Two undersized": ibid., pp. 87ff.
10. "This is a wooden": quoted by T. Pitkin, op. cit., p. 107.
11. "If more mills": quoted by *The New York Times*, October 18, 1905.

Chapter 14 *New Restrictions*

1. "I took hold": and following excerpts from W. Williams's scrapbook no. 2, WWP.
2. "I felt then": F. H. La Guardia, op. cit., p. 65.
3. "To those who": John Walker Harrington, "Ellis island, by Liberty Darkened," *The Forum*, March 1927, pp. 331–340.
4. "And that is why": W. Williams's scrapbook no. 2, WWP.
5. "Consular inspection": J. Weber, op. cit., (North American Review).
6. "best material": E. Steiner, op. cit., p. 76.
7. "Not all of them": W. Williams's scrapbook no. 2, WWP.
8. "In the detention": E. Corsi, op. cit., p. 77.
9. "At the present time": letter quoted by T. Pitkin, op. cit., p. 106.
10. "Prior to the expiration": W. Williams's scrapbook no. 2, WWP.

Chapter 15 *Bureaucrats Declare War*

1. "Ellis Island": Frederic C. Howe, *The Confessions of a Reformer* (New York: C. Scribner's Sons, 1925), p. 253.
2. "I believe it would": "For a Better Ellis Island," *The Outlook* October 21, 1914, pp. 402–403.
3. "seven hundred and fifty men": "The New Ellis Island," *The Immigrants in America Review*, June 1915, pp. 10–12.

4. "The first thing we did": *The Immigrants in America Review*, op. cit., p. 10.
5. "You believe then": *The Immigrants in America Review*, op. cit., p. 10.
6. "During the next" and following excerpts: F. Howe, op. cit., pp. 255ff.
7. "Commissioner Howe has": "Turning Ellis Island Inside Out," *The Survey*, October 17, 1914, p. 63.
8. "By proposing": quoted by T. Pitkin, op. cit., p. 118.
9. "That he is fostering": *The Survey*, August 5, 1916, p. 486.
10. "The tide was coming in": quoted by E. Corsi, op. cit., p. 118.
11. "Visiting the little": "Ellis Island Cool Under Showers of Shrapnel," *The Survey*, August 5, 1916, p. 486.
12. "In two particulars": President Wilson's first veto message of 1915, United States 63rd Congress, 3d session, *House Doc. No. 1527*, quoted by E. Abbott, op. cit., p. 214.
13. "This movement against": Howe, op. cit., pp. 273f.
14. "In these proceedings": Howe, op. cit., pp. 274f.
15. Fiorello H. La Guardia: quoted by T. Pitkin, op. cit., p. 123.
16. "There was no demand": *The New York Times*, June 4, 1919.
17. "It is impossible": ibid., June 5, 1919.
18. "On the way": Howe, op. cit., pp. 326f.
19. "From the armistice": *The World*, November 25, 1919.
20. "I am not an anarchist": Cosntantine M. Panunzio, *The Deportation Cases of 1919–1920* (New York: Da Capo Press reprint, 1970), pp. 61–62.
21. "An official said": E. Corsi, op. cit., pp. 199–200.
22. "When I came to": quoted by C. Panunzio, op. cit., p. 75.

Chapter 16 *The Beginning of the End*

1. "All have participated": Cecillia Razovski, "The New Pilgrims," *The Survey*, October 30, 1920, p. 155.
2. "At Ellis Island": D. Brownstone, I. Franck, and D. Brownstone, op. cit., p. 194.
3. "a perfect miracle": Ian C. Hannah, "Arriving as an Immigrant," *The Survey*, October 30, 1920, p. 154.
4. "they put all the women": D. Brownstone, I. Franck, and D. Brownstone, op. cit., p. 207.
5. "The detention room": Marion C. Calkins, "The Jaws of the Machine," *The Survey*, October 30, 1920, p. 156.
6. "In addition to this": Marion C. Calkins, "The Jaws of the Machine," *The Survey*, October 30, 1920, p. 157.
7. "We have managed": quoted by T. Pitkin, op. cit., p. 134.
8. "Well, they opened up a seder": D. Brownstone, I. Franck, and D. Brownstone, op. cit., p. 216.
9. "When the inspector": ibid., p. 216.
10. "Imagine the ships": E. Corsi, op. cit., p. 288.
11. "ascertaining how many": *The New York Times*, June 10, 1921.
12. "They were very crude": quoted by D. Brownstone, I. Franck, and D. Brownstone, op. cit., p. 205.
13. "able administrator": "Ellis Island Stuck Fast," *The Survey*, October 15, 1922, pp. 75f.

14. "Mr. Tod is a gentleman" and following excerpts: A. C. Geddes, *Despatch from H.M. Ambassador at Washington reporting on Conditions at Ellis Island Immigration Station* (London, 1923), pp. 1–12.
15. "has to deal with": ibid.
16. "I had taken home": Philip Cowen, *Memories of an American Jew* (New York: The International Press, 1932), p. 174.
17. "The food is of good quality": A. C. Geddes, op. cit.
18. "Here by our country's permission" and following excerpts: Henry C. Curan, *Pillar to Post* (New York: Charles Scribner's Sons, 1941), pp. 299ff.
19. "Secretary of Labor": *The New York Times*, July 20, 1924.
20. "I have seen many jails": H. Curran, op. cit., p. 294.
21. "Is it time" and following excerpts: John Walker Harrington, "Ellis Island, By Liberty Darkened," *The Forum*, March 1927, pp. 331–340.
22. "become so indigenous": quoted by T. Pitkin, op. cit., p. 152.
23. "He had publicly": E. Corsi, op. cit., pp. 93f.
24. "evident astonishment": ibid., p. 97.
25. "In my own mind": ibid., p. 309.
26. "Such wholesale raids": ibid., p. 309.
27. "Voskovec had been" and following excerpts: Andy Logan, "A Reporter at Large: It Doesn't Cost Them a Cent," *The New Yorker*, May 12, 1951, pp. 56–77.
28. "What frightened me most": quoted by J. Morrison and C. F. Zabusky, op. cit., pp. 277f.
29. "This detention station": quoted by T. Pitkin, p. 175.
30. "In all but a few": *The New York Times*, November 12, 1954.
31. "They made their way": ibid., November 13, 1954.

All materials credited to the New York Public Library are courtesy of Astor, Tilden, Lenox Foundations.

All photographs credited to the National Park Service are courtesy of The Statue of Liberty National Monument/American Museum of Immigration on Liberty Island.

ABOUT THE AUTHOR

Mary J. Shapiro was born in Buffalo, New York and educated at Manhattanville College and New York University. She is the author of *A Picture History of the Brooklyn Bridge*, an annotated collection of prints and photographs; *How They Built the Statue of Liberty*, a children's book; and three walking-tour guides to New York City. She lives in Manhattan with her husband, Barry, and sons, Michael and Eben.